HILDEGARD
OF BINGEN

HILDEGARD
OF BINGEN

The Woman of Her Age

Fiona Maddocks

DOUBLEDAY

New York   London   Toronto   Sydney   Auckland

PUBLISHED BY DOUBLEDAY
a division of Random House, Inc.
1540 Broadway, New York, New York 10036

DOUBLEDAY and the portrayal of an anchor with a dolphin are
trademarks of Doubleday, a division of Random House, Inc.

First published in the United Kingdom by
HEADLINE BOOK PUBLISHING, 2001
a division of Hodder Headline, 338 Euston Road, London NW1 3BH

Library of Congress Cataloging-in-Publication Data
Maddocks, Fiona.
Hildegard of Bingen: the woman of
her age/Fiona Maddocks.
p.   cm.
Includes bibliographical references and index.
1. Hildegard, Saint, 1098–1179. 2. Christian saints—Germany—Biography
BX4700.H5   M33   2001
282'.092—dc21
2001028601

ISBN 0-385-49867-5

Printed in the United States of America

June 2001

First Edition in the United States of America

1   3   5   7   9   10   8   6   4   2

For Tom, Arabella and Flora

Picture Credits

CONTENTS

PREFACE

Why read a book about Hildegard of Bingen? And why write one? One answer is enough: she was an extraordinarily gifted individual who, for all her apparent remoteness in time and place, illumines our own times and shines a light on the past. We can ask little more of history. This German abbess's power and influence seeped into every crevice of twelfth-century life. That she also happened to be a woman who only found her voice in mid-life merely adds to the richness of her story, though for others with a more directly feminist preoccupation that fact would be of critical importance.

Today she is best known for her music. Yet her compositions form only a small part of her story. She was a polymath: a visionary, a theologian, a preacher; an early scientist and physician; a prodigious letter writer who numbered kings, emperors and popes among her correspondents. She was an artist not only in the musical and literary sense but in painting and, it would seem, architecture. She even invented her own coded language. Her boldness, courage and tenacity made her at once enthralling and haughty, intrepid and irksome. By contrast, the ills and terrors caused by, or perhaps even causing, her spectacular and overwhelming visions often rendered her helpless and torpid.

Fortunately, since the twelfth century witnessed a flowering of scholarship, an extravagant amount of source material exists in the form of Hildegard's own writings (still obscure to a general reader though helpful modern editions begin to emerge), her letters and contemporary biographical accounts. To avoid constant explanation of these important but drab sounding documents, I have listed them at the front of the book, together with a glossary of key people and places. Her works are listed with a short description in Appendix I. If only to avoid the Russian novel effect, I urge readers to glance at these at the start.

The task of encompassing her myriad spheres of interest only underlines my own inadequacies. Hundreds of books have already been written about her. With what entitlement does this present study appear? Ideally one should be a specialist in twelfth-century Germany, in medieval Latin and ecclesiastical history, in the history of science and medicine, botany and biology, mineralogy and petralogy, zoology and theology, mysticism, music, painting and monastic architecture.

Not surprisingly, scholars usually prefer to examine aspects of her life or work in depth, particularly her theology, while virtually ignoring the rest. A few, notably Peter Dronke at Cambridge, who first pioneered an interest in Hildegard in the English-speaking world in the 1970s, and more recently Barbara Newman in America and Sabina Flanagan in Australia have dared to pull together all the strands. Their work is warmly recommended. Still, each has his or her own strengths and obsessions.

At the other end of the spectrum, Hildegard has featured in steamy (or, rather, quietly simmering) novels, TV documentaries and anecdotal popular histories. These have their place but leave too many questions unanswered for the enquiring general reader. Moreover, as a quick look at the Internet shows, she has become the darling of crankish cults and New Age zealots, Creationists and Greens, women's movements and alternative doctors.

I have tried to steer a route between the extremes of fashionable enthusiasms and scholarly minutiae and have written instead with the freedom of one who simply enjoyed the quest and wanted to tell the whole story.

ACKNOWLEDGEMENTS

Thanks are due to Doug Young, who had the idea, and to Celia Kent at Headline for their endless patience and enthusiasm; also to Lavinia Trevor for making the connection. John Pull at the Library of Congress, Washington, first gave me a glimpse of the size of the enterprise by sending a list of Hildegard citations running to dozens of pages. So much for obscurity. Sister Benedicta Ward SLG, Reader in the History of Christian Spirituality at Harris Manchester College, Oxford, scrutinised the manuscript with painstaking attention and, I felt, some kindly awe at my ignorance. Her wit, sagacity and stern annotations saved me from many a scholarly slip but I am responsible for those which remain. She also made invaluable suggestions concerning the bibliography.

Professor Roderick Swanston, Reader in Historical and Inter-disciplinary Studies at the Royal College of Music, London, chewed rigorously over the chapter on music, which arrived back covered in red ink and with many stimulating suggestions, especially about the origins of Western music (no small matter). I have endeavoured to address them without, I hope, burdening the reader with technical detail but providing enough for those who want it. I have also done my utmost to ackowledge all sources and attributions, but I apologise to any I may have overlooked. The staff at the Bodleian Library, Oxford, always tracked down the books I needed. Alice Wood pointed out connections between Hildegard's medical writings and modern homeopathy. Francesca Currie read the manuscript at a late stage and asked some timely and penetrating questions which proved invaluable.

Sister Ancilla Feerling at the St Hildegard Abbey, Eibingen, allowed me to interview her and freely to publish the results. Those acquainted with the Catholic faith will find many of her observations about the world of a convent familiar. I have included them nevertheless (as an appendix) to demonstrate the continuity, and in some respects discontinuity, of the Benedictine vocation. Her decidedly unceremonious attitude towards her famous patron was of surprise and interest.

Especial thanks are due to my ever supportive friends and family, who now know more about the quiddities of monastic life than is necessarily good for them. My children agreed uncomplainingly to a summer holiday in Bingen when a beach (or indeed almost any other destination) might have appealed more. My husband, Tom Phillips, read and commented meticulously on the manuscript at each stage with a devotion way beyond the bounds of marital or editorial duty. Without him it would never have been written.

Hildegard of Bingen (1098–1179)
Biographical Sources

Vita Sanctae Hildegardis (The Life of Saint Hildegard)

This is the chief biographical source. Written by two monks, Gottfried of Disibodenberg, who wrote Book One in 1173–5 when Hildegard was still alive, and the more scholarly Theodoric of Echternach, who took over after Hildegard (and Gottfried) had died. Theodoric completed the task c. 1180–90, using additional material by a third monk, Guibert of Gembloux (see below), as well as invaluable autobiographical passages by Hildegard herself, thought to have been dictated in the 1170s during a critical illness when she believed she was dying. The complex structure, sometimes retelling events in three different versions, the main narrative breaking off at 1155 (still early in Hildegard's career) and the mix of biography, autobiography and hagiography make the Vita an interpretational minefield, but a priceless eye-witness source and an unique document of its kind from this period. The simplified account of its provenance given here only hints at the maze of complexities still awaiting scholarly clarification. It is referred to throughout this book as the Vita. Extracts used are taken chiefly from Jutta and Hildegard: Biographical Sources, translated and introduced by Anna Silvas.

Letter from Guibert of Gembloux to the monk Bovo

An unfinished life of Hildegard, sometimes referred to as the Hildegard-Vita, by Guibert, a monk from the Benedictine abbey of Gembloux, in Flanders (now Belgium), who stayed at her Rupertsberg monastery 1177–80 and was there at the time of her death. He incorporated his incomplete account into a long letter to his friend and fellow Gembloux monk Bovo, who is of importance to us only as the recipient of this letter. More vividly written and not always consistent with other sources, Guibert's version is strong on atmosphere and colour, weaker on facts. Towards the end of his life he returned to the subject of Hildegard, making revisions and embellishing the monks' Vita Sanctae Hildegardis, though the information is not always reliable.

Hildegard's Letters

Still in the process of being edited, Hildegard's correspondence of nearly four hundred letters is discussed in Chapter 9 and referred to throughout the text. These documents, often written as sermons (in the epistolary tradition of the time), provide not only a rich gloss on her theological thinking, but also cast light on her character and mode of thought and delivery.

Vitae domnae Jutta inclusae (Life of Mistress Jutta, the anchoress)

Referred to here as the Vita Jutta, this life of Hildegard's fellow anchoress, teacher and later abbess, Jutta of Sponheim, has only recently surfaced as an essential source and is still being assessed. It throws new light on Hildegard's childhood and does not always match other sources concerning her early years. It is thought to have been written around the time of Jutta's death (1136), perhaps by the monk Volmar, who appears to have been secretary to both women.

People and Places

Cuno – Abbot of Disibodenberg from around the time of Jutta's death (1136) until his own death in 1155. Officially Hildegard's superior, he had authority over her, not always happily, during the most critical time of her life, when she won papal approval for her visionary writings and founded the new Rupertsberg monastery.

Disibodenberg – Monastery at the junction of the rivers Nahe and Glan, approximately thirty kilometres from Bingen, on the site of an old Christian cult. St Disibod, an Irish bishop/hermit had settled there in the seventh century. Hildegard was taken to the monastery as a child when it was being rebuilt, and stayed for nearly forty years, becoming abbess. Ruins survive, largely dating from a later period.

Eibingen – Site of Hildegard's second monastery across the Rhine above Rüdesheim. She visited it regularly but never lived there. Today the St Hildegard Abbey, built in 1900–4, stands on the hill one and a half kilometres above the parish church of Eibingen (C20), site of Hildegard's modern-day shrine. None of the original monastery remains.

Heinrich, Archbishop of Mainz – A seemingly charismatic and highly political figure of some note. He was instrumental in helping Hildegard gain papal approval from Pope Eugene III at the Council of Trier. He consecrated the rebuilt abbey of Disibodenberg in *c.* 1146 and also Hildegard's new Rupertsberg monastery in 1152, and gave some of the nuns the veil. The following year he opposed the election of Frederick I and was removed from office. He became a Cistercian monk and died soon after.

Jutta of Sponheim – Noble woman whose birthdate is uncertain, but she was probably about six years older than Hildegard. She founded the women's cloister at Disibodenberg, where Hildegard spent the first half of her life and took instruction from Jutta. Died 1136.

Rupertsberg – Site of Hildegard's new monastery at the junctions of the rivers Rhine and Nahe at Bingen, dedicated in 1151 and destroyed by the Swedes in 1632.

Volmar – Monk of a similar age to Hildegard who became her secretary (following normal monastic practice for a leader of a community) and assisted her in writing down her visions. He is thought to have been the author of the *Vita Jutta*, and as scribe of Disibodenberg, may also have written the chronicles of the abbey. Died 1173, six years before Hildegard.

Chronology

1066   Norman Conquest
1076   Start of Investiture Crisis
1079   Peter Abélard b.
1085   Domesday Book
1088–1130 Abbey of Cluny reconstructed
1090   Bernard of Clairvaux b.
1093–1130 Durham Cathedral built
1095   Council of Clermont; First Crusade
1098   **Hildegard born**
1098   Siege of Antioch
1099   Crusaders captured Jerusalem
1099   Pope Urban II d. (Pontificate 1088–99)
_c._ 1100   _Chanson de Roland_ written down
1100   Geoffrey of Monmouth b. (d. 1154)
1106   Henry IV, German Emperor (since 1056) d., succeeded by Henry V
_**c.** 1106_   **Hildegard to Disibodenberg**
_c._ 1120   _Rubáiyát of Omar Khayyám_
1121   Peter Abélard condemned unheard at the Council of Soissons
_c._ 1122   Eleanor of Aquitaine b.
1122   Concordat of Worms, re Power of Rome. End of Investiture Crisis
1122   Peter the Venerable becomes eighth Abbot of Cluny
1123   Frederick Barbarossa b.
1125   Henry V d. End of Salian Dynasty (from 1024)
1135   Henry I of England d.
1135   Chrétien de Troyes b.
1136   **Hildegard becomes abbess after death of Jutta of Sponheim**
1137   St Magnus Cathedral, Orkney under construction
1138   Start of Hohenstaufen Dynasty (to 1254)
1140   Peter Abélard condemned for heresy at Council of Sens
1142   Peter Abélard d.

1142	First Latin translation of Qur'ān, commissioned by Peter the Venerable at Cluny
1147–9	Second Crusade. Defeat of German army on Turkish territory 1147
c. 1147–8	**With eighteen nuns Hildegard founds her own abbey at Rupertsberg near Bingen**
1149	Church of Holy Sepulchre, Jerusalem, dedicated
1152	Frederick Barbarossa becomes King of Germany (d. 1190)
1152	Henry II Plantagenet m. Eleanor of Aquitaine
1152	**Consecration of Rupertsberg monastery**
1153	Bernard of Clairvaux d., canonised 1174
1154–9	Pope Hadrian IV (the English Pope, Nicholas Breakspear)
1155	Frederick Barbarossa crowned Emperor
1158	Bologna University granted charter by Frederick Barbarossa
1159–81	Popes Alexander III, Victor IV. Start of Papal Schism
1160–79	**Hildegard travels along Rhine preaching**
1164	Antipope Paschal III
1165	**Foundation of community at Eibingen**
1168	Antipope Callistus III
1170	Thomas Becket murdered, Canterbury. Canonised 1173
1170	Fibonacci, Italian mathematician b.
c. 1170	Earliest known version of *Tristan und Isolde*
1174	Leaning Tower of Pisa under construction
1175	**Death of Hildegard's secretary, the monk Volmar**
1179	**Death of Hildegard of Bingen, 17 September**
1179	Lateran Council, Pope Alexander III against Albigensians (Cathars)
c. 1181	Francis of Assisi born
1187	Jerusalem recaptured by Saladin
1189–92	Third Crusade

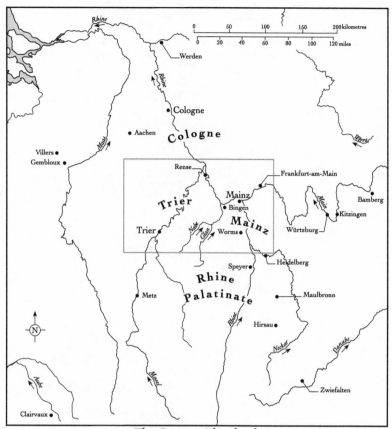

The German Rhineland.

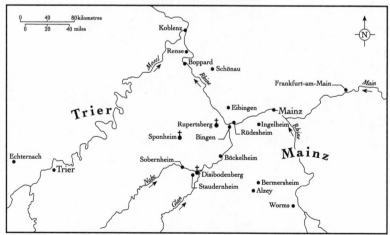

Rupertsberg, Disibodenberg and nearby abbeys.

HABEAS CORPUS

On 21 March 1852, a handful of people gathered around a coffin in the church of Eibingen, a small village surrounded by fertile vineyards above Rüdesheim on the banks of the Rhine. Among them was the parish priest, a sensitive-looking man in his mid-forties, with soft wide eyes and a sharp chin, named Ludwig Schneider. A local physician from Bingen, on the opposite bank of the river, was there too. The others had come to bear witness. On this occasion, Father Schneider's purpose was not burial. Nor was the doctor there to bid a final farewell to a much-loved patient. Under orders from the diocesan court of Limburg, these men had a more unusual task ahead of them. They were to open the casket and examine its contents, believed to be the mortal remains of a woman who had died almost seven hundred years before.

Inside, wrapped in a violet-coloured silk shroud, were nearly sixty bones, immediately identifiable as the well-preserved skeleton of a female. The skull was covered in a silk hood. Through this assemblage of bones, the spinal column was discernible. A pocket sewn into the skullcap contained strands of gold-grey hair. A parchment, tied to the cloth, bore an inscription in gothic lettering: *Caput sancte Hildegardis* ('Head of the blessed Hildegard'). Three more locks of hair were discovered in a pouch. In addition, the mummified remains of a heart and tongue were encased in boxes specially shaped to fit these two vital organs. Part of a nun's black and brown habit had been buried with the body. Attached was a note describing it as the 'choir cap of the blessed Hildegard'.

For the next five years extensive investigations, scientific by the standards of the day, were carried out on the coffin and its contents. By coincidence, in Paris at the same time, the literary remains of Hildegard were also being sifted. As part of his phenomenal *Patrologia Latina*, the celebrated French scholar-priest Jacques Paul Migne completed a first modern edition of Hildegard of Bingen's texts. His epic industry, consisting of 221 volumes of Church Fathers (and a small number of Mothers), which appeared between 1844 and 1864, is in itself an enthralling tale. The self-promoting, inexhaustible and tenacious Abbé Migne, a flesh-denying workaholic, ran a Catholic publishing sweat-shop in Paris in the mid-nineteenth century, with low wages, a rule of silence and conditions so harsh he was reported to the Préfet de Police. His editions are largely borrowed, some would say plagiarised, from earlier sources and abound with errors still in the process of being untangled by scholars. Volume 197, devoted to the works of Hildegard, published in 1855 and still referred to today, signalled a stirring of interest (laced with lightly veiled mysogynist disdain) in this remarkable twelfth-century iconoclast.

Two years after the examination of the remains, perhaps mindful of a growing fascination with his local prophet, the Bishop of Limburg, Peter Joseph Blum, announced himself satisfied. A combination of clinical examination, wish-fulfilment and guesswork gave him the answer he sought. These bones, he declared, buried in an unknown place in the twelfth century, transferred in the thirteenth, twice briefly on view when the coffin was opened in the fifteenth, moved to Cologne during the Thirty Years War of the seventeenth and which had survived war and pillage in the years thereafter, were the true remains of Hildegard of Bingen, mystic, composer, herbalist, poet, pioneer spirit of the Middle Ages and a German saint.

Thus in 1857 the first procession of the relics of Hildegard took place. In the same year, with impeccable timing, the Prussians demolished the surviving remains of her Rupertsberg monastery at Bingen to make way for a new railway track. The rock on which the towers, apse and choir stood was blown up.

The vaulted crypt beneath the high altar, metres from where a dozen trains now rattle by each hour and where Hildegard's bones once rested with those of St Rupert, caved in and vanished for ever. The monastery's solid walls, nevertheless, whose construction she had overseen in 1150, provided a sturdy, ready-made foundation for the railway embankment. Blackened with soot, they still stand firm.

In Eibingen Father Schneider inscribed every bone in the coffin with the authenticating words *Os Stae Hildegardis, 1858*. His modest but important role in her rehabilitation was complete. Little could he have realised that over the next century and a half her cult would grow and prosper, surpassing the extraordinary power it had known in her own lifetime; that abbeys and churches throughout Germany, Holland, Austria, and as far afield as Japan, New Guinea and the Bahamas would ask for fragments of these relics to furnish their own shrines to the blessed Hildegard. The dry bones he was handling were charged with meaning and were about to put on immortality.

CHAPTER ONE

BIRTH OF HILDEGARD

*From earliest childhood I have not even for one single
hour lived free from anxiety.*

(HILDEGARD, LETTER TO BERNARD OF CLAIRVAUX, 1146–7)

No one knows the exact date of Hildegard's birth. Her family name can only be surmised. She herself, perhaps indulging a taste for the harmony of round numbers, gives 1100 as the year she entered the world. All the records, however, point to 1098. Some writers like to claim her as a summer baby. Her place of birth is equally the subject of dispute. To describe her as being 'of Bingen' is itself an anachronism, though the name has stuck. It merely identifies the sprawling town on the Rhine which has now engulfed the site where once her Rupertsberg monastery stood. She might just as easily be called Hildegard of Rupertsberg, or of Disibodenberg, or of Rüdesheim. Many older books, following an error perpetrated in a sixteenth-century biography,[1] give her birthplace as Böckelheim on the Nahe, a southern tributary of the Rhine. That the German Emperor Henry IV was held captive in the castle there when Hildegard was a child added desirable romance to the location. Her first biography in English, written in 1914 by Francesca Maria Steele, pictures the infant Hildegard playing in the castle grounds, looking up at the window of the room in which the Emperor was imprisoned, hearing tales of how he had sold his boots for food.

The currently preferred view is that she was born in Bermersheim, near Alzey, in the same wine-growing region of the Rhinehessen, a short journey from the powerful bishoprics of Mainz, Speyer and Worms. The great pink and ginger sandstone cathedrals of these cities, like those of Durham, Ely and Santiago de Compostela, the abbey churches of Cluny and Silos, and the pilgrim basilicas of Conques and Moissac were under construction at the time. Their slender turrets and twin bell towers, massive piers, galleries, arcades and foliate carving, especially at Speyer, typify the Rhineland Romanesque style of the early twelfth century. This region of Germany was close to the heart of imperial power, a fulcrum of economic and ecclesiastical energy. Since antiquity, the green, fertile, rolling landscape had attracted new settlers – Celts, Romans and Franks – drawn by the moderate climate and gentle, wooded terrain. Traces of exoticism have left their still-visible mark on buildings, including the mysterious presence of small conical white dwellings using quarried stone, similar to the *trulli* of Apulia in southern Italy whose origins date back to neolithic times. A few churches retain the oriental-styled domes and elaborate octagonal towers modelled on churches or mosques encountered during campaigns to the East. The First Crusade against the Muslims had begun three years before Hildegard's birth, sweeping kings, bishops, soldiers and pilgrims towards the Holy Land.

Germany, split by civil strife and a complex, rumbling dispute between kings and popes over the appointment of bishops (dubbed the Investiture Crisis), sent fewer soldiers on the First Crusade than did France or England. Yet their departure still made an impact. The annals of the monastery of Disibodenberg, which would shortly become Hildegard's home, record this exodus in violent detail:

> *Moreover the Gospel witness confirmed it, 'And Jerusalem,' said the Lord Jesus, 'shall be trod down by the nations until the time of the nations is fulfilled'* [Lk 21:24]. *Whereupon not only country people but even kings, dukes and other powerful ones of the world were stirred, and I shall go on to greater things: bishops, monks and the other orders of the Church were moved to make this journey. At length when all these mentioned were agreed in purpose, kingdoms were left empty by their rulers, cities by their pastors, villages by their inhabitants. Not only men and*

boys, but many women also took part in this journey. Indeed females went forth on this venture dressed as men and marched in armour . . .

When all who had crossed themselves to make this journey [on Crusade] had assembled, they entered into a scheme that wherever they found Jews, they would draw them in to Christianity, either willingly or forcibly . . . Many, however, were killed and their wealth seized by the Christians. The distress was so dreadful that the Jews were driven to stab and kill each other with knives. The men did not spare their wives nor their relatives; they put to death their mothers, sons and daughters.

And so, pressing on with the journey to Jerusalem, they reached a city of Pannonia which is called Mersberg, where a great part of them were killed. And deservedly! Since men were marching together with women as mentioned above, unclean deeds of fornication and abomination transpired among them. For this reason they well deserved the wrath of God.[2]

In 1099, when Hildegard was one year old, Jerusalem fell to the Christians. The Crusades were to remain a feature of life (if with dwindling force) for the next three centuries. Fighting was the great game of Europe and warriors were celebrated by name as the sporting icons of their day in epic verse such as the *Chanson de Roland* (written down *c.* 1100). In other crucial respects the Europe of the late eleventh century, much of it still covered in forest, bore little resemblance to the continent we know today. The idea of a nation state hardly existed until the nineteenth century. Germany itself was united neither by a particular language nor a firm geographical identity. The only common tongue was Latin, which was still the official written language for science, diplomacy, the law and, underpinning all, the Church. The continent consisted of a network of feudal loyalties and ecclesiastical sees and a mosaic of ethnic groups. A change of monarch might almost go unnoticed: at one time Germany, Italy and Burgundy were all under one ruler; Aquitaine passed between France and England without undue trouble. Leadership stemmed from a web of jostling warlords and potentates, above whom were the Holy Roman Emperor and the Pope. Then came kingdoms, corporations, duchies and archbishoprics, traces of which survive as, for example, in the arbitrary boundaries of English shires.

Cultural and economic horizons were not as narrow as might be assumed. Trade was thriving. Great mercantile routes criss-crossed Europe, bringing grain, wax, honey, wood and furs from the east; silk, damask, porcelain and ivory from the south. The Rhine linked the important commercial areas of Flanders and the Rhine delta to the Lombard cities south of the Alps. Trade companies and guilds emerged. Methods of travel and navigation were improving: maps grew more sophisticated; the compass, borrowed from the Chinese, came into use; technical refinements to sailing eased hazardous sea voyages. Merchants risked their lives when travelling long distances over sea and land, from England to Germany to the Baltic, Riga, Samarkand and as far as China, exchanging sturdy wool and herring for rare luxuries, spices and incense. Salt was of vital importance, first brought by the Romans from the French coast, Lorraine and the Rhineland along the ancient *Hellweg*, the salt road through north and central Germany. In Bingen itself the narrow Salzstrasse, which was once lined with salt storehouses where the precious commodity was conserved after its arrival by barge on the adjacent Rhine, still survives.

Despite war, hardship and disease, Europe's population was on the increase. The climate in this period was moderate (temperatures were similar to those of the late twentieth century, though they were to drop sharply in the interim).[3] Towns developed into conurbations, the drift from the land had begun. By the thirteenth century Mainz, barely fifty kilometres to the south of Hildegard's home, and Cologne, just to the north, were two of Europe's largest cities. Yet those people with trades – bakers, millers, goldsmiths – maintained their smallholdings and vineyards and grew much of their own food, fearful of renouncing all links with the land because of uncertainty about their urban future. The agrarian landscape, too, had changed. New crop systems and better tools led to improved harvests. Reclaimed land was used for growing cereals, pulses and root vegetables, a staple diet, supplemented by fifty kinds of freshwater fish. Meat from livestock, mainly salted, was eaten in moderation, less frequently than game. Houses, usually made of timber, were dark, damp and cramped, with earthen floors and low, narrow doors. Homes of the gentry, to which Hildegard's family belonged, might have exotic textiles and wall hangings brought back from the Crusades, but most people relied on wool and linen of the homeliest varieties.

We know neither the whereabouts nor the appearance of the house in which Hildegard was born on the eve of the new century. Several hundred years later historians, with orderly hindsight, were to call this period of new Christian fervour, intellectual endeavour and artistic enterprise the 'Renaissance of the twelfth century'. Treated with the caution appropriate to such generalisations, it remains a useful label. Indeed, looking back at this age of cathedral-building and pilgrimage, of new monastic orders and the first awakenings of humanism, it seems as if every facet of life was subject to reform, examination, classification and evolution. Those living it, however, must have struggled to salvage any shred of order or certainty. Years later, in a vision, Hildegard was to recall the time of her birth as a moment of great unrest, when Christians were lax in observing their faith and the Church was at risk from destruction by heretics. It was then, she wrote, that, 'with sighs, I chose God as my parents'.

CHAPTER TWO

CHILDHOOD AND CLOISTER

I was only in my third year when I saw a heavenly light which made my soul tremble, but because I was a child I could not speak out.

(HILDEGARD, *VITA II, II*)

Her father and mother had separated her from their other offspring; in a way they had abandoned her to hope in God's mercy alone...

(GUIBERT'S LETTER TO BOVO)

This Year that is 1108, construction began of the new monastery at Disibodenberg. Burchard ... first Abbot of the community of St Disibod, placed the first foundation stone on the second day before the Kalends of July [30 June].

(CHRONICLES OF DISIBODENBERG, 1108)

Hildegard was the tenth and last child of Hildebert of Bermersheim and Mechthild of Merxheim. They owned extensive estates in the Rhinehessen region and appear to have been middle-ranking and well connected but untitled. A later writer, Trithemius (1462–1517), one time Abbot of Sponheim, describes Hildebert as 'a just and devout man employed with other knights of the Court of Sponheim, in fighting'.[1] Here, Hildegard spent her first eight years. Few details are known about her early life, or her family, though records and charters provide a sketchy picture. Three brothers and four sisters have been identified. Two remain unknown. Drutwin, her eldest brother, is mentioned with her father as witness to a document in 1127, but no further details survive. Hugo (also referred to sometimes as her eldest brother) became Praecentor of Mainz Cathedral and had dealings with Hildegard later in life when she had founded her new abbey at Rupertsberg, near Bingen. His name appears on a Rupertsberg document in 1158. A third brother, Roricus, also entered the Church, becoming a canon at the Tholey monastery on the Saar. His name appeared in the death registry at Rupertsberg. Of her four sisters, even less is known beyond their names though the last, Clementia, is thought to have joined Hildegard's convent as a nun. Given the path Hildegard's life was to follow and the little time she spent with them as a child, the close link she maintained with her family is surprising.

In 1106, at the age of eight, the freedoms of her early childhood came to an abrupt halt. At birth, her parents had promised her as a tithe to the Church, a tradition but by no means an obligation concerning the tenth child. The practice, also called oblation, was common among well-born, pious families, even those with fewer children from whom to choose. Some children entered monasteries at an even younger age. The Venerable Bede became an oblate at the age of seven; the mystic Gertrude of Helfta was handed over as a five-year-old to Cistercian monks. More than a century after Hildegard, Thomas Aquinas's family sent him away to Monte Cassino at the age of five but his aristocratic mother allegedly kidnapped him and forced him to stay at home for a year.

At this early point in her story, sources conflict over precisely what happened to Hildegard. Her own words in the *Vita* are frustratingly vague: she says she was 'offered for a spiritual way of life' in her eighth year. Nearly four decades later in *Scivias* (II, V) she would argue against child oblates, urging parents not to commit a child against his will 'until he has reached the age of reason'. Her own sufferings notwithstanding, she appears to have accepted her fate. We know that she was given over to the care of Jutta, a woman of noble birth acquainted with Hildegard's family. Until less than a decade ago, most scholars have accepted that Hildegard joined her as a recluse or oblate at eight, took the veil at fourteen and remained with Jutta until the latter died in 1136, when Hildegard herself became abbess.

In 1991 a life of Jutta came to light, written in the traditional hagiographic style of the Middle Ages. Despite all the learned hermeneutics and intelligent guesswork concerning Hildegard, especially in the last twenty years of the twentieth century, this *Vita Jutta* is the first concrete scholarly evidence for more than a century which changes accepted readings of her childhood years.[2] It transforms our view of Hildegard's early biography. The absolute reliability of this evidence cannot yet be judged, but it renders most standard works on Hildegard to date open to question, at least in the chronology and experiences of Hildegard's early life. Crucially, it suggests that Hildegard may not have been wrenched from her parents and thrown into the strict enclosure of an anchorage at the age of eight as has been assumed. Instead, she may have spent time on Jutta's family estate at Sponheim, only entering the monastery at the age of fourteen or fifteen, when Jutta was about twenty, possibly with Uda of Gollheim, a noble and devout widow who was in turn Jutta's mentor.

Given her pivotal role in Hildegard's life, we owe it to Jutta to give as full an account of her circumstances as is now possible. This new information confirms that at the time of their enclosure Jutta herself achieved some renown, attracting pilgrims just as her young pupil would many years later. The difference, however, is that she left no body of written work for posterity. Today, Jutta's modest celebrity depends entirely on the well-established evidence that she not only perceived the remarkable, visionary ability of the young Hildegard, but also encouraged her pupil to pursue her gifts. Of particular significance was the clear evidence that Jutta led Hildegard towards the monk Volmar, a name to note since he was to become her secretary and her most faithful ally for nearly the duration of her life. This same Volmar was almost certainly the author of the *Vita Jutta*, probably acting at the behest of Hildegard herself and Cuno, Abbot of Disibodenberg. The work's exact date is unknown, but is around 1140 or shortly after. Cuno, who had become abbot in December 1136, a few days after Jutta's death,[3] had shared a close spiritual friendship with her. In the *Vita Jutta* he is described as pouring out 'an unstinting rain of tears' over the body of Jutta, like many others 'racked by the overwhelming ardour of [his] affection'.[4] Years later, however, he was to cause Hildegard some of her greatest tribulations.

Jutta was the daughter of Count Stephen of Sponheim in the Rhinehessen. He died when she was three. Her mother was Sophia, of 'illustrious Bavarian stock'. The family may have been distantly related to Hildegard's. As already noted, it is possible that Hildegard's father was attached to the court of the Counts of Sponheim. Soon after her father's death, Jutta was 'handed over to be instructed in the learning of the sacred scriptures', an indeterminate description which gives no clue as to who provided this instruction, and whether it took place at home or elsewhere. When she was twelve, she suffered a severe, unspecified illness. Awaiting recovery, she prayed that if she survived she would give her life to God. This proved harder than expected. Handsome, clever and rich, she found herself the toast of the region. 'But when she recovered from this illness, she was the delight of everyone for this young woman was of comely appearance. Many nobles and wealthy landowners were coming to her, even from far-off places, panting to be joined to her in the marriage union.'[5]

Determinedly spurning these breathless suitors, she swore 'to know nothing of the marriage bed', though not without difficulty. The monk Guibert of Gembloux, writing nearly forty years later (when he visited Hildegard at the end of her life), gives a more embellished account of the young Jutta's travails, information perhaps derived from speaking to Hildegard or merely exaggerated in the retelling. Like that of Volmar, Guibert's name will appear several times in these pages. His writings tend to be enlivened with detail and anecdote, which make him an excellent raconteur but not always the most trustworthy source. He describes her struggles graphically:

> [Jutta] triumphed over all that would entice and divert her and clasped celibacy vigorously; she wrenched it from her heart so that she might not dally in any way about it . . . she put up an unflinching resistance to all the base-minded who told her unseemly stories and who stood in the way of her vow, crying out in imprecation to them: 'Get away from me, you detestable purveyors of an oil which shall never anoint my head' [Ps. 140:5].[6]

Obscurity shrouds the simple matter of Jutta's exact age, and whether or not she had already embarked on the life of a recluse, or anchorite (a term sometimes feminised as anchoress), when the young child joined her. Here, the *Vita Jutta* sheds both light and confusion. It seems certain that she was only fourteen herself and by now under the religious instruction of the widow Uda when the eight-year-old Hildegard came into her care in 1106. Soon after, around 1110/11, Jutta's mother died. Jutta already had a burning urge, like thousands of others at the time, to go on pilgrimage, a desire intensified by her mother's death. She had plans to 'slip away' when a moment arose. Jerusalem, recaptured in the First Crusade (1099), Rome and the newly rebuilt Santiago de Compostela were obvious destinations. Indeed, members of her own family, an uncle half a century earlier and more recently her great-aunt had both died on similar quests. Little wonder her brother Meinhard, now head of the family, forbade her from going.

Thus advised by Meinhard and with the spiritual guidance of one Bishop Otto (who would later give Hildegard the veil), Jutta decided instead to renounce the world. She chose to take the vows of an anchorite and to live in solitary confinement among the monks at the nearby Benedictine house of Disibodenberg, a monastery hugging the low Mount Disibod at the confluence of the Glan and Nahe rivers. According to Guibert, she looked around at other monasteries first, but chose Disibodenberg for its pious reputation and for its seclusion from 'the disturbance of a noisy crowd'. Considering the monastery had been in declining use for nearly a decade, this was a radical decision.

It was at this point, Guibert continues, that Hildegard's parents, hearing of the 'holy virgin's enterprise', decided to send their daughter to Disibodenberg as well.

> So they both came in their longing to the venerable servant of the Lord [Jutta] *and begged her earnestly to be so generous as to take to herself their daughter, whom they had set apart for holy celibacy and divine service, so that*

she might stay with her always. Just as they had not
hesitated to make their petition, so there was nothing to
delay their obtaining what they sought, for it seemed she
embraced the companionship of the girl as consolation sent
her from heaven.[7]

A pious and richly gilded plaster relief made in 1895,[8] in
preparation for the 800th anniversary of Hildegard's birth,
shows a luxuriantly dressed little girl, with fur tippet and ornate
gold robes with pink lining, being handed over to a benign and
maternal-looking nun (aged about thirty-five). Her aristocratic
parents stand behind her stoically, and another figure holds a
small chest containing her belongings or her useful dowry. The
mood is more that of a child being left by rich parents at a
smart prep school. This depiction, anachronistic and romantic
as it is, has a certain force. You would not guess, however,
that she was about to be committed to the care of a girl only
six years older than herself, living among a small number
of monks in a dilapidated and isolated hillside monastery and
to be put in a cell and literally walled off from the world,
supposedly for life.

Taking the new evidence of the *Vita Jutta*, Jutta appears to
have become an anchorite only when Hildegard (and possibly
one other girl) was enclosed with her on 1 November 1112.
That same year the fourteen-year-old Hildegard took the veil.
All other versions prefer the earlier date of 1106. The aristocratic
practice of donating to the Church, in life and death, was
widespread, among noble women as well as men. In addition to
money, they bequeathed belongings, as much to secure a
memorial of their lives as to endow the particular religious
foundation. Queen Matilda of England (d. 1083), wife of
William the Conqueror, left a luxurious cloak to be reshaped as
liturgical vestments. One European empress donated the silk
mattress on which she slept during her final illness to raise
funds for a charity for lepers. The Sponheim family was no

exception. Jutta's father, Count Stephen, was noted for his gifts to the Church. Her grandfather, Count Eberhard, had provided funds to build and to maintain the church at Sponheim and its adjoining monastery. Family members were encouraged to take holy orders. One son (Jutta's nephew, Craffto) went so far as to marry, then thought better of it and became a monk. His wife, whether under duress or by choice, joined a convent near Trier. It was entirely in keeping, therefore, that Jutta's family endowed the cell at Disibodenberg in which their daughter, sister or niece was to be immured.

The potent image of two young girls voluntarily shutting themselves off from the world fires the imagination. Not surprisingly, accounts vary wildly concerning their precise circumstances. Some insist that Hildegard was alone in a cell with Jutta; others that she was not enclosed at all, but merely living with the monks of Disibodenberg. (A very young woman and a child living freely among monks seems unlikely.) With this double chronology, glossed over and conflated variously by all Hildegard's biographers past and present, we must keep an open mind.

We can only form a picture of Hildegard's life at Disibodenberg by example. Her own passing accounts of that time, and those of the monks who wrote her biography, give frustratingly little detail. However, the practice of anchorage (from the Greek 'to withdraw') was widespread in the early twelfth century. Enclosure had been central to the religious life, for monks and nuns, for several centuries. The outside world was considered superfluous to the needs of abbey life. The 36th Rule of St Benedict states: 'There is no necessity for the monks to go about outside of [the abbey], since that is not at all profitable for their souls.' For women, prey to the violent attentions of marauding Saracens, Vikings or Magyars, virtue was at stake, safety a determining factor. In the late fourth century, St Jerome wrote a letter warning of the dangers of women unprotected in the world: 'Go not out from home, nor wish to behold the daughters of a strange country . . . Diana went out and was ravished. I would not have you seek a bridegroom in the highways . . . Narrow and straight is the way that leadeth to life.'[9]

The double monastery of Wimborne, Dorset, was typical of many with its high, thick walls from which none should escape. Once out, the general rule was that there was no return. Excommunication ensued. Accounts exist of nuns letting themselves down by rope and trying to return by the same method. St Caesarius of Arles (470–542) was responsible for shaping the rules of enclosure for women. He might have been writing for Jutta herself: 'If a girl leaving her parents desires to renounce the world and enter the holy fold to escape the jaws of the spiritual wolves by the help of God, she must never up to the time of her death go out of the monastery, nor into the basilica where there is a door.' Women in convents, even those not strictly enclosed as anchorites, had little freedom. Jutta and Hildegard, indeed, may well have been observing the local Council of Mainz ruling of 813 that all nuns and canonesses must observe enclosure. In general, women were not permitted to travel except in exceptional circumstances such as 'meeting the emperor', presumably considered as remote a likelihood as Cinderella going to the ball and therefore a safe condition. Even the abbess, who on occasion would be involved in fund-raising and the recruitment of suitable novices, had to be accompanied and to gain permission from a male superior. Strict enclosure, however, though an ideal of the Benedictine life, was not enforced until 1298, when any flexibility of movement was removed by the influential decree known as *Periculoso*. The need for formal segregation came as much from the nuns' desire for protection from a violent world as the Church's wish to curb their influence or behaviour.

Monks, who were not limited by the same severe restrictions, had an easier time. The very fact that they were urged to stay away from taverns and hostels, to eschew banquets and never to embrace a woman suggests that some of them must have experimented with these pleasures. The psychological effect of incarceration on nuns did not escape the notice of the bishops who ruled over them. In an almost gleeful letter to the celebrated St Radegund of Poitiers, who headed an order of nuns obedient to the model of Caesarius, a group of prelates showed little mercy for deviance, making their attitude to women plain:

> *If therefore any nun driven insane by the prompting of a mind diseased, shall seek to bring to the shame of such opprobrium upon her vows, her glory and her crown, and, at the Devil's urging, like Eve expelled from Paradise, shall venture forth from the cloisters of her convent . . . to visit this place and that, to be bustled and trodden under foot in the vile mud of our public streets, she shall be cut off from our communion and shall be stricken with the awful wound of anathema . . .*[10]

Details of practice and ceremony differed, but the central tenets of the Divine Office were common in outline throughout Catholic Europe. Anchorage was a form of hermitage. The aim was to achieve total removal from the world for the remainder of the self-elected person's life. The anchorite usually occupied a special building constructed near or adjacent to a church, walled up with no free access. Some recluses were chained and fettered, the paraphernalia as well as the language of imprisonment characterising the procedure. Every aspect of the self, of the individual, was to be mortified.

To whatever degree and in whichever version we elect to follow, and whether alone with Jutta or with one (or even two) other girls, Hildegard certainly encountered the privations of enclosure. Though she and her biographers skim over the details, their choice of words is telling. In the *Vita*, the monks record her entering the monastery of St Disibod 'in order to be buried with Christ and with him rise to immortality'. In his short and incomplete account, her last secretary, Guibert of

Gembloux, refers to her 'prison' or 'mausoleum'. Peter the Venerable considered anchorites as being dead to the world, and the world dead to them in turn; thus, after their vocation they should cover their eyes and faces in a thick veil 'like a shroud'. 'Enclosed in this cloister of salvation, or rather buried alive in this sepulchre, they waited to change a temporary prison for the freedom of eternity, to change burial for resurrection.' The sixteenth-century account of Hildegard's life by Trithemius calls the place she lived with Jutta a 'cloister or little cell'. Certainly this disturbing combination of imagery, of the cell and the tomb, was common to anchorage. Incarceration of the mind and the body was part of the ideal, to reach a state as close to death in life as could be achieved.

Sequestration permitted a life of prayer as well as an escape from life's temptations. Abbot Hugh of Cluny called the cell *gloriosum hunc carcarem* ('this glorious prison'). In the same year as he preached the First Crusade, 1095, Pope Urban issued a charter warning that no one should molest the nuns of Marcigny, who were 'dead to the world', but leave them free to strive towards finding their 'eternal spouse'. Most chilling in its depiction of being buried alive is the *Regula Monachorum*, probably dating from the ninth century and inspired by the earlier example of St Jerome: 'The thing that is most frightening for those that are lying in the burial mound is the grave robber who sneaks in at night to steal precious treasure. Thieves dig this up, to steal with infinite skill the treasure that is inside. Therefore the tomb is watched over by a bishop whom God installed as the primary guardian in his vineyard.'

The practice was widespread in England, where a rewarding amount of documentary evidence has survived. In his *Liber Confortatius* (1080) Goscelin, a Benedictine monk, celebrates Eve, a nun of Wilton Abbey with whom, as far as one can judge and within the constraints of chastity, he was besotted. He describes her cell as a place entirely free from 'anger, quarrels, dissensions, contentions, emulations, envy, jealousy, scandal, homicide, the passion of flesh and the furor of war'.[11] Nevertheless, Brother Goscelin seems to have inveigled himself into her austere life sufficiently to fall in love with her, and to be racked with torment at her subsequent departure to another convent in France, calling her the joy of his life. Aelred, Abbot of Rievaulx, advised his anchoress sister to keep religious hours, pray, recite the offices, eat, work and sleep, but to avoid close friendships, especially with men. St Anselm, later Archbishop of Canterbury, wrote two letters of instruction to anchoresses *c.* 1103–7. He had particularly harsh words for the daughter of Queen Margaret of Scotland, who, like Hildegard, had been an oblate since childhood, albeit a reluctant one who eventually wanted to leave to marry Henry I. Matilda claimed that her aunt, the abbess, had made her wear the veil, not for love of God but to keep her from the lust of Normans. She railed against the 'little black hood' and 'tore it off and threw it on the ground and trampled on it and in that way, although foolishly, I used to vent my rage and the hatred of it which boiled up in me'.[12] St Anselm finally permitted her to go. But to another nun, who had wished to marry a man who then died, he was harsh in the extreme, exhorting her to 'Go now, sister, place yourself with him in the bed in which he now lies; gather his worms to your bosom, embrace his cadaver. Kiss his nude teeth, for now his lips have been consumed by rot . . .'[13] The most celebrated instruction to anchoresses, however, was the *Ancrene Riwle*, first known as the *Ancrene Wisse* and then revised, written by an anonymous English Augustinian canon *c.* 1220[14] and soon translated into French and Latin.

In as much as these various manuscripts specify the initiation ceremony, a heady mix of grief at loss and joy at a new beginning, their descriptions tally. In keeping with this vision of death in life, the anchorite's ceremony of giving up one world to begin another entailed full burial rites. Descriptions suggest in disturbing detail what the young Hildegard may have encountered when, tapers flickering and blazing in the dim light, she entered the cloister on a short, dark All Saints' Day, 1 November 1106 or 1112.[15] The lengthy and intricate ritual for a female was as follows:

- The postulant, in simple shroud and barefooted, lies prostrate, either on the cold stone floor, or on a specially prepared covering of leaves and branches.
- A passage of scripture is read by two clerics, often from Isaiah.
- The bishop blesses the recluse with holy water and incense.
- She then stands to be given two lighted candles by a priest, one indicating love of God, the other of one's neighbour.
- The witnessing congregation stands for the gospel reading.
- The postulant's sponsors (presumably Hildegard's parents or godparents, or a priest representing them) lead her to the high altar to make their petition.
- Meanwhile, during the postulant's procession through the church, the monks chant the *Veni creator* ('Come creator spirit').
- The postulant genuflects three times at the altar, saying, '*Suscipe me Domine*' ('Receive me Lord . . . do not confound me from my expectations').
- She then places the two candles at the altar and returns to her place, waiting prostrate through the readings and homily.
- The congregation prays together for the postulant who is about to be enclosed.
- A mass for the Holy Spirit is celebrated.
- The choir chants the funeral antiphon 'May angels lead you to paradise' and psalms from the Office of the Dead.
- The rites of the dying begin, followed by prayers.
- The celebrant (the bishop or priest) sprinkles the recluse's cell/sepulchre with holy water and incense, blessing it in preparation for the arrival.
- The recluse enters the cell, singing the antiphon 'Here will I

stay forever; this is the home I have chosen'.

- The bishop sprinkles dust over the recluse, chanting, 'From the earth you formed me', the Office of Extreme Unction.
- The choir continues singing Psalm 139, 'Yahweh, you examine me and know me'.
- Before withdrawing from the cell, the bishop instructs the recluse to rise and obey the Lord.
- The entrance to the cell is blocked up, or the doors locked as a last symbolic act of finality.
- The congregation completes the ceremony with further prayers for the dead.

Guibert, ever keen to supply his reader with colour, gives an account which tallies with the ritual of enclosure described above. Again, he may have derived his evidence from a cocktail of Hildegard's own memories, accepted tradition and poetic licence. He paints a dark picture:

> *The fixed date of their induction came and many persons of both high and low degree came to be in attendance. According to the ritual of those laid to rest in the most solemn funeral liturgy, with burning tapers – which warned her to go out with lamps alight to meet the bridegroom at his midnight coming* [Matt. 25:6] – [Jutta] *was interred by the Abbot and brothers of the place as one literally dead to the world together with her spiritual daughter Hildegard then in her eighth year of age and another handmaid of Christ of the same name but of lower birth, her niece who was to minister to them. Crying out with all the longing of her heart she said:* 'This is my resting place forever, here shall I dwell for I have chosen it' [Ps. 131:14] and again, 'I shall go up into the place of the wonderful tabernacle' [Ps. 41:5] and this too: 'Let us enter the house of the Lord with rejoicing' [Ps. 121:1].
> *She did not, however, enter her burial-place lifeless and*

barren, but as the scripture says, in abundance [Job 5:26].
*So, like a crop of wheat harvested in due season, an
immense yield of produce eventually springs from the root
of her planting, which, cultivated by the Heavenly Father,
has clearly revealed itself up to this very hour. Surely there
has also been fulfilled in her what the Lord says about
himself in the Gospel: Unless a grain of wheat falls into the
ground and dies, it remains alone; but if it dies, it yields a
great harvest* [John 12:24–5]. *For Jutta, having died to
the world and withdrawn from it, was more fruitful in her
one spiritual heir and daughter Hildegard, as can be seen
today, than if she had been given in marriage and had
brought forth a greater number of offspring through
generation of the flesh.*

*And so with psalms and spiritual canticles the three of
them were enclosed in the name of the most high Trinity.
After the assembly had withdrawn, they were left in the
hand of the Lord. Except for a rather small window through
which visitors could speak at certain hours and necessary
provision be passed across, all access was blocked off not
with wood but with stones solidly cemented in.*[16]

In this manner, in style and solemnity, though she never
referred to it herself, we may imagine the young Hildegard of
Bingen bade farewell to her home, her parents, her brothers
and sisters, her childhood friends, and entered a life of seclusion
in the hillside cloister of St Disibod, hidden above the junction
of two fish-filled rivers in a lush land. In this place, she was to
spend nearly forty years of her life.

CHAPTER THREE

DISIBODENBERG

O mons clause mentis . . . Tu in absconso latuisti.
(*Oh mountain of a cloistered mind . . . You dwelt in a
secret place.*)

(SEQUENCE FOR ST DISIBOD FROM HILDEGARD'S
SYMPHONIA ARMONIE CELESTIUM REVELATIONUM)

*Jutta carefully fitted her out for a life of humility and
innocence, and, instructing her in the Psalms of David,
showed her how to play the ten-stringed psaltery. For
the rest, except for some simple psalm notation, she
received no other schooling in reading or music.*

(*VITA* I, I)

Compared with many of the famous, more imposing monastic ruins, such as Tintern or Rievaulx or Jumièges, Disibodenberg is a private, shrouded place. It lies two kilometres above the featureless small town of Bad Sobernheim, which seems disturbed by no greater event than the chime of the bells from one of the two churches. You approach Mount Disibod along a winding tunnel of trees which climbs gently through a green, sheltered landscape. Horizons are close, vistas unseen. Ancient trees and new saplings grow densely against the slopes. The final ascent, through a field of sheep and an apple orchard, is unexpectedly steep. Underfoot, the pine needles and accretion of rotting leaves make a soft, silent path. Still you see nothing of the monastery, hidden by woodland on the crown of the hill. Where once the abbey's squat octagonal tower must have been visible above the tree-line, now all but a few stones, a solitary façade, have tumbled to the ground.

By the time you sight the monastery wall, the sense of pilgrimage is unexpectedly powerful. Broken pillars and shards of columns, unidentifiable slabs and weather-smoothed fragments grow out of the landscape, covered with dark ivy, powder-grey lichen and bright, fresh moss. Watercolour painters of the eighteenth century would have thrilled at the sight of this most mysterious of ruins, in which shaped stone and raw nature unite. Indeed, an anonymous ink and wash drawing *c.* 1790, when more of the choir, apse and arcades of the abbey church survived, captures that romantic mood perfectly. The best-preserved building, the hospice, is the image of Disibodenberg most commonly reproduced, misleading as a key to Hildegard's circumstances since it post-dates her by

Disibodenberg Abbey. Anonymous copper engraving 1620/21.

nearly two centuries. On a still, damp autumn day, the only sound is of thousands of leaves dripping and plopping to the ground. Through the mist, you see nothing of the land around. The place gives out an air of oppression, of nowhere to go.

Two features immediately impress the visitor. One is the confined site on which the monastery was built, with abbey church and chapels, refectory, dormitories, kitchen crammed within the limited area of the mound, with no open space. In size, one of the smaller Oxford or Cambridge colleges offers a useful comparison. We see plainly why, years later, Hildegard left this place where there was no room to expand to found her own monastery. We sense, too, a profound air of claustrophobia which surely exacerbated the series of unexplained illnesses, many clearly psychological in origin, Hildegard suffered throughout her years at Disibodenberg. All this, however, forms a later part of our story. The other conspicuous feature, in contrast, is the awe-inspiring scale of the church, whose shape and proportions are easily visible. Today a vast, three-forked oak rises out of the nave at the narthex end. (Nature or nurture? In the Benedictine revival of the 1880s, when this tree must have been a sapling, the oak was chosen as a symbol of the revitalised order.) The rounded apse, the two aisles, the two steps up to the high altar (on whose site a stone table has been erected), the spacious transept and great columns, of which enormous four-foot-square piers survive, indicate the grandeur of the building whose erection Hildegard witnessed nine hundred years ago. A recent model reconstructing the abbey shows six buttresses and an upper and lower tier of windows. The shouts and curses of stonemasons, the hammering and sawing of carpenters, the rattle and screech of cart, pulley and winch would have been constant. Amid all this disruption, the monks, together with Jutta and Hildegard, had to observe the Divine Office, study and labour.

Set apart, behind a wall next to the abbey church, archaeologists have identified what some presume to have been the women's cloister. The foundations indicate two small rooms, with a yard or garden limited in size by its position at the edge of the hill. No information exists to tell us what degree of contact Hildegard and Jutta, shut away behind this wall, may have had with the monks. Nothing shows what access they had to the church, and whether they received their food and the sacrament through a window or a door, freely or with strictly limited access. In keeping with other hermitages, the small building probably had some sort of opening or grille through which contact could be made. Guibert describes a small window 'through which they spoke to visitors at certain hours and through which the necessities of life were passed'. He also says the cell was blocked up with wood wedged in by a stone to prevent easy access. Other accounts of enclosed women itemise the elaborate procedures for keeping the inmates apart, from ditches and walls to a *fenestra versitilis*, a kind of revolving hatch which meant visitor and anchorite could not see each other but through which food could be passed.

Disibodenberg took its name from a wandering Celtic monk, Disibod (of whose life, many years later, Hildegard was to write an account[1] and who appears in her sequence of songs, *Symphonia*). He was an Irishman who left his home in *c.* AD 600 and travelled to the Rhineland to preach, settling on what is now Mount St Disibod. The monastery's history during the tenth and eleventh centuries is blotted with abandonment, expulsion and reconstruction, culminating in the departure of all the monks from 1098 to 1105 when the latest Archbishop of Mainz (Ruthard) had been forced into exile by Henry IV for supporting the Pope. These dimly comprehensible happenings are recorded in the Disibodenberg chronicles, an almanac of key events and ecclesiastical appointments. This document also provides occasionally vivid snatches of detail about life beyond the monastery walls in the first half-century of Hildegard's life, including the weather, strange omens such as the comet of 1106 and the earthquake and eclipse of the moon of 1117.

We learn, too, of the founding of the Cistercian order, described as 'a band of monks who are clothed not in black but in grey attire', and of book production in Canterbury under the scholastic St Anselm. Of special interest is the receipt in 1143 of relics from the bodies of 'the eleven thousand virgins' martyred with the fourth-century English princess St Ursula in Cologne, a legend which, in its portrayal of perfect virginity, inspired Hildegard later in her sequence O *Ecclesia*. The mass grave had been discovered in 1106 by Henry IV's workmen, who were fortifying the city walls. There appear to have been an ample number of bones, enough to provide relics to religious institutions in the surrounding countryside (though the dubious origins of the legend led to the Vatican suppressing Ursula's feast day in 1969). Curiously, the chronicles end in 1147, a crucial year for Hildegard, as we shall discover – a coincidence prompting speculation that the author of the chronicles, like that of the *Vita Jutta*, was once again Volmar (who, given his new and time-consuming task of secretary to Hildegard, would have been forced to abandon the chronicles).

The monastery struggled to life again early in the twelfth century, just before the advent of Hildegard and Jutta, with monks from Mainz and Hirsau and funding from local wealthy families. We must assume that when they arrived its buildings were in a bad state of repair, the monastic institution in disarray and the hillside cloister certainly no place of comfort for a young woman and a small child. Around the same time, Archbishop Ruthard of Mainz (1089–1109) called a new group of Benedictine monks to Disibodenberg and work began on the building of a massive new abbey church. The foundation stone was laid in 1108, and the tomb of St Disibod consecrated in 1138. Eventually, in 1143, the building was dedicated by the Archbishop of Mainz. Thus Mount Disibod was a site under construction for almost the entirety of Hildegard's stay, and hardly therefore a place of quiet retreat.

These early years at Disibodenberg are the part of Hildegard's life we know least about. We may assume she saw little, if anything, of her parents. The responsibilities of family and work, not to mention the difficulty of travel, would surely have inhibited frequent visits, even supposing they were permitted or customary. Much scholarly ink has been spent in speculation about the effects of maternal separation on the young child, drawing on her later visionary writings on the motherhood of God for evidence. Some writers have even examined the possibility that Hildegard may have been breastfed because of a reference by her to the 'time of my mother's milk' (though it seems likely that this form of words was merely a metaphor to indicate babyhood). Common sense suggests she must have turned desperately to Jutta for a mother figure. The rest is a diversion which cannot usefully be pursued here. What child can seriously be relied on for a description of being breastfed? Nevertheless, in her first book of visions, *Scivias* (I, IV), she poignantly describes the loss of her mother in painfully alive terms:

And when I had said these things, I went away by a narrow path and hid myself from sight of the North in a small cave, bitterly weeping for the loss of my mother and also for all my sorrows and all my wounds. And so many tears did I shed, weeping and weeping, that my tears soaked all the pain and all the bruises of my wounds. And behold!

A most sweet fragrance touched my nostrils, like a gentle breath exhaled by my mother. Oh what groans and tears I poured forth then, when I felt the presence of that small consolation . . . And I said, 'O mother, O mother Zion, what will become of me? And where is your noble daughter now? Oh how long, how long, have I been deprived of your maternal sweetness, in which with many delights you gently brought me up!' And I delighted in these tears as if I saw my mother.

At the age of fourteen or fifteen, Hildegard took the veil (when, according to the chronology of the *Vita Jutta*, she also entered the hermitage). The celebrant was Bishop Otto of Bamberg, acting for Archbishop Adalbert of Mainz (1110–25), who because of his loyalty to the Pope was being held prisoner by Emperor Henry V at the time. We can surmise much about the structure of her daily life, since it would have been built round the performance of the Divine Office, the unchanging pattern of the religious life as ordered by the Rule of St Benedict, who founded his first monastery and in effect Western monasticism in the sixth century. The day allowed eight hours of sleep, three or four hours of prayer, four hours of study and eight of manual labour. Prayers took place according to an ordained timetable, which varied slightly according to the season. Matins, recited shortly after midnight, was the longest service; all 150 psalms were intended to be read at Matins within the course of a week. Daytime offices were shorter than those at night. A single meal was permitted in winter, two in summer. Portions of food were strictly rationed, greed regarded as a punishable sin.

The monastic day was as follows:

2 a.m.: Matins (one and a half hours)
Sleep till dawn
Dawn: Lauds
Needlework, or study
6.30 a.m.: Prime
8.15 a.m.: Terce
12 noon: Sext (followed in summer by lunch and two hours' sleep)
2.30 p.m.: Nones (during winter followed by the only meal of the day)
5 p.m.: Vespers (followed in summer by second meal)
7.15 p.m.: Compline (followed by bedtime)[2]

The principal obligations, some of which would severely challenge Hildegard's loyalty in years to come, were stability of residence (*stabilitas loci*), obedience to the abbot and to the community, commitment to life according to the rule, work, prayer, moderation and silence. Chatter was discouraged, jokes forbidden. The idea of Hildegard and Jutta sharing girlish laughter in their male-dominated institution seems remote. Indeed, levity scarcely enters the picture. You have to search hard to find humour in the works of Hildegard of Bingen. Chapter VI of Benedict's Rule makes matters clear: 'As to jokes (*scurrilitates*), vain words and such which cannot fail to provoke laughter, we condemn them for ever and everywhere, and we do not permit the disciple to open his lips for such discourse.' Humility, evinced by keeping one's eyes down, was the highest goal: 'Lord, I am a sinner, and am not worthy to lift my eyes towards heaven . . . I am always bent down and humbled.'

For the remainder of her life, Hildegard would bemoan the inadequacy of her education, calling herself unlearned, ignorant and simple. The *Vita* only describes her having learned from Jutta the basics of the religious and moral life, and the singing of the psalms. The likelihood is that she learned simple Latin, and the tenets of the Christian faith, but was not instructed in the Seven Liberal Arts, which formed the basis of all education for the learned classes in the Middle Ages (the Trivium of grammar, dialectic and rhetoric plus the Quadrivium of arithmetic, geometry, astronomy and music). These disciplines were required for entry to the Church or government. Monastic women would have acquired an *ad hoc* smattering, learning the Latin psalms by rote and making the most of what a particular *magister* or *magistra* had to offer. Hildegard certainly did this, and her frequent denial about the extent of her learning does not entirely ring true. She knew enough Latin to read extensively, if not to write it with scholarly fluency. Jutta also taught her pupil how to sing and to carry out her duties as a choir-nun. Given Hildegard's later reputation as a composer, we should note that Jutta is also credited with teaching her the ten-stringed psaltery, though this may be a version of the familiar trope (following St Augustine) in which the instrument was likened to the Ten Commandments. The *Vita* confirms that Jutta trained her 'in learning and singing the sacred songs of David', adding that in other respects she 'received no other schooling, either in reading or in music'.

A comparison with Hildegard's great pioneering forebear of the tenth century, Hrotsvit of Gandersheim, offers insight into the level of education sometimes reached by monastic women. This Saxon canoness, hymned as the first known dramatist of Christianity, the first Saxon poet and the first woman historian of Germany, was probably well versed in the works of Horace, Ovid, Lucan, Boethius and Virgil as well as liturgical texts and lives of the saints and martyrs. She made her own versions of comedies by Terence, replacing pagan impiety with language more appropriate to the cloister (though some have accused her writing of having explicitly sadomasochistic undertones). Excusing 'female frailty' and 'relying on heavenly grace and not on my own powers', Hrotsvit claimed to have found all she required in the abbey library and produced no fewer than eight legends, six plays, two epics and a short poem some of which have enjoyed modern acclaim. The library of Disibodenberg, with its chequered history, may not have possessed such broad resources.

It is tempting to wonder what sort of devotion a child can have to the religious life, committed without choice at the age of eight. The evidence repeatedly suggests Hildegard recognised her own exceptional gifts, and their attendant troubles, from an early age. Nor even now is it considered abnormal for a child to recognise a vocation so young. A study of nuns in the late twentieth century,[3] in which each describes her vocation, is remarkable in this respect. A high percentage knew their religious destiny at a young age, or else in adolescence. One, at the age of seven, 'made a master plan for life . . . to enter the convent when I grew up and give my life to the service of God'; another recalls having 'first heard God's call to the religious life' at the age of eight; a third was addicted to the ritual, 'the symbolic paraphernalia, music and mysterious language' by the age of nine. We should not automatically dismiss accounts of the child Hildegard's prodigious spirituality as hagiographic excess on the part of her biographers.

Two aspects of Hildegard's history, however, did set her apart from others, and were to do so for the remainder of her life: her frequent illnesses, and the visions which, as she soon realised herself, others did not experience. Both pre-date her arrival at Disibodenberg, and might have persuaded her parents that their decision to tithe her to God was more than appropriate. As mentioned earlier, the *Vita Jutta* suggests that she may have spent her early years in the monastery with a widow, Uda of Gollheim, either instead of or as well as Jutta. Possibly Uda took on the role of teacher, cook, housekeeper and matron to the two young women whose lives would have been fully occupied in liturgical and educational matters. All three women may have engaged in sewing and embroidery for church purposes. The famous English anchoress Christina of Markyate made slippers for the Pope. Adornments of various kinds – vestments, altar cloths, hangings – would have been required for the new abbey church. The monks' coarse wool or linen tunics and cowls needed mending, and washing too, though lay clerks may have shared these tasks. Food, even if prepared in the monastery kitchen rather than by the women themselves, had to be gathered. The staple diet consisted of vegetables, fruit and bread. Cooked dishes could be made from eggs, fish, cheese or beans. On meat the Benedictine Rule is precise: no flesh of four-footed animals should be eaten except by the sick or invalid.

Jutta's biographer gives vivid accounts of her struggles to pray as a result of her self-denial. What effects did these excessive acts of piety have on the young Hildegard? The fact that Hildegard recalls the later years of her childhood and youth – the period she was enclosed with Jutta – as more difficult and fraught than her infancy cannot be ignored. Nothing in Hildegard's own biographical writings suggests she took an extreme attitude towards physical self-denial, even though fasting was considered the worthiest form of ascetic rigour. The patristic writers asserted that Adam's chief sin was gluttony, and taste 'the mother of all vice', a view still taken seriously a century after Hildegard by Thomas Aquinas. Fasting was thought to temper lust (made worse by eating meat), offer purification, exorcism, relief from mourning and general penitence. The fourth-century writer known as pseudo-Athanasius considered it especially salutary for virgins: 'Fasting . . . cures disease, dries up the bodily humours, puts demons to flight, gets rid of impure thoughts, makes the mind clearer and the heart purer, the body sanctified, and it raises man to the throne of God.'

In the circumstances, it is a wonder women ever ate at all. Countless descriptions survive of female saints wasting away. Men were prone too – St Simon Stylites, for example, refused all food for the duration of Lent – but the instances are fewer. A certain scepticism should be employed, since evidence of mortification of the flesh was a convention in all hagiographical writings, each perhaps borrowing their more lurid details from another. Nevertheless, such tendencies are well corroborated. St Francis of Assisi is recorded, more than once, as having argued over this issue with St Clare, finally instructing her to abandon her fast for fear of death. The biographer of Catherine of Siena (who started refusing food as a teenager when she fell out with her parents over her religious vocation) recounts a mode of behaviour which today might be called bulimic: after eating nothing, she then consumed large quantities on the feast of the Ascension. Nor was outward appearance accepted as the only source. It was known, for instance, because of the emptiness of her intestines and her lack of need for excretion, that the peasant saint Alpais really did live on nothing but sacramental bread and wine for forty years.

Jutta, in a further display of piousness, insisted on standing through hours of prayer, often in bare feet, 'so that from this labour she became afflicted by a serious debility'. She obeyed the warning of Solomon, who said, 'diligently work your field so that afterward you may be able to build your house [Prov. 24:27]', chastising her body and subjecting it to servitude, 'crucifying it along with its vices and passions'. She gave herself up as a living sacrifice in vigils, prayers and continual fasting. In practice this entailed depriving herself of sleep, inflicting wounds on her body and wearing a hairshirt and an iron chain. Many in holy orders died as the result of similar practices, which were often taken as certain evidence of sainthood in subsequent applications for canonisation.

In addition, Jutta dressed in rough, lowly attire and was content to eat only the leftovers at table. Today her behaviour might be diagnosed as a form of anorexia nervosa (a connection given scholarly credence by Caroline Walker Bynum in her book *Holy Feast and Holy Fast*). Whether we share this conclusion or not, the link between near-starvation and holiness is well documented. St Benedict's Rule, in any case, preached dietary moderation. The religious calendar instructed several days of fasting, in Lent and elsewhere. Abstinence was both a penance and a sign of devotion, often practised collectively within a community. Dry eating – that is, only bread, salt, water, a limited intake of fruit and vegetables – was common. Some, particularly hermits, ate only raw food. Food was probably more lavish at all-male institutions, therefore regarded as a serious vice, a form of lust at its most potent. The feast was a mainstay of medieval life. Monasteries were not immune to its pleasures. Mouthwatering accounts survive of monastic feasts consisting of meat, game, fish, fowl and shellfish, often one stuffed into another. Small birds such as crane and lark were a speciality; imitation meat was concocted from fish; green dye from spinach was used to brighten up colour. Appearance was crucial. An English recipe for roasted peacock states that feathers and tail should be wound round the body of the cooked bird so that it might be served 'as if the bird were still alive'.

Jutta's obsessions, it is clear, were not merely those of a healthy vegetarian and led to some conflict with her monks. On occasion she was 'obliged by order of her elders to abstain from extreme behaviour'. The *Vita Jutta* describes her frailty after refraining from eating meat for eight years, after which she was 'laid low by a serious weakness. Thereupon by command of the lord Abbot Adilhum[4] she was ordered to use meat. She was still humbly begging to be excused from this when, unexpectedly, a kind of water bird rather large in bulk, occasionally heard in the area before but never seen, came and settled at her window at twilight one evening.' The account goes on to tell how the bird, to the amazement of all, remained there. They read it as a sign.

> When the said father [Adilhum] found out about this, he
> drew deep sighs, dissolved into tears and said 'Heaven has

*refuted my hardness of heart since for so long I have put off
compassion for her infirmity.' He then commanded that
she must take refreshment with the gift that heaven had
sent her. She then humbly yielded to him, but she requested
that she should not be put under obligation by such an order
from him or his successors except for unavoidable necessity,
when it would be otherwise impossible for her to recover
her strength. This she obtained – though she knew that by
decree of our holy Father Benedict food of this kind was
permitted for the sick that they might recover their strength.*

In contrast to Jutta, Hildegard's attitude to food was healthy
in its moderation, springing largely from common-sense notions
of balance which still have validity today. Following St Benedict,
she frequently warns against excess in any guise, either partak-
ing of food or its denial. Abstaining from eating, especially when
the person concerned is 'fickle and imprudent' or 'preoccupied
with immense and serious sufferings', can cause a variety of
pustules, abscesses or tumours which may have a fatal outcome.[5]
Self-induced vomiting, meanwhile, is dangerous to the health
and never beneficial, threatening the blood vessels and upsetting
their balance 'in such a way that the vomit will not find the
proper way out'.[6] She warns men against sexual greed by using
a food metaphor: '[A man] should not behave like someone
stuffing himself with food like a glutton who disregards proper
mealtimes but rather, like someone who observes proper mealtimes so that he is not a glutton.'[7] Her entire theology is based
on the harmony of the created world and its relation to God.
Thus, she states that 'God fashioned the human form according
to the constitution of the firmament and of all the other
creatures, as the founder has a certain form according to which
he makes his vessels.' Similarly the proportions of the human
head are compared with the world: 'The sphere of the human
head indicates the roundness of the firmament, and the right
and balanced measurements of our head reflect the right and

balanced measurement of the firmament.'[8] These two examples from the *Liber divinorum operum* exemplify a key thread running through her work and thought.

However problematic the evidence, the frequent mention of one or more others in the enclosure suggests Hildegard may have had a more sociable time than at first would seem the case. It explains, too, how an anchorage, where recluses had supposedly sworn to stay for life, might gradually grow into a small convent attached to the monastery. The presence of an anchorite in a region attracted fame and celebrity. They were often consulted – through their little barred windows or revolving hatches – on matters holy and secular. They were discouraged, however, from teaching children or turning the place into a school. Thus Hildegard's relationship to Jutta, essentially that of pupil and teacher, would not have been welcomed by everyone. The older woman's reputation attracted several noble young women to a religious life. In this way, she appears gradually to have abandoned strict commitment to a life of seclusion, and instead agreed to become abbess of Disibodenberg.

The *Vita Jutta* is of little help in explaining how this profound change in circumstances came about. Only the chatty Guibert furnishes us with explanation, showing how Jutta's celebrity as a woman of wisdom and a pious anchorite drew pilgrims to her:

> For indeed noble men and women began to flock to her, offering their daughters to her that they might take up the habit of the holy religion and the life of professed virginity, and for their support they contributed vineyards, properties and estates. These petitions and requests of theirs she handed on to the Abbot and the brothers of more mature age. With their counsel and permission, she agreed to receive the maidens and the gifts offered with them. When the entrance to her tomb was opened up, she brought inside with her the girls who were to be nurtured under the

guidance of her disciplined guardianship. It was on this occasion that what was formerly a sepulchre became a kind of monastery, but in such a way that she did not give up the enclosure of the sepulchre, even as she obtained the concourse of a monastery.

The clear intimation, therefore, is that Jutta in fact remained enclosed to the end of her life, as her original vows intended. Given the varying degrees of seclusion, the possibility that within a segregated area of the monastery she was nevertheless free to come and go, and to run a small convent, makes it hard to judge whether she was cut off from the world, or that she had renounced her anchorage. We know that she was visited by people from all walks of life who sought her advice. The truth probably lies in between: detachment from the world outside, relative liberty within. In other words, Jutta managed the remarkable, almost contradictory feat of being an anchoress and running a community, with Hildegard as her trusted support and, in every sense, her lady in waiting.

CHAPTER FOUR

VISIONS

I saw all this and then – I refused to write. Not out of stubbornness, but out of a sense of my inability, for fear of the scepticism of others, the shrugging of shoulders, and the manifold gossip of mankind, until God's scourge threw me on the bed of illness. There, finally, overcome by much suffering, I set my hand to write.

(SCIVIAS, DECLARATION)

Our literal interpretation of [Hildegard's visions] would be that she experienced a shower of phosphenes in transit across the visual field, their passage being succeeded by a negative scotoma.

(OLIVER SACKS, MIGRAINE: UNDERSTANDING A COMMON DISORDER)

In 1136, 'her forty-fifth year', Jutta died. Hildegard was thirty-eight. As the Disibodenberg chronicles report: 'In this year on Dec. 22, Lady Jutta of holy memory died, 24 years enclosed in Mount St Disibod, the sister of Count Meginhard of Sponheim. The holy woman was enclosed on 1 November and three others with her, that is to say Hildegard and two of the same name; whom she took pains to imbue with holy virtues as long as she lived.' The *Vita Jutta* has shed new light on the manner of her death and its coming. Extraordinarily, it records that Jutta had been forewarned of the timing of her death more than two decades earlier by an old woman called Trutwib, a devout widow who was staying at Disibodenberg on the precise day Jutta (and Hildegard) were to enter anchorage. As Trutwib approached the courtyard of the guesthouse, a vision appeared before her and spoke: '"You must know that the lady Jutta who today is to be enclosed in this place, shall happily spend twenty-four years here, and in the twenty-fifth year pass happily from this world. That you may give all credence to my words, you must know that in a short while from today you yourself are to die."'[1]

Accordingly, the poor, astonished old woman died within a few days, but not before having communicated to the newly immured Jutta what fate lay before her. As the years passed, Jutta began to prepare for her imminent death, 'keeping watch for the coming of her Spouse' lest the Lord take her when she was asleep. In the last year of the number granted, her strength began to fade. She engaged in lengthy fasts and vigils, crying out to the Lord to take her and longing 'to be dissolved and to be with Christ'.[2] At dawn on 2 December, Jutta saw a vision of a tall, handsome man who revealed himself as St Oswald, an

English king venerated at Cluny and Disibodenberg and commemorated by the Venerable Bede. He told her, with comforting words, the exact date of her death. The *Vita Jutta* gives a moving account of her final hours, which appear to have involved the whole of the women's community and in which Jutta was self-denying to the last:

> *After she had been burning in an acute attack of fever for twenty days she comforted her disciples, ten of them in number, with her soothing counsels. Since she knew the time of her call was drawing near, she asked for Viaticum* [Holy Communion given to the dying to assist them on their journey] *and received it, which she had been accustomed to do almost every day she was lying ill. When she sensed that the hour was almost at hand for her to be led forth from the body, she asked them to read to her the Passion of the Lord. When this was finished she counselled all who were present to give themselves to the prayers and the psalmody, praying, like her, unceasingly.*
>
> *In the silent hours of that very night, she surprised everyone there by asking that the holy veil be brought to her quickly. Having placed it on her head, she asked that she be placed on a hair-mat strewn with ashes, earnestly appealing to the bystanders then, as she had before, that they not hinder her by their weeping from moving forward towards her Creator. Thus placed on her hair-mat in a place convenient for the arrival of the brothers she entreated by a sign that the brothers be called. When they had prayed the litanies over her, she then forti-fied herself with the sign of the holy Cross and gave up her holy soul.[3]*

Hildegard and two others 'who were more advanced in a holy way of life and more privy to her secrets than the others' attended to her body. Significantly the *Vita Jutta* reports that Jutta had begged them, after her death, not to allow her corpse to be 'openly uncovered for washing'. Reading the meticulous account of the laying-out process, it becomes evident why:

> So putting out the others, they gave themselves in privacy to the task of arranging the limbs of her holy body. They declared that they were struck back by the light of the brightness of her dead body. They marvelled at the snowy whiteness which shone from her, to which we too can testify, for through the Lord's compassion we were deemed worthy to take part in her passing and funeral. These disciples of hers, watering the body of their mother and magistra with heartfelt tears, carefully examined it. Among innumerable other marks of her passion they discovered a chain which she had worn on her flesh had made three furrows right round her body. Thus it became clear in her dead flesh what her soul had wrought while living in the flesh, now that her heavenly spouse was inviting it to come from Lebanon to be crowned [Song of Songs 4:8] in his heavenly kingdom.

This account of Jutta's sufferings might have been based on the description of the female ascetic's existence by the fourth-century Church Father John Chrysostom, who wrote that 'even at a tender age [they go] without food and sleep and drink, mortifying their flesh, sleeping on the ground, wearing sackcloth, locked in narrow cells, sprinkling themselves with ashes and wearing chains'.[4] The hagiographic tradition of describing the body in meticulous detail is well established. That extreme ascetic, Bernard of Clairvaux, sometimes paralysed for lack of food, had a bad stomach and is said to have reeked perpetually of stale vomit. Aelred of Rievaulx's biography, by his fellow monk and secretary Walter Daniel, describes the great English Cistercian as having 'flesh clearer than glass, whiter than snow, as though his members were those of a boy five years old, without a trace of stain, but altogether sweet . . . Perfect in every part of his body the dead father shone like a carbuncle, was fragrant as incense, pure and immaculate in the radiance of his flesh as a child.'[5] Jutta's biographer may have stolen the poeticisms from else-where, yet such observations were never made about Hildegard, who seems not to have aspired to the higher flights of ambitious asceticism. Jutta was buried 'in a place where she might be trodden upon by passers by', at first probably in the floor of the monks' chapter house at Disibodenberg. Later her remains were exhumed and reburied in front of the altar in the Lady chapel.

Thus that same year, after nearly three decades of providing patient support, Hildegard was appointed abbess, her nuns accountable only to her. At last, though answerable to the monks and Abbot Cuno (1136–55), she had a degree of autonomy. In medieval life, spiritual authority was the one real avenue for women to obtain leadership, just as the religious life was the only chance for them to enjoy a degree of privacy and the opportunity to educate themselves offered by access to the monastic library. Strictly speaking, Hildegard seems never to have been granted the title abbess, but rather prioress or *magistra*, apparently because of the informal status of her community within Disibodenberg. Neither a women's house nor a double monastery, it had no right to use the title abbess, though in all practical and external respects she performed that duty and is widely referred to by that name (except, on occasion, by those wishing to score superiority of rank over her, which later in her life some liked to do).

A surprising silence hangs over Hildegard's reaction to Jutta's death. Could the very absence of verbal outpouring from one who articulated her views so copiously on all other aspects of life imply a coolness towards her companion and *magistra*? It is plain that only after Jutta's death, released from her role as pupil, did Hildegard find a mode of self-expression. For the duration of her life to that point, from the age of three 'when I saw an immense light that shook my soul', she had experienced visions which she kept secret from the world. While still with her parents, she realised that what she saw was visible to her eyes only. 'When I became exhausted I tried to find out from my nurse if she saw anything at all other than the usual external objects. And she answered "Nothing," because she saw nothing like I did. Then I was seized with a great fear and did not dare to reveal this to anyone.'[6] As a child she is even supposed to have predicted the markings on a calf still in the womb. She told no one of all this, but Jutta noticed her unusual qualities and 'confided it to a monk well-known to her'. This monk was almost certainly Volmar, the assumed author of the *Vita Jutta*. Soon his life would change radically. He was to become Hildegard's secretary, a post he held for nearly forty years until his death in 1173, six years before her own.

Hildegard, however, was not ready to act on these intimations, still suppressing all and apparently making herself ill as a result. This secret burden dominated her life, yet still she hid it from others. As a young woman, or, in her words, 'When I was twenty-four years and seven months old', she had had a stormily prophetic vision which racked her physically:

> I saw an extremely strong, sparkling, fiery light coming from the open heavens. It pierced my brain, my heart and my breast through and through like a flame which did not burn; however it warmed me. It heated me up very much like the sun warms an object on which it is pouring out rays. And suddenly I had an insight into the meaning and interpretation of the psalter, the Gospel and the other Catholic writings of the Old and New Testaments, but not into the meaning of the sentence structure and the hyphenation; also I had no understanding of the events of the times.[7]

Her implication here is that this divine light, whatever its origin, enabled her to understand the scriptures beyond the level of her education and normal comprehension but not without anxiety. She says, 'Out of fear of people I dared not tell anyone.' At times, she 'cried out like a child' despite herself but refrained from saying precisely how these imaginings came to her. Most alarming, as a child, was her discovery that others about her did not see what she saw.

It was William James, the Bostonian philosopher, who in his *Varieties of Religious Experience* (1901–2) helped restore the idea of the supernatural, shunned by theologians in the eighteenth century, philosophers in the nineteenth and psychologists in the twentieth as a topic for serious debate. (As an aside, we might add that his brother, Henry, was to explore the matter of seeing and believing from a more sinister point of view in his novella *The Turn of the Screw*.) His penetrating observations on the capacity of any receptive mind, religiously disposed or not, to experience what might be called 'the mystical' is still a valid starting point for interpreting Hildegard's visions, though he does not refer to her by name. His chief proposition was that our 'normal waking consciousness' is but one form of consciousness, 'whilst all about it, parted from it by the flimsiest of screens, there lie potential forms of consciousness entirely different . . . How to regard them is the question.' As an example, he compared the Mystic Consciousness with the Drunken Consciousness, arguing that alcohol 'stimulates the mystical faculties of human nature, usually crushed to earth by the cold facts and dry criticisms of the sober hour'. In other words, both states of being are part of a larger metaphysical whole. This is not for a moment to suggest that, despite her advocacy of the virtues of wine, Hildegard received her visions in a haze of alcohol, yet the comparison helps us picture a state of mind in which supernatural or hallucinatory sensations might occur.

To people in the Middle Ages, more attuned to the metaphysical workings of the psyche, Hildegard's experiences would have been considered extraordinary rather than abnormal, part of the religious experience at its most elevated. Accepting the fact of mystical seeing, the matter and means of the experience had to be identified. The eleventh century had embraced visionary monastic reformers like St Peter Damian (d. 1072) and St Bruno (d. 1101) whose mystical perceptions were known by their writings, following in a tradition dating back to St Augustine which as yet included few women exemplars. Hildegard was the first known to us today in a strong line of female medieval mystics, many of them German, including in her own time her fellow Benedictine Elisabeth of Schönau, Mechtild of Magdeburg, Mechtild of Hackborn and the sisters Margaret and Christina Ebner in the following century. Her exact contemporary, the English Christina of Markyate (1096/8–1160), had a particularly colourful life. Forced by her parents into marriage, she vowed to remain a virgin and rejected her husband's advances. Her desperate parents attempted to get her drunk and ordered her bridegroom back to rape her. After a series of calamities, she escaped to a hermitage *virgo intacta* and proceeded to have visions. One explanation (until it became politically unfashionable) for this sudden rush of visionary women has always been the natural passivity of mystical experience, supposedly suited to the female condition of receptive submissiveness. The sexual analogy is not irrelevant, nor the related image of women as receptacles or vessels. The active corollary of the visionary gift was that it enabled women to have a voice, where the rest of religious life, preaching, administering the sacraments and so on, firmly shut them out. Among the growing numbers of women renouncing the world and entering convents and anchorages, some would surely have possessed the attributes (spirit visitations, second sight, etc.) which have been such a potent ingredient of the spiritual life of so many cultures.

Hildegard's insistence on *how* her visions occurred had a significance not easily appreciated today. Without recourse to the extensive history of mystical thought, we should distinguish between the various kinds of visionary experience, from vivid imaginings recollected in tranquillity (Wordsworth's 'pensive mood' which allows the daffodils to 'flash upon that inward eye/ Which is the bliss of solitude'), to optical hallucinations or disturbances, to concrete images visited upon a passive recipient. Words used by Hildegard to describe what she saw, generally referred to as *lux vivens*, include 'perceptions', 'illumination', 'reflection of the living Light', 'visionary insight'. In contrast to most other visionaries, she 'saw' when she was fully awake, rather than in a state of ecstasy induced by fasting, hysteria or any other mix of psychological and physical conditions. This was of prime importance. At the end of her life, she described the experience in a letter to Guibert of Gembloux using language similar to that first used in the preface to *Scivias* nearly forty years earlier: 'I do not see with external eyes, and I do not hear it with my external ears; I do not perceive with thoughts of my heart nor by any medium of my five senses, but rather only in my soul, with open eyes, so that I never experience the unconsciousness of ecstasy, but, awake, I see this day and night.'[8]

The Scottish-born mystic Richard of St Victor, Hildegard's contemporary and an inspiration to Dante a century later, called mysticism 'the science of the heart'. Others have named it the 'eye of the soul'. He made a distinction between physical and spiritual types of seeing, which he argued closely and, to a lay person, arcanely in his commentary on the Revelation of St John. Ordinary physical sight is readily understood. He identified a second kind of ordinary sight which possessed a hidden meaning (as when Moses saw the burning bush). In the third (symbolic) type it is the eyes of the heart which see heaven-sent figures and signs.

As far as we can tell, Hildegard came into the third category, seeing figures and signs with an inner eye. The important factor, which she herself considered remarkable and returned to in letters and her theological writings throughout her life, was that her ordinary sight was not interrupted, her visions not the result of daydream or trance or hallucination. What she saw came from the eyes of her soul, not the eyes of her body. The ever-curious Guibert asked, with natural tabloid instinct for detail, whether she received the Lord's words in German, her native tongue, or in Latin, with which she was familiar though not, as she often tells us, at a scholarly level. She appears not to have given Guibert a direct answer, but the implication, from her insistence that her own learning was inadequate for the tenses and syntax, and from her comments elsewhere, is that they occurred in Latin. Clearly this was a matter of interest at the time. Another later visionary, Suso (d. 1385), was subject to the same inquiry, though in his case God spoke to him in German.

Why did Hildegard so determinedly keep her principal gift a secret for more than four decades? In the *Vita*, the monks speculate that she held back 'out of womanly timidity, fear of what people might say, and the rash judgements of others'. It is true that in this she had no female role model. A combination of lack of self-esteem, in later years perhaps more a pretence than a reality, and a dread of retribution from the Church would have been enough to silence anyone. Following St Paul's injunction, women were not allowed to preach. The ruling male clergy were understandably nervous of women finding a voice, quickly discrediting them as foolish, depraved witches suffering from hysteria. Accordingly, women were taught silence and humility as the only way to honour God. Should any display signs of assertion, she was promptly equated with Eve. It was Eve's boldness, after all, which had brought down Mankind. If men, as the early Church Fathers considered, were evil merely from the waist down,[9] women were rotten from head to toe. Little wonder Hildegard portrayed herself as a weak, unlearned creature, a simple vessel of God. The Church permitted her no other view of herself. Two centuries later, in what had become a familiar convention, Julian of Norwich used precisely the same terms of self-reproach, calling herself a mere woman, 'ignorant, weak and frail'. The more mould-breaking and audacious Hildegard's behaviour was to become over the next four decades, the more useful this alibi became – for such, in part, we must allow it to have been. She, too, like other women mystics of the time, sought a male ally to support her (Volmar). Without the protection of the Church, physically and morally if not financially, she would have had no means of survival. Outside the Church, too, women were dependent on fathers, husbands, sons, for their well-being.

In addition, those men who spoke out – famously Peter Abélard and others – had suffered. The progressive and inquiring Abélard, arguing from a radically different point of view from Hildegard, had been condemned, unheard, at the Council of Soissons in 1121. He was briefly imprisoned, his book on the Trinity burnt. Twenty years later Bernard of Clairvaux denounced him again at the Council of Sens in 1140/1. Abélard was forced to recant. Again, his books were burnt. Hildegard's theology, by comparison, was reactionary and in most respects conventional. Merely not being a man could have been trespass enough. Women, forbidden to preach, incurred opprobrium for daring to express themselves at all, rather than for the content of their writings. One, Marguerite de Porete, was burned at the stake, while her book, thought to have been written by a man, was celebrated far and wide.

Finally, at the age of forty-two, shortly after being appointed abbess, the pressure on Hildegard became intolerable. In the midst of another prolonged and severe bout of illness, the call came. We are fortunate to have her own account of the cataclysm which disrupted her private world order:

> And behold! In the forty-third year of my earthly course, as I was gazing with great fear and trembling attention at a heavenly vision, I saw a great splendour in which resounded a voice from Heaven saying to me,
>
> 'O fragile human, ashes of ashes, and filth of filth! Say and write what you see and hear. But since you are timid in speaking, and simple in expounding, and untaught in writing, speak and write these things not by a human

mouth, and not by the understanding of human invention, and not by the requirements of human composition, but as you see and hear them on high in the heavenly places in the wonders of God. Explain these things in such a way that the hearer, receiving the words of his instructor, may expound them in those words, according to that will, vision and instruction. Thus therefore, O human, speak these things that you see and hear. And write them not by yourself or any other human being, but by the will of Him Who knows, sees and disposes all things in the secrets of His mysteries.' And again I heard the voice from Heaven saying to me, 'Speak therefore of these wonders, and being so taught, write them and speak.'

It happened that in the eleven hundred and forty-first year of the Incarnation of the Son of God, Jesus Christ, when I was forty-two years and seven months old, Heaven was opened and a fiery light of exceeding brilliance came and permeated my whole brain and inflamed my whole heart and my whole breast, not like a burning but like a warming flame, as the sun warms anything its rays touch.[10]

At the same time, God's voice as revealed in the vision led Hildegard to the monk Volmar (unnamed) – he who had supported Jutta – so that he might help her in writing down what she saw: 'And she found such a one that loved him, knowing that he was a faithful man, working like herself on another part of the work that leads to Me. And, holding fast to him, she worked with him in great zeal so that My hidden miracles might be revealed' (*Scivias*, Declaration). This friendship, even though we know so little about it, was to become one of the great blessings of her life. As for her state of physical collapse, Hildegard attributed it precisely to the fact that she was an elected being of God, and in this chosen role must inevitably suffer. According to Hildegard's own understanding (as shown to her by God), she had been stricken low, lying immobile, as if dead for the very reason that she was an elected being of God. The history of mysticism throws up numerous examples of seers collapsing, psychically or physically, as part of the visionary process.

Later writers have regarded this period of suffering as a time of temptation, purgation and cleansing. Elisabeth of Schönau, a correspondent of Hildegard, claimed an angel had beaten her until she agreed to admit to her visions. Catherine of Siena, whose methods of purgation were excessive and beside whom Hildegard appears a model of restraint, was visited repeatedly by fiends uttering obscenities and tempting her with lust. Hildegard may have been fully conscious when she had her visions, but she seems to have fallen into some sort of cataleptic trance beforehand. Her own accounts of her physical suffering are told in powerful language. She speaks of her womb convulsing, extinguishing her bodily powers until she no longer knew herself, unable to see or move. Her monk biographers describe her suddenly rising from her bed and pacing the anchorage from corner to corner, 'all the while unable to speak'. Elisabeth of Schönau, Hildegard's contemporary, went into a trance, was unable to speak and often lost consciousness when her visions occurred. A later mystic, St Teresa, describes how, in a trance, it is impossible to speak or open your eyes, the hands become cold and stiff 'and straight as pieces of wood'.

From another culture, early in the twentieth century the Indian visionary Krishnamurti wrote of an acute pain at the nape of his neck and a state of semi-consciousness which preceded his visions, regularly occurring at 6.30 each evening:

> I toss about, groan and moan and mutter strange things, in fact almost behave like one possessed. I get up, thinking somebody is calling me, and collapse on the floor; I rave considerably, see strange faces and light. All the time, I have a violent pain in my head and the nape of my neck and can't bear the touch of anyone. Also during that time,

I become very sensitive, can't bear a sound however small it may be. I feel so tired and exhausted while the whole thing is going on. Sometimes the whole thing becomes very acute, and force has to be used to keep me down and other times it is quite mild. After it is over, I remember some parts of the scene I had been creating; then I have my food and retire to bed.[11]

His brother Nitya, in a letter, gave an identical account of Krishnamurti's experience, adding that his pain centred 'mostly in the spine, so we have surmised that his *kundalini* is being awakened'. In Yoga philosophy, a force called *kundalini* or 'serpent fire' resides in the base of the spine. Its release, often with excruciating pain, also liberates powers of clairvoyancy.

Oliver Sacks, the British neurologist, has put forward a convincing case for Hildegard's visions, and their attendant illnesses, as resulting from migraine attacks. That she appears to have been chronically ill throughout her life points to the likelihood of such a condition, rather than to a series of different disorders. The visual disturbances, nausea, rushing and roaring sensation, abdominal pain, trance-like drowsiness, muscular weakness, epileptic-like attacks and pallor Sacks lists among symptoms certainly tally with those attributed to Hildegard and which she herself described. Oddly she makes no mention of headaches, but as Sacks points out, it is a mistake to define migraine in such narrow terms. In *Causae et Curae* Hildegard identifies migraine, caused by a preponderance of black bile, as just another form of headache affecting parts of the head rather than its entirety. The abruptness of her description suggests she did not connect the malady with her own catalogue of afflictions, though she does admit that it is hard to cure 'because it is difficult to calm black bile and the bad humours simultaneously'. In his study of the condition, Sacks cites as unique Hildegard's account of the aura which precedes an attack. He observes, too, that it was not so much that her visions were rare, rather that she had the ability to open herself to them, as other grumbling sufferers would not:

> *Invested with this sense of ecstasy, burning with profound theophorous and philosophical significance, Hildegard's visions were instrumental in directing her towards a life of holiness and mysticism. They provide a unique example of the manner in which a physiological event, banal, hateful or meaningless to the vast majority of people, can become, in a privileged consciousness, the substrate of a supreme ecstatic inspiration.* [12]

Sacks was not the first to make such a connection. The theory of Hildegard having suffered migraines was first developed early last century by Charles Singer, who identified key features of her visions in this context:

> *In all, a prominent feature is a point or a group of points of light, which shimmer and move, usually in a wave-like manner, and are often interpreted as stars or flaming eyes. In quite a number of cases one light, larger than the rest, exhibits a series of concentric circular figures or wavering form; and often definite fortification figures are described, radiating, in some cases, from a coloured area. Often the lights gave that impression of working, boiling or fermenting described by so many visionaries.* [13]

One Hildegard scholar and migraine sufferer, Madeline H. Caviness, has argued that Hildegard's medical condition makes it all the more likely that she had a direct hand (always a matter of dispute) in the celebrated illuminations for the Rupertsberg *Scivias*, 'since she was the one with migraine and knew these effects at first hand'. [14]

Let us pause, for a moment, from visionary puzzlings to consider the more practical aspects of how Hildegard and her newly appointed secretary Volmar might have worked together. In the existing contemporary, or near-contemporary, depictions of Hildegard, she is seen with a wax tablet and stylus in her hand. The frequently reproduced image (seen on the cover of this book) of Hildegard receiving the lashing flames of Divine revelation from on high prompts several questions. What is Hildegard incising on her wax tablet? Is it a memorandum or a fully developed account of her vision? Is it a first draft, later transcribed to parchment? How does this relate to Volmar, peeping from behind a pillar in wait? Did she read her initial rushed thoughts to him and leave it to him to shape into formal prose? To what extent was he a co-author? What materials and techniques might have been used?

The last is easier to answer than the rest. Disibodenberg, like other monastic institutions, would have had a scriptorium, or writing room, in which books were made. There being no other method of reproduction, the copying of the scriptures and works of the Church Fathers (Augustine, Ambrose, Boethius and so on) for the monastery library was a full-time occupation. Around 1100, a good monastic collection might have numbered two to three hundred books. By 1200, Durham had 546 volumes; by 1250 the Sorbonne had around a thousand. Furthermore, making books, an act of piety as well as of practical use, helped monks honour the Rule of St Benedict, which instructed that part of the day should be spent in manual labour. Most were produced anonymously, though some carry the signature of the monk (or nun) who made it, usually as a picture or a riddle, since expressions of individuality were not encouraged. Eadwine, the scribe of Christchurch, Canterbury, in the 1140s, was rare in singing his own praises ('Fame proclaims your writing forever, Eadwine').

Nuns and monks often shared the work of copying, though usually the women were at the service of men. An astronomical treatise made in 1154 shows a portrait of the illuminator, Brother

Sintram, with his scribe, Guta, canoness of the sister house of Schwarzenhann. In the depiction of Hildegard with Volmar, and with her nun Richardis, the roles are subtly reversed. Disibodenberg was well placed for Worms, Metz and Trier, all cities famed as centres of scholarship where books were translated, copied and illuminated. The works of all the great Christian thinkers of the day (such as Abélard, Peter Lombard and Bernard of Clairvaux) and recently translated works from Greek and Latin, Jewish and Arabic sources would have been borrowed and copied for their libraries. We do not know what was available to Hildegard, but her scientific writings, especially, demonstrate a wide range of knowledge and familiarity with works from outside as well as within the Christian tradition.

Most of these books would have been written in the formal, rounded pre-Gothic script known as Carolingian minuscule (named after Charlemagne). Those monks making books for their own use might have used an abbreviated, more informal style. Vellum, in short supply but long-lasting and recyclable, was prepared from the autumn slaughter of sheep, cows or goats, thus efficiently reducing the number having to be fed throughout winter. Disibodenberg, judging from its terrain, would have had a good flock of sheep. The preparation was elaborate. Scribes or lay clerks had to soak the skin in alum and lime and stretch it on a frame. They cut it to size, pricked it with an awl and rubbed the skin with pumice to remove grease. The process of ruling up the page, working out how many words could appear on each page and how many bifolia (double sheets folded into quires, later sewn together) would be needed was exacting. Quills, the main writing implement, were made from the primary wing feathers of geese, crows or swans. They were inconvenient, messy and needed frequent resharpening. A twelfth-century account of ink-making describes the boiling of bark from hawthorn wood with water and wine until it becomes thick and black. Another method was to boil oak galls and iron salts, so that this potent mixture would burn into the writing surface. Amendments could be made by scratching out the error with a knife, one of the scribe's most vital tools.

Who made Hildegard's corrections? The recent growth of interest in women's history, not well represented in this period since most surviving documents derive from monasteries and were written by monks, has led to heated debate over the extent to which Hildegard wrote her own works and allowed them to be edited or embellished by her male secretaries. Hildegard's manuscripts show two main kinds of correction: regarding Latin syntax and regarding content. Even if Volmar was permitted to adjust grammar or spelling, he is unlikely to have been allowed to tamper with meaning. Hildegard's repeated lament is that she was *indoctam*, unlearned, a mere vessel of God through whom the complexities of scripture and language became clear. Guibert says she was 'uneducated as to learning in the grammatical art . . . having a knowledge of the psalter in the manner of women, reading scripture simply, without the sharpening of wit of their senses'. He also suggests that Volmar 'clothed her naked and unpolished words with fitting style'. The *Vita* describes how 'she wrote down in her own hand or from her mouth dictated the contents in their disarrayed state to a certain faithful male attendant. He then rendered their cases, tenses and conjugations according to the exactness of the grammatical art which she did not have, but he presumed to add nothing at all to them, nor tried to interpret their sense of meaning.'[15]

Was this emphasis on Hildegard's inadequacy merely a useful foil? From the point of view of the Church's attitude towards women daring to speak, the more ignorance she could claim, the safer her position. True, her scholarship may have had a less rigorous grounding than that of her male colleagues. Perhaps this subterfuge, if such it was, is best exposed by the fact that Hildegard was invited to speak and sermonise to learned monks, which surely would not have been possible without some good command of Latin. She may have preferred, however, simply to devote herself to the bigger purpose rather than to the mechanics of its expression, by canny choice rather than lack of education. Great leaders customarily rely on subordinates to enact plans, presidents on speech writers for the articulation of their policies, writers on copy editors to spot errors. Management structures have always been based on a hierarchical division of thinkers and doers. Why should Hildegard, busy running a monastery, consulting dignitaries, writing letters and seeing visions, have had any wish to correct her own grammar when others could do it for her?[16]

We must consider, too, the manner and speed at which Hildegard's often highly allusive and enigmatic visions occurred. She may have been unaware of any precedent for her divine communications. Scanning back through the subsequent literature of mysticism, the marvel is how consistent certain factors prove, especially the helplessness of the individual to challenge or prevent the experience. Thus in the seventeenth century the highly emotional Madame Guyon, not among the more sophisticated or intellectual of mystics, describes finding the need to take up her pen and write as if by invisible command, often at the most inconvenient moments. 'In writing I saw that I was writing of things I had never seen . . . I was given light to perceive that I had in me treasures of knowledge and understanding which I did not know that I possessed.' The words flowed so thick and fast that one of her longest works was completed in a day and a half. Similarly William Blake, in a letter, spoke of his *Milton* and *Jerusalem* arriving with comparable expedition: 'I have written the poems from immediate dictation, twelve or sometimes twenty or thirty lines at a time, without premeditation and even against my will. The time it has taken in writing was thus rendered non-existent, and an immense poem exists which seems to be the labour of a long life, all produced without labour or study.'

If we take into account the sheer volume of material Hildegard produced in her lifetime, especially given her full-time preoccupation with the external world as well as that of the spirit, it seems likely she and Blake had much in common, and that the long-suffering Volmar may have been burdened by an outpouring of words, scratched on wax tablets at immense speed. Scribes of the Middle Ages frequently begged relief from their labours, preferring to work in summer because of the better light and warmth for work which required sitting bent over a desk for hours. It was not uncommon for monks to plead cold hands and cramped joints as an excuse not to copy the manuscript of a visiting traveller. An interim measure was the quicker task of scribbling on to a wax tablet, later committing the work to vellum. One twelfth-century writer asks his reader to remember the labour which has gone into the volume before him, work which is 'heavy; it makes the eyes misty, bows the back, crushes the ribs and belly, brings pain to the kidneys, and makes the body ache all over . . . As the sailor finds welcome in the final harbour, so does the scribe the final line.'

After the writing had been completed, the text was passed to another hand to add rubrics (titles and initial letters in red). The table of contents, in the first version (but not in later copies), could only be added later when the work was complete. From the amendments and interpolations in the earliest surviving copy of Hildegard's works, the Ghent manuscript of *Liber divinorum operum*, at least one scholar has concluded that the 'first parchment copy' could have been copied straight from one of Hildegard's wax tablets,[17] and that it was not written continuously from beginning to end. To a modern reader, these subtleties of scholarly inquisition seem impossibly remote. Yet such small shreds of evidence cannot be ignored, any more than we can discount Beethoven's sketches for his symphonies or Ezra Pound's pruning of T. S. Eliot's *The Waste Land*. They take us back directly to Hildegard herself. Her gainsayers prefer to argue an absence of proof for Hildegard having any true authorship over the works attributed to her. The general reader must register such findings and decide whether or not they matter. This is scholarship in progress, with findings as yet inconclusive.

Once the text was finished, the manuscript was passed to an artist for illumination, itself another lengthy procedure. Bernard of Clairvaux frowned at the luxurious gold plate and elaboration of his fellow monks at Cluny and ordered that manuscripts should be written in one colour only, without illumination. Hildegard, not averse to small pleasures, evidently had few such qualms. No one knows who executed the remarkably vivid and apocalyptic illuminations for her visions, especially those of *Scivias*, to which we shall return, but it is impossible not to think she had a guiding hand. We do know that the loyal Volmar was helped in his task by Richardis, daughter of the Countess of Stade in Saxony. Richardis, Hildegard's acknowledged favourite, was later to provide us with the most vivid insight we possess, not always favourable, into her mistress's character.

CHAPTER FIVE

PAPAL APPROVAL

Who is this woman who rises out of the wilderness like a column of smoke from burning spices?

(POPE EUGENE III, QUOTING SONG OF SONGS, 3:6)

For the man is the sower, but the woman is the recipient of the seed.

(SCIVIAS, I, II)

Her appointment as abbess (or pro-abbess as, strictly speaking, she should be called) revolutionised Hildegard's life. Just how remarkable this transformation was cannot be emphasised too strongly. She was now in her early forties, from our perspective a woman in her prime poised for fulfilment. From the vantage point of the 1140s, however, with life expectancy short, the picture was different. Abbot Cuno, in charge at Disibodenberg, may have regarded the task of overseeing a small group of nuns, hidden away in the relative obscurity of this quiet hillside, as an ideal way for this unusual and obdurate woman to see out her twilight years. If so, how wrong, how naïvely misguided, he would prove. Had Hildegard, like Jutta, died in middle age, she would have left us nothing except a few written visions and a song or two. There would be no cult, no story. Instead, an entirely new existence, of burgeoning creativity and industry, fame and celebrity, lay ahead of her.

Until that moment, from the age of eight, her every move had been governed by monks and elders, rules and restrictions. Any notion of self-expression was quelled, by herself or others. Her one aim in life was obedience, submission, silence, self-denial, in effect to make herself invisible to the world. This is still the expectation of those enclosed in holy orders. Now, for the first time, she had a degree of independence, a voice, a means of utterance. After years of pent-up silence, how masterful, loquacious and richly fertile that self-expression was to grow. According to the *Vita*, she now began writing music for the first time, songs for her nuns to sing as part of the Divine Office. Far more important, thanks to establishing a *modus vivendi* with Volmar, her first visionary work was under way.

Entitled *Scivias*, which might be translated as 'Know the Way' (almost a Latin equivalent of Tao), it remains today her best-known work. Ten years in the making, this three-part account of Creation, Redemption and Salvation would transfigure her existence. It consists of twenty-six visions, including illuminations. Alone it would have guaranteed her a place in theological history. Yet *Scivias* was merely a beginning. Five more major works, nearly 400 letters and eighty songs were to follow over the next four decades.

Word of Hildegard's community quickly spread. The monks, eclipsed by her flourishing reputation yet beneficiaries of it, cannot have been wholly delighted. Disibodenberg had not been built or intended as a double cloister. The sisters were there by default, an adjunct to the monks, who enjoyed their own petty importance as an outpost for the primping prelates of Mainz. They had extended their hospitality to the noble Jutta and her young oblate out of a combination of duty and expedience, squeezing her cell into a corner out of view but happy to enhance their own good standing in the region with an in-house anchoress. Now they were being upstaged by women. By 1140, two years after Jutta's death, the number of nuns residing on the cramped site had risen from a dozen to eighteen. All were of noble lineage. Of the few whose names we know, two were from Jutta's family: her cousin Richardis of Stade, and her niece Hiltrud, Hildegard's childhood friend. Strictly speaking, Hildegard and her nuns were answerable to the monks and Abbot Cuno. The chain of command led up through the monks and the abbot to the Archbishop of Mainz. Later, when the time came for Hildegard to found a new monastery, this hierarchical edifice would house and cause a festering dispute. Yet already, despite the monks, Hildegard had established her own, often quite contrary, way of doing things. Status emboldened her. Always insisting that she acted as the 'mouthpiece of God', constantly pleading her own feeble femininity, her actions had begun to court publicity. The behaviour of the nuns, their lavish dress and immodest deportment, as we shall see, broke St Benedict's rules and drew adverse attention.

Nevertheless, Hildegard remained profoundly anxious about her visions, originally a private matter between herself and Volmar. Her secretary had in turn confided in Cuno, which led to a flurry of events. That their sequence remains vague is immaterial, since together they all led to one outcome: the recognition of Hildegard as a seer and prophet. First Cuno, at once nervous of harbouring a possible heretic and doubtless a little boastful about having a visionary under his very nose, reported the abbess's strange visitations to Heinrich, Archbishop of Mainz (who had recently consecrated the abbey church at Disibodenberg, at last completed after nearly forty years). Never one to miss an opportunity for preferment, but also impressed with Hildegard's evident powers, Heinrich informed Pope Eugene III, who sent envoys to Disibodenberg to investigate for himself. The notion of a delegation of prelates thundering across the Palatinate, straining up the final steep climb and arriving breathless at the monastery gate demanding to see the abbess has a certain absurd filmic quality. Nevertheless, the Pope's intention was serious: heresy undermined papal authority and all theological writings were in one sense political. The Pope's envoys were satisfied with what they found, confident of Hildegard's authenticity. They even borrowed the half-finished *Scivias* to show the Pope, 'and reported what they had heard to him and all his attendants, who had been waiting most expectantly'.[1]

About the same time, 1147, Hildegard wrote one of her first surviving letters, to Bernard of Clairvaux, by now one of the most august and venerable of Church leaders. Why did she unburden herself to him? She was forty-nine; he was nearly sixty. Clearly she felt the need of a higher authority to endorse her writings and visions. His reputation as a spiritual firebrand, built up over his thirty years as a deeply ascetic Cistercian, made him a formidable figure throughout Europe. By all

accounts, his extreme holiness and evangelising wisdom notwithstanding, he was not a sympathetic character, a fiery zealot
with little empathy for those who disagreed with him, notably
the theologian and logician Peter Abélard. Bernard was
Abélard's chief opponent in one of the most keenly fought
doctrinal duels of the time (which led to Abélard's excommunication). Hildegard's letter shows a tone of genuine diffidence
which would become uncommon as her own sense of authority
developed and her voice grew more strident. It is not surprising
that she should have had qualms about disturbing a man whom
she did not know and who, in addition to all his other burdens,
was trying to organise a Holy War, gathering men 'into Christ's
army to fight under the banner of the cross against pagan
savagery' (as she put it). She confessed everything, in phras-
eology which was to form the basis of other tellings:

> *Father, I am greatly disturbed by a vision which has*
> *appeared to me through divine revelation, a vision seen not*
> *with my fleshly eyes but only in my spirit. Wretched, and*
> *indeed more than wretched in my womanly condition, I*
> *have from earliest childhood seen great marvels which my*
> *tongue has power to express but which the Spirit of God has*
> *taught me that I may believe. Steadfast and gentle father, in*
> *your kindness respond to me, your unworthy servant who*
> *has never, from her earliest childhood, lived one hour free*
> *from anxiety. In your piety and wisdom look in your spirit,*
> *as you have been taught by the Holy Spirit, and from your*
> *heart bring comfort to your handmaiden.*

The letter continues to relate how, despite her poor education
and lack of knowledge, she understands the deep meaning of
these visions, which she has dared share with only one man, 'a
certain monk' (Volmar), because of the 'many heresies abroad in
the land'. She begs consolation from Bernard because she has
seen him in a vision, 'like a man looking into the sun, bold and

unafraid', and implores him to reply. She goes on to describe the severe malady which she has suffered as a result of her silence:

> *In the meantime, because I have kept silent about this vision, I have been laid low, bedridden in my infirmities, and am unable to raise myself up.*
>
> *Therefore I weep with sorrow before you. For in my nature, I am unstable because I am caught in the winepress, that tree rooted in Adam by the devil's deceit which brought about his exile into this wayward world. Yet now, rising up, I run to you. And I say to you: You are not inconstant but are always lifting up the tree, a victor in your spirit, lifting up not only yourself but also the whole world unto salvation. You are indeed the eagle gazing directly at the sun.[2]*

She concludes with an image of the fruitful womb of the Virgin being like a honeycomb (alluding to bees as a symbol of the Immaculate Conception and of the Holy Ghost) and a final request for a speedy reply, urging him to 'be a mighty warrior for God'. Bernard's abrupt response even today has the familiar feel of a standard letter from the desk of one in high office. That she received a reply at all was surely exceptional. He writes: '. . . I have made some effort to respond to your letter of love, although the press of business forces me to respond more briefly than I would have liked.'

The 'press of business' to which he refers was no doubt the not inconsiderable matter of the Second Crusade, which Bernard preached at Pope Eugene III's behest at Vézelay in 1146, in the presence of King Louis VII and his wife, Eleanor of Aquitaine. Some 200,000 men and a number of noble women, including Eleanor herself (a disciple of Bernard at that time, as well as mother of a two-year-old child), were marching forth to the Holy Land at that very moment, though the prophet of Clairvaux himself declined to take part. The ensuing disaster was to dent Bernard's reputation. Later, in an address (*De consideratione*) to

Eugene III, he sought justification for having obeyed God's command, arguing that 'this sad and unexpected outcome cannot be blamed on the foolhardiness of the leader'. No wonder he kept his letter to Hildegard brief. In a more personal tone and not without admiration, he urges her to recognise 'this gift as grace and to respond eagerly to it with all humility', while pleading his own poor abilities in advising on such matters. To conclude, he beseeches her to pray for his community.[3]

The two separate matters of Bernard's letter and the papal inquiry came together, to Hildegard's incalculable benefit (as reported in the *Vita*) at the Synod of Trier, which took place between November 1147 and February 1148. Eugene III had been a pupil of Bernard. Whether because of the call to arms of the Second Crusade or to support the Pope, Bernard was in the Rhineland and attended the Synod. Hildegard was not present, and no account exists of the two ever meeting (Trithemius, writing Hildegard's life three centuries later, claims they met at this time, but he is alone in this view. A fanciful engraving also depicts them together at Trier). Eugene III read passages from *Scivias* to the assembled prelates, at which point Bernard intervened and spoke in favour of Hildegard. It is rewarding to picture the assemblage of bishops, cardinals and clergy in their ornate robes listening to the Pope with growing scorn, only to have their scepticism silenced by the endorsement of the holy Bernard. The Pope, who had recently given his blessing to the innovative writings of Odo of Soissons, may have found Hildegard's views orthodox in comparison. In any case, he sanctioned her work and encouraged her to continue with her prophetic mode of thinking and writing.

The monks of Disibodenberg must have begun to ask themselves whether, in some sense, a plot had misfired. Far from being discredited, or put in her place, Hildegard had become the focus of the attention of the Pope himself. As a result of the Synod of Trier their abbess, until then only a minor local celebrity, was suddenly famous. Already her advice was being sought far and wide from every level of society. A letter written shortly after the Synod by Bertolf, an abbot who was present when the Pope read from *Scivias*, celebrates 'the fame of your virtue' and her womanhood: 'Indeed you have far exceeded your sex by having surpassed with manly spirit that which we were afraid even to approach.'[4] Jealousies began to surface. Of all the various contemporary biographies written about Hildegard and the many surviving letters to her, only one is openly antagonistic. As a source of information about how Hildegard was viewed, and how she ran her convent, it is invaluable.

The correspondent is Tenxwind, superior of a foundation of canonesses at nearby Andernach on the Rhine. It was probably written in or around 1150 (or, it can be argued, later in Hildegard's life when the Rupertsberg convent was at the height of its wealth and celebrity). With polite but lightly veiled malice, Tenxwind attacks Hildegard on several fronts. This celebrated letter is known to have been revised, and may have been neutered by her hagiographers in the recipient's favour. Nevertheless, its blade remains sharp, its rhetoric skilful. Once you appreciate the degree of hostility underlying the flattery, the document becomes perilously comic, like Mistress Quickly writing to Falstaff. First Tenxwind praises the saintliness of Hildegard, 'mistress of the brides of Christ', reports of whose holiness, endowed by an angel from on high, have spread far and wide, even to the lowly sisters of Andernach. After a preliminary sentence or two in this ingratiating vein, she aims her tweezers and tugs. 'We have, however, also heard about certain strange and irregular practices that you countenance.'

These irregular goings-on concerned the manner in which Hildegard's nuns adorned themselves, as brides of Christ, with flowing hair, jewels and crowns. Such behaviour wholly contradicted the Rule as written by St Benedict and feminised by Caesarius of Arles in his sixth-century Rule for Nuns, which states plainly: 'Let them have all their clothing in a simple and

respectable colour . . . There is never to be anything covered
or decorated with embroidery or needlework . . . Let not
your apparel be notable, nor should you aspire to please
in your clothing . . .'[5] For nuns, having their head shorn,
usually four times a year, was mandatory. Hair worn
flowing and uncovered was permitted among upper-class
secular women but not the lower orders. Tellingly, it also
signified female authority. The thirteenth-century English
Ancrene Riwle followed well-established convention when it
forbade women jewellery, 'neither ring, nor brooch, nor ornamented girdle, nor gloves, nor any such thing that is not proper'.
St Clare, follower of St Francis in the same century, urged her
nuns 'to wear cheap garments out of love for the most holy and
beloved child who lied wrapped in such poor swaddling clothes'.

Closer to home, Hildegard's ally, Bernard of Clairvaux, in
his famous *Apologia* attacking the Cluniacs' lax way of life, had
spelled out his attitude: 'Soft clothing is a sign of moral flabbi-
ness: the body would not be decked out with such care had not
neglect first left the soul unkempt and bare of virtues.' Hildegard
was indeed walking perilously. In her second visionary book,
the *Liber vitae meritorum*, she sees the virgins in paradise dressed
in gowns of purest gold and decked with precious jewels,
wearing on their heads 'golden crowns studded with gems and
entwined with roses and lilies'. The Rupertsberg Codex of
Scivias, too, has many illustrations of women in golden crowns
with flowing hair, notably those representing Ecclesia (the
Church) and her counterpart Synagoga (Synagogue, or 'Mother
of the Incarnation'). In the same work Hildegard exemplifies
Chastity as 'clothed in a robe more full of light than crystal'.
Tenxwind's equally graphic picture conjures a garden of earthly
delights straight out of Hieronymus Bosch or Botticelli, full of
Rossetti's Blessed Damozels. The monks must have thought
themselves in a seventh heaven. Tenxwind writes:

They say that on feast days your virgins stand in the church

with unbound hair when singing the psalms and that as
part of their dress they wear white, silk veils, so long they
touch the floor. Moreover, it is said that they wear crowns of
gold filigree, into which are inserted crosses on both sides
and the back, with a figure of the Lamb on the front, and
that they adorn their fingers with golden rings. And all this
despite the prohibition of the great shepherd of the Church,
who writes in admonition: Let women comport themselves
with modesty 'not with plaited hair, or gold, or pearls or
costly attire' [I Tim. 2:9].[6]

Tenxwind then criticises Hildegard's unashamed habit of
allowing only noble women in to her convent, absolutely
rejecting 'others who are of lower birth and less wealth'. With
barely disguised smugness and a pretence of confusion, she
admonishes her counterpart with apt quotations from the
Scriptures. Her letter closes with an exquisite show of bemused
humility, the grovelling tone reminiscent of a punctilious correspondent in the letters page of *The Times* challenging the brash
audacity of a star columnist:

O worthy bride of Christ, such unheard of practices far
exceed the capacity of our weak understanding, and strike
us with no little wonder. And although we feeble little
women wholeheartedly rejoice with all the esteem due your
spiritual success, we still wish you to inform us on some
points relative to this matter. Therefore, we have decided to
send this humble little letter to you, saintly lady, asking by
whose authority you can defend such practices, and we
devoutly and meekly beseech, worthy lady, that you do not
disdain to write back to us as soon as possible. Farewell,
and remember us in your prayers.

As we might expect, Hildegard remained unmoved by this
verbal onslaught. Her long reply addresses the criticisms in

full. Throughout, infuriatingly for the recipient no doubt, her tone is composed, soothing and placatory. Nevertheless, the language is extravagant in comparison with that of the severe Tenxwind, with frequent reference to her cherished notion of *viriditas*, a singularly Hildegardian concept translated variously as greenness, vigour, youthful freshness. She praises woman-kind in all her beauty and variety: 'O, woman, what a splendid thing you are! For you have set your foundation in the sun, and have conquered the world.'

On the question of apparel Hildegard claims, with precious little scriptural evidence, that these rules of physical propriety apply only to married women (who have already succumbed to the serpent), not to virgins who can still equate themselves with Eve before the Fall. As St Jerome wrote: 'Eve in Paradise was a virgin: it was only after she put on a garment of skins that her married life began. Paradise is your home. Keep therefore as you were born . . .' His last remark suggests nothing can have been further from his mind than that these pure virgins adorn themselves in tiaras and flowing white robes. Hildegard, how-ever, maintains that a married woman is like a plant deflowered by winter, her innocent beauty ravaged; she should only wear a crown or golden ornaments 'at her husband's pleasure, and even then with moderation'. Conversely, or perhaps conven-iently, a virgin is free of such strictures, for she stands in the 'unsullied purity of paradise, lovely and unwithering, and she always remains in the full vitality of the budding rose'. Con-juring her proof as if from thin air, she asserts that 'A virgin is not commanded to cover her hair, but she willingly does so out of her great humility, for a person will naturally hide the beauty of her soul lest, on account of her pride, the hawk carry it off.' Citing the Revelation of St John, Hildegard sums up:

> *Thus through the permission granted her and the revelation*
> *of the mystic inspiration of the finger of God, it is appropriate*
> *for a virgin to wear a white vestment, the lucent symbol of*

*her betrothal to Christ, considering that her mind is made
one with the interwoven whole, and keeping in mind the
One to whom she is joined, as it is written: 'Having his
name and the name of his Father, written on their foreheads'*
[Rev. 14:1] *and also 'These follow the Lamb whithersoever
he goeth'* [Rev. 14:4].

Near the end of her life Hildegard elaborated her theory of
the symbolism of dress for consecrated virgins in a letter to
Guibert of Gembloux, who, years later (in 1175), audaciously
wrote to the seventy-seven-year-old woman asking whether it
was 'by divine revelations or merely for the sake of ornamentation that you have your virgins wear crowns'. Furthermore, he
had heard that not all the crowns were the same and begged an
explanation as to the various distinctions between them. In her
reply, Hildegard attributed her symbolic use of crowns to a vision:

*I saw that all the orders of the church have distinct emblems
according to their celestial brightness, but that virginity has
no such distinguishing emblem save the black veil and the
sign of the cross. And I saw that a white veil to cover a
virgin's head was to be the proper emblem of virginity. For
this veil stands for the white garment which man once had,
but subsequently lost, in Paradise. Furthermore, upon the
virgin's head is to be set a circlet of three colours joined into
one. For this circlet stands for the Holy Trinity. To this circlet
four others are to be joined: in the front bearing the Lamb of
God; the right, a cherubim; the left, an angel; and the one
behind, man. For all of these are pendants to the Trinity.
This sign given by God will bless God, for He once clothed
the first man in the whiteness of light. All of this is fully
described in* Scivias, *as well as other volumes, according to a
true vision, and I continue my writing up to the present day.*[7]

On the sticky matter of social snobbery in her convent,

she proves equally adroit. She believed, like many at the time, that mankind existed in hierarchies like the angels. The notion that human beings might be born equal seems not to have troubled her. In this respect, and in a different age, it is hard not to side with Tenxwind. Hildegard finds evidence in the animal kingdom, arguing that different species should be kept apart and that muddling them all together would lead to problems of ambition and rejection. She argues the same point in the *Physica*, condemning animals or fish which breed outside their kind as acting against nature, 'as we can notice in eels' (a creature ineluctably suggestive of a serpent). The celebrated vision, in *Scivias*, of the people carrying milk in vessels and making cheeses, some thick and strong, others thin, weak and curdled, is explained as exemplifying the inequality of human seed and the variety of people made from it. Moreover, using apocalyptic imagery, she paints a black picture of what might ensue if high- and low-born live under one roof. She omits to mention that noble women come with better dowries:

> God also keeps a watchful eye on every person, so that a lower order will not gain ascendancy over a higher one, as Satan and the first man did, who wanted to fly higher than they had been placed. And who would gather all his livestock indiscriminately into one barn – the cattle, the asses, the sheep, the kids? Thus it is clear that differentiation must be maintained in these matters, lest people of varying status, herded all together, be dispersed through the pride of their elevation on the one hand, or the disgrace of their decline, on the other, and especially lest the nobility of their character be torn asunder when they slaughter one another out of hatred. Such destruction naturally results when the higher order falls upon the lower, and the lower rises above the higher. For God establishes ranks on earth, just as in heaven with angels, archangels, thrones, dominions, cherubim and seraphim. And they are all loved by God, although they are not equal in rank.[8]

Scholars, properly more concerned to establish facts than to read character, have been surprisingly respectful of Hildegard's rhetoric in this famous and telling exchange, one or two raising an eyebrow at its blithe confidence but most happy to accept the fascinating document as it stands, without scepticism. Yet it is impossible not to gasp at her temerity. As ever, she signs off with the plea that 'these words do not come from a human being but from the Living Light'.[9] The same alibi which once seemed so modest (disavowal of personal responsibility for visionary gleams) now serves an arrogation of luminous power. Whether the genesis is human or divine, the logic is rocky. Her comparison of a married woman to a plant withered by winter collapses under scrutiny since spring and rebirth, as Hildegard observes again and again, are essential to the natural process. Using animals as a metaphor for humans is still more preposterous (and to us, perhaps sinister), since humans are of one species, animals of many.

No one can argue, though many try, that Hildegard was a liberal. In all her thinking, however novel and innovative its mode, she was a reactionary, a soulmate to the conservative and mystical Bernard of Clairvaux rather than to the scholastic and questing (though not always progressive) Peter Abélard. Nowhere is this more evident than here. She regarded women as of secondary importance to men, except in her own, divinely inspired case. We must beware of transposing these deep-rooted beliefs, typical of their era, to our own times. Her negative attitude towards Jews, expressed in *Scivias* and elsewhere, was in keeping with Orthodox and Christian thought in the Middle Ages. It is perhaps no coincidence that several centuries later the revival of interest in Hildegard at the time of the 750th anniversary of her death in 1929 was linked to a stirring of interest not only in the Catholic Church but also in German national identity at the end of the Weimar Republic. Indeed, some recent commentators have hinted darkly at such a connection. To burden Hildegard with the consequences of that revival is as foolish as to blame Wagner for the policies of Hitler. To acknowledge a hint of authoritarianism running away with itself, and its moral dangers attendant, none the less seems unavoidable.

CHAPTER SIX

THE MOVE TO RUPERTSBERG

Since an anchoress's small dwelling could scarcely house them all, she was soon engaged in a quest for more spacious quarters to which they might transfer. She was shown by the Spirit a place where the river Nahe flows into the Rhine, a hill dedicated in days of old to the name of St Rupert the Confessor . . . [Her abbot and the monks] were unenthusiastic . . .'

(*VITA*, I, V)

What good is it for well-born and wealthy girls to pass from a place where they lacked nothing into such penury?

(*VITA*, II, V)

Within three years of the critical Synod of Trier, Hildegard had the world at her feet. She was fifty, and had acted as abbess (though still holding the title unofficially, as she always would) for a decade. Disibodenberg lacked space, but life there was familiar and comfortable by the standards of the time, thanks to the increasing number of dowries brought by noble nuns whose families naturally wanted to protect their daughters' institution with wealth. Hildegard had papal approval and her work could continue in freedom. The burden of being confined with Volmar and Richardis in the scriptorium for hours on end, while also maintaining numerous public and spiritual duties, was glamorised by the trappings of fame, though she may not have expressed it in such terms. A steady stream of august international figures began to pay homage and seek counsel from this 'poor little woman' who had caught the Pope's imagination so vividly.

The *Vita* says that 'crowds of people of both sexes came flocking to her', not only from the locality but 'from every part of threefold Gaul and from Germany'. Her celebrated powers of prophecy enabled her to divine the inner minds and consciences of those who visited her. She knew what the timid wanted to say before they opened their mouths. She recognised the dissemblers, who came 'as if to try her out' and were chastened by her astuteness. She blessed the physically sick, advised the spiritually infirm and welcomed those in need, friends or strangers. She even agreed to subject herself to cross-examination by some of the many Jews in the area (Mainz had an important rabbinical school and a large Jewish community at the time), apparently coercing them into Christianity, 'urging them on to faith in Christ with words of devout warning'.[1] Her eighteen or twenty nuns, nearly double the number at the time of Jutta's death, must have hoped for a period of certainty and calm, their well-regulated existence brightened by the dash of celebrity their abbess attracted. Life might have continued in this manner indefinitely. They surely assumed it would.

Hildegard had other aims. Or, as she affirmed, God had another purpose for her, revealed to her in yet another spell-binding and debilitating vision. He wanted her to build a new monastery. Given the conditions at Disibodenberg, her growing aspirations and her desire for independence, she must already have debated with herself the need to move her sisters else-where, away from the men and with more space. She may, too, have considered forty-odd years long enough to remain in one place. Immediately 'the virgin of God learned of the place they were to move to', she announced her intentions to Abbot Cuno and the monks. The place decreed was Rupertsberg, a small mountain about thirty kilometres away, roughly a day's journey, where the river Nahe joins the Rhine at Bingen. Hildegard would have passed this conspicuous site on which a ruined monastery stood, at the meeting of two rivers and at the start of the great Rhine gorge, on journeys to Mainz, or possibly visiting a nearby property owned by the Disibodenberg monks. (Even the unquestioning observer must otherwise wonder how she had such a precise geographical location in mind.) When they heard of her intention, the monks expressed their alarm with disparaging criticism. Why on earth would this foolish abbess wish to move 'from a lushness of fields and vineyards and from the beauty of that place [Disibodenberg] to an arid place with no conveniences'? Their derision, provoked by envy, was under-standable. The idea of losing not only the fame, but also the wealth which this troublesome woman brought them was too much to countenance. Hildegard was well aware of their attitude, as this autobiographical passage of the *Vita* reveals: 'They were shocked and conspired among themselves to block us so that it should not come about. They were even saying that I was deceived by some kind of vain imagination.'[2]

The *Vita* provides two separate accounts of Hildegard receiving God's instruction and sharing it with her fellow monks and nuns. They differ in exact chronology. Both, however, emphasise the sudden and acute malaise which overcame her as she attempted to suppress or delay her intentions, whether out of her own uncertainty or in an attempt to win over the obdurate monks. Once again, we see the by now well-established link in Hildegard's life between major event and onset of illness. In a vivid description of her physical state (closely paralleling similar accounts by mystics of later times) she describes a malady so extreme that she goes blind and cannot raise herself from her bed, let alone walk. In her words:

> I could not see any light because of a clouding over of my eyes, and I was so oppressed down by the weight of my body that I could not raise myself. So I lay there, overwhelmed by intense pains. Why I suffered like this was because I did not make known the vision in which it was shown to me that I must move with my young women from the place where I had been offered to God, to another place.

Only when Abbot Cuno saw the extent of her suffering, 'sick and utterly paralysed like a pile of stones', did he acknowledge that her instruction came from God. Unwillingly, he consented to her outrageous plan and promised support. As a woman founding a monastery, she was rare but not alone. The English visionary Christina of Markyate established a priory *c.* 1145. Some had more modest aims. The thirteenth-century English chronicler Matthew Paris, in his *History of the Abbots of the Monastery of St Albans*, relates that in 1140, 'next to the woods not far from a river . . . two holy women, having made an extremely poor dwelling from the branches of trees woven together with pieces of bark and twigs, had begun to lead a life of vigil and prayer under marvellous abstinence'.[3] Cuno's change of heart was no doubt hastened not by such examples (which he is unlikely to have known) but by the unhappy experience of one particular fellow monk, Arnold. This former lay brother voiced his trenchant objection to the women's project and incited dissent among the other brothers. On monastery business near the intended site at Bingen, he was suddenly struck down with a mysterious illness so intense that he 'despaired of life itself'. This nasty episode and its surprising outcome led Arnold to a swift change of heart:

> *His tongue swelled up so grossly that he could not close his mouth over it. But he asked by signs, as best he could, to be carried to the church of St Rupert. As soon as he vowed there that he would not stand in the way any longer but would strive to help all he could, he immediately recovered his health. He began to be of assistance . . . and with his own hand cleared the vineyards around the site where the houses suitable for receiving nuns were being built.*[4]

Hildegard too, once she had the Abbot's approval, made an equally miraculous recovery. Cuno, completely outmanoeuvred, visited her in her cloister and gave her permission to embark on her move to 'the dwelling place prepared for her by heaven'. At this 'she rose up very sprightly as if she had not at all been disabled for so long a time. Amazement and wonder seized all who were present.'

So in 1148 or 1150, Hildegard and her nuns left Disibodenberg to embark on a new life at Bingen. Thenceforth Hildegard's name became associated with that place, even though the site of her monastery was on a steep hill, the Rupertsberg, on the opposite (west) bank of the Nahe. For geographical purposes, however, the two names are interchangeable. The *Vita* reports how the women departed from 'the place of the original dwelling' with sadness and tears, but their spirits quickly lifted when news of their coming spread to the nearby villages. Peasants and nobles, young and old, rushed out to greet them like royalty, 'with much dancing and singing of the divine praises'. If the journey was a time of promise, however, the arrival was another matter. Once again Hildegard found herself setting up home in a monastic ruin, this one established by the mother of St Rupert and deserted centuries before. Whereas when Hildegard arrived at Disibodenberg as a child, reconstruction was well under way thanks to the endeavour of others, here the enterprise was hers alone. As yet little had been done. Only a deserted chapel and a few farm buildings remained, with some makeshift temporary accommodation for the women. Apart from an ex-soldier and his family, no one lived there. Every aspect of the building work, the designs, the facilities, was her responsibility. How could she expect her well-born nuns, accustomed to a degree of order and comfort in their lives, to feel equally enthusiastic at the prospect of living on a building site, lacking necessities (as the *Vita* tells us) and short of money? In addition, the Disibodenberg chronicles record a great famine in this period, 'from which people died', followed by 'an immense flood' in the Rhineland.

For the first time, Hildegard had a crisis of her own making among her hitherto compliant women. Many were disaffected, sharing the dismay of the monks, perhaps tiring of their abbess's perpetual struggles and, as they might have judged, her overweening ambition. She may have taken comfort in the knowledge that such trials were the penalty of leadership. Abélard had met similar resistance from his abbot when he left Saint-Denis to found the Paraclete in a barren land, his followers forced to leave their spacious dwellings and luxurious food to live in huts, eat herbs and sleep on straw. When Héloïse and her nuns went to the Paraclete, they too endured privation. Bernard had a similar experience when he set out from the parent house of Cîteaux in 1115 with a dozen monks, short of food, salt, clothes and money, to found Clairvaux in the grim valley of the River Aube in the Champagne region. None the less during his influential abbacy, sixty-eight daughter houses were established, scattered throughout France, Flanders, Germany, Spain, Portugal, Sweden, Italy and England.

Hildegard may not have had such grand intentions, or have envisaged quite such rancour. Some nuns left for other monasteries. With a hint of satisfaction, their abbess later judged that they had lived to regret it: 'Some of [the noble young women] afterwards lived so negligently that many said their works showed that they had sinned against the Holy Spirit and against that person who spoke from the Holy Spirit'.[5] The girls' parents, too, showed anger at seeing their money – or, more often, property – given for one foundation and now redirected to another, their daughters forced to endure appalling conditions in the process. Some withdrew support. Indeed, the financial circumstances in which the Rupertsberg changed hands and in which nuns' dowries were appropriated from Disibodenberg caused their abbess administrative burdens for years to come. These time-consuming battles are not easily comprehended today, with our sketchy knowledge of the mechanics of twelfth-century finances. Yet they reveal Hildegard's sharp, if not ruthless, attitude to business and her careful forward planning. The move, prompted though it might have been by a heavenly vision, took effect in a real world of property and politics.

Before leaving Disibodenberg, in order not to seem as though she had 'taken over and occupied what properly belonged to another', she had bought the Rupertsberg site but only after first ensuring that she obtained the freehold. This she had done by persuading one of her keen supporters, the widowed marchioness Richardis von Stade (mother of her favoured nun, Richardis, and related to Jutta), to speak on her behalf to Heinrich, Archbishop of Mainz, and win his support. Accordingly, Hildegard was able to buy the land from the canons of Mainz Cathedral and Count Bernard of Hildesheim and his brother, who owned it. A later document dated 1195 gives the purchase price as twenty marks. The funds came from a combination of gifts and property, with Jutta's brother (Count Meinhard of Sponheim), Emperor Conrad III's sister Gertrude and Hildegard's own brothers, one of whom was by now a cleric at Mainz, among the contributors. In addition, one sum came from a widow 'for her daughter on entry', in other words as a guarantee of the girl's future place in the convent. While a dowry was an accepted part of a young woman's admission to holy orders, advance payment may have bordered on irregular practice. Gradually, as the women started to show their worth, local support grew and the carping decreased. Rich families began to request the burial of their dead in the convent grounds (the cemetery lay to the north of the convent church, over-looking the Rhine). Another common monastic habit entailed the exchange of cash for prayers for the souls of the departed, recorded in the accounts as assets 'conferred for the souls of the faithful'. In the final year of her life, the question of burying lay people would trigger a painful last crisis in Hildegard's eventful career. For the moment, the practice confirmed the status of the Rupertsberg and provided welcome income.

The Rupertsberg was rededicated on 1 May 1151. Issuing documents from the Archbishop of Mainz followed a year later. At the same time, the nuns were also given the mill at Binger Loch, the famously turbulent stretch of the Rhine immediately below the Rupertsberg, still hazardous to navigate. The implica-tion is that the mill, vital for the self-sufficiency of the monastery, would also provide income, 'with all its catchment and the whole extent of its waters, with its roads and paths, with its area for halting, its exits and approaches'. If someone had stood guard at each 'approach' and 'exit' extracting tolls, the Rupertsberg coffers would soon have started to fill. In any case, within a few years Hildegard's abbey owned extensive lands, including what is presumed to be her own home village of Bermersheim. The Archbishop of Mainz's document also reports giving 'the holy veil to certain young women', suggesting new members had already joined the Rupertsberg, undeterred by its early tribulations and still makeshift buildings. Already, if the charter is to be believed, the nuns had settled in to an austere way of life, Tenxwind's accusations of indulgent self-adornment nowhere in evidence. On the contrary:

> For certain faithful virgins, conquering the inducements of the flesh, and refusing lawful marriage so that they might deserve to be joined indissolubly with the Son of God, have extinguished in themselves all natural heat by the shower of heavenly grace, and have transferred from another place to the above mentioned place, as revealed through the Holy Spirit.[6]

Well aware that she would need a supply of priests if she and her nuns were to celebrate the mass, and perhaps as a sop to the irate monks, Hildegard agreed that Disibodenberg would remain the authority for their spiritual needs. The first, urgent battle was to wrench Volmar from the reluctant Cuno, who no doubt found his skills as secretary, teacher and archivist too valuable to renounce lightly. Hildegard's wrath is barely containable in this outburst to Cuno: 'If some of you, unworthy ones, said to yourselves, Let's take some of their freeholds away – then I WHO AM say: You are the worst of robbers. And if you try to take away the shepherd of spiritual medicine [Volmar] then again I say, you are sons of Belial, and in this do not look to the justice of God. So that same justice will destroy you.'[5] Here, as on many occasions in Hildegard's more frenzied outbursts, the 'I WHO AM' is not easily distinguished from the she who was, when the Almighty and his vessel appear, seamlessly, to have become one. The peevish Cuno gave in to this prophetic bullying. In order to settle all these matters, however, particularly those concerning the sensitive question of the nuns' endowments and the financial independence of Rupertsberg, Hildegard realised that she had no choice but to make a short return visit to Disibodenberg, a place of which by now she may have considered herself well rid. Before she could tackle this tricky business, she had more pressing tasks. In addition to continuing work on, and soon completing *Scivias*, the Rupertsberg monastery urgently needed rebuilding . She was in danger of losing more women, or failing to attract the new novices and their dowries for whom the new, enlarged premises were intended.

What do we know about the physical appearance of the Rupertsberg monastery? Today its remains are buried and inaccessible beneath railway tracks, highways and houses. Only the solid foundation walls are visible, built into the hill. The *Vita* gives no detail. The reconstruction is not mentioned. Our main visual evidence is an engraving (below) after a detailed drawing by Daniel Meissner dating from before his death in 1625 and therefore shortly before the monastery's destruction by the Swedes in 1632. By the time John Gardnor (1720–1808), an art teacher and one-time parish priest from Battersea, south London, travelled down the Rhine in 1788, the building

Rupertsberg Abbey. Engraving after a drawing
by Daniel Meissner before 1625.

had become a romantic ruin in the landscape, as his two aquatints from that period show. Like Disibodenberg, the monastery and its surrounding walls, outhouses and farm buildings were constructed tightly on the crown of a hill. The Rule of St Benedict, in the interests of self-sufficiency, instructed that there should be necessities such as a mill, gardens, stables, workshops, as well as church, dormitory, infirmary and cemetery, all of which the Rupertsberg possessed. The abbey church, with its round apse, nave, two aisles and double towers, tallies in style with the great tradition of Rhenish cathedral building of the Romanesque period. One modern source, unsubstantiated, gives these measurements: nave, 30m long × 7m wide; each aisle 4.35m. We may assume it was built with the coarse local pink sandstone of the region, the masonry filled with rubble. Materials are likely to have survived from the ruins of the earlier monastery. If not, the chosen riverside position would have made transportation of new stone by water relatively easy. The very absence of any description suggests that they used what they found already.

We have no information concerning Hildegard's role, but given her immense energy and her capacity for determination, she was certain to have been fully engaged in every detail. From the rich array of architectural imagery in the third and final part of *Scivias*, written shortly after her arrival at Bingen, we can discern her preoccupation with the enterprise. Language and imagery alike speak of walls, chancels, vaults, pillars, ladders, often given precise measurements. In one vision she refers to a tower 'not yet finished, but [which] was being diligently constructed, with great skill and speed, by a great many workers'. The illustrations in the Rupertsberg *Scivias* accordingly portray castellated towers, ramparts and walls. The celebrated Lucca manuscript of the *Liber divinorum operum* also depicts an array of Romanesque churches with circular apses in the Rupertsberg style. This extract from Vision Six in the third book of *Scivias*, describing the Stone Wall of the Old Law, is typical:

And after this I saw the wall of the aforementioned building, which ran between the north and west corners, and its inner side was all arched like a chancel, except that it was not open like chancel arches but unbroken, and each arch had the picture of a human being in it. And on the outer side of this wall I saw two smaller walls extending from the north to the west corner, and joined to these corners at each end like a vault. The height of these two lesser walls was three cubits.

Moreover, Hildegard would have been expected to act as overseer. In the Middle Ages, patron and master stonemason, in effect the architect though not usually named as such, worked closely on site, whether for castle, cathedral or manor house. The death of either usually cut short the project. Kings and clerics alike expected to initiate and participate in matters of design and choice of material. An account survives from 1140 of Abbot Suger worrying about where he would find wood for the beams of Saint-Denis because of the shortage of forests in the area. Unable to sleep after Matins one night, Suger determined to sort the matter out himself. Setting off early with carpenters and measurements, he trawled the neighbouring forests. By Nones, pushing his way through thick forests and thorn bushes, he had found the twelve beams he wanted. 'We had them carried to the holy basilica and placed them with joy on the roof of the new work . . .'[7] Work on Saint-Denis stopped abruptly when Suger died in 1151, the year Hildegard was embarking on her own building work. Word of Abbot Suger's daring experiments with Gothic architecture in Saint-Denis, so robustly condemned by the austere Bernard of Clairvaux, appears not yet to have reached the Rhineland, which clung to the Romanesque style for another century. Hildegard may have learned by the example of Bernard (by now wasting away, dropsical and close to death which eventually came in the summer of 1153). The Cistercians had a reputation as innovative builders of cathedrals and abbeys to the greater glory of God.

In addition to their practical need to house their expanding order, they prized manual labour as a form of prayer. In 1133 Bernard had engaged labourers, called 'mercenaries', to work with the monks on new buildings at Clairvaux. At the same time his brother, Achard, had supervised many Rhineland monasteries and may have been known to Hildegard.

For several years (though a relatively short time for a build-ing on this scale, as Guibert later remarked) the Rupertsberg would have swarmed with male workers, predominantly from one of two groups: the stonemasons in all their hierarchy, from cutters and dressers to carvers and carriers working with chisels, compasses and set squares; and the carpenters. Vigilance was required to segregate the nuns. Caesarius of Arles' Rule for Nuns had made provision for every eventuality, even the arrival of the odd-job man:

> And when the buildings must be remodelled or doors or windows must be constructed, or any repairs of this sort are needed, such artisans and workers as are necessary to do the work may come in with the provider, but not without the knowledge or permission of the mother. And the provider may never enter the inner part of the monastery except for those reasons explained . . . and never without the abbess or at least some other very respectable witness, so that the holy women have their private place as is fitting and expedient.[8]

Architectural drawings, plans and models were not un-known, but not commonly preserved, and none survives from the Rupertsberg. A plan of Christchurch Monastery, Canterbury, from the 1150s shows an elaborate water circula-tion system. Hildegard, too, would no doubt have ensured the best available plumbing for her sensitive, well-bred women. Indeed, we know that the facilities were good for the time from a valuable and uniquely detailed description by Guibert, written when he visited the Rupertsberg in 1177. After praising the manner in which the abbess nurtured her 'daughters', to which we shall return, he draws attention to her achievement in founding and reconstructing the place. He speaks, too, of there now being accommodation for fifty nuns:

> *Besides this there is another marvel to consider here: that though this monastery was founded but recently – a short space of time ago, that is twenty-seven years – not by any of the emperors or bishops or the powerful or the rich of any region, but by a woman who was poor, a stranger, and sick; yet it has made such progress in its religious character and in its resources that it is skilfully laid out, not with grand but with commodious and dignified buildings most suitable for a religious community, with running water distributed through all the workshops. Furthermore, not counting guests whom we are never without, and the administrators of the house of which they have several, the monastery provides enough for the expenses of food and clothing of fifty sisters without any shortfall.*[9]

Prominent and eye-catching from its elevated site on the banks of the Rhine and the Nahe, the Rupertsberg would have been a famous landmark of its day, more public, visible and accessible than the secluded Disibodenberg could ever have been. The site is indeed so prominent that a thousand years earlier the Romans had chosen the place to build a citadel, Bingium, between two trade routes. Seven hundred years after Hildegard, between 1877 and 1883, at this exact point in the river on the opposite bank, the huge 'Germania' monument was erected, towering 225 metres above the Rhine as a symbol of the re-established German Empire. The equestrian statue of Kaiser Wilhelm I surmounts the sculpted figures of Bismarck and the ranks of German princes, sovereigns and commanders-in-chief at its base. Were they but flesh and blood not bronze, they would find themselves looking out in perpetuity towards the junction of the two rivers where the abbess built her monastery. Between them Hildegard and God had made a smart move.

CHAPTER SEVEN

THE RICHARDIS AFFAIR

St Benedict's Rule on what kind of man [woman] the abbot [abbess] should be: *Let him not make any distinction of persons in the monastery. Let him not love one more than another, unless he find him better in good work or obedience . . . Therefore let the abbot show an equal love to all, and let the same discipline be imposed on all in accordance with their deserts . . . Above all let him not have greater solicitude for fleeting, earthly, and perishable things, and so overlook or undervalue the salvation of souls committed to him.*

(RULE 2)

For while I was writing the book Scivias *I bore a deep love for a certain noble young woman, daughter of the above mentioned marchioness [Richardis von Stade], just as Paul loved Timothy. She joined herself to me in loving friendship in everything, and comforted me in all my trials, until at length I finished that book.*

(*VITA* II, V)

In the midst of the public turbulence clouding her life at the time of the move to Rupertsberg, Hildegard had another matter on her hands. It was personal in nature, overwhelming in impact and harder to resolve. Throughout the *Vita* and in letters, we glimpse moments of turmoil in Hildegard's life, but the image flickers elusively, lost in the language of scriptural convention or the mirage of symbolic visions. Only once, around the year 1150, just before or after leaving Disibodenberg, did her defences fall and her feelings overcome her. In providing insight into her emotional life in all its rawness, no comparable episode exists. The danger to a reader today, because of its uniqueness in satisfying our need to understand Hildegard's occluded personality, is to exaggerate its importance or misconstrue its nature. Let the facts stand alone. The existence of an extensive correspondence allows the story to tell itself.

During the ten years since she had started writing down her visions, Hildegard's daily existence revolved increasingly around two people. One of course was Volmar, her secretary. The other was the young nun who assisted them, Richardis von Stade, daughter of the noble woman of the same name who had intervened on Hildegard's behalf to secure the Rupertsberg, and a distant cousin of Jutta. The surviving image of the three of them working together suggests its own potent story. Of her relationship with Volmar, one might justifiably speculate that for a man and woman to work in intimate circumstances for so many years, a *modus vivendi* must have been reached early on, perhaps after a crisis on the part of one or other. Their friendship managed to survive for thirty years, through times of trouble, until Volmar's death in 1173, only briefly interrupted when Abbot Cuno initially refused to release him to join her at Rupertsberg. From a letter written to Hildegard near the end of his life, the only one which survives, we witness Volmar's quiet admiration and loving affection for his 'sweetest mother' and 'reverend lady'. Of a similar age, they had grown old together, he the willing shadow to her bright light. Yet many years earlier the *Vita Jutta*, which in all probability he wrote, suggests he may once have had anxieties of his own. The writer gives examples of Jutta's understanding towards those who struggled with temptation. Since crises of the soul were private matters between the individual and his confessor, not shared with the community, he may perforce have been drawing on his own experience. He says that 'one of the faithful was very hard pressed as he struggled with a temptation of the flesh against the spirit. He thought that it would be a help to lay his distress before this handmaiden of Christ, trusting that he would gain relief, if only he uncovered to her his wound. And his hope did not prove false.'

He then relates how another 'certain brother' had voiced 'certain things very inimical to his salvation'.[1] Following Jutta's imprecations, the brother was temporarily struck dumb, only recovering three days later. If we share the view that the *Vita Jutta* was written early in the 1140s by someone who already knew of the (still clandestine) visions of Jutta's successor, it is reasonable to conclude that Volmar wrote it when his partnership with Hildegard in the scriptorium was just beginning. How normal his confusions might have been, finding himself confined with a woman for the first time in his life, engaged in work of great personal revelation and intensity. Of Hildegard's feelings towards him, frequently expressed in the loving terms of a close, private friendship ('that man whom I had sought and found'), again one can only surmise. That these encounters may once have kindled intimations, at least, of sexual feelings is, though a matter for conjecture, not necessarily one of mere prurience. Throughout her writings she displays a rare natural sympathy with the pleasurable aspects of 'lust'. Nor is she always quick to condemn, while not condoning either. In a letter to Archbishop Eberhard of Bamberg, she proposes that God must have delighted in what he had created, that despite the Fall human nature was His supreme achievement, and that Creation looked to Him 'like a lover'. Something must have stirred her imagination beyond the talk of women in the hospice or guest house. Yet despite the lurid fantasies, hot sweats and subsequent flagellations of a recent novel about Hildegard entitled *Scarlet Passion*, in which Volmar and the alluring Heinrich, Archbishop of Mainz are objects of the repressed nun's unconsummated desire, there is no evidence at all that Hildegard might for a moment have contemplated breaking her vows. Her relationship with Volmar stands out as an example of loyalty, trust and, according to monastic necessity, perfect propriety. The *Vita* gives no suggestion of any moral weakness in Hildegard. Her only frailty allowed by her biographers is her susceptibility to illness with an attendant implication of depression. In contrast, Aelred of Rievaulx's biographer describes the venerable Cistercian having to go to the extreme lengths of constructing a secret brick chamber under the floor of the novice house into which water flowed and where, 'when he was alone and undisturbed [he] immersed his whole body in the icy cold water [to] quench the heat in himself of every vice'. Hildegard's contemporary visionary and friend, Elisabeth of Schönau, endured forceful visions in which she was instructed by an angel to thrust her hand into a pile of filth. The angel then compares this deed to the pollution caused by lust which is not satisfied by carnal action, seeming to imply, at the very least, thoughts of impurity, or masturbation. Elisabeth begs, urgently, to learn whether virginity can be lost by the lust of temptation alone.

Hildegard's all-consuming friendship for the other key figure in her life, Richardis von Stade, is more tangled. Apart from a short, unembellished passage in the *Vita*, our source is an exchange of several letters. The impetus for this correspondence was Richardis' decision to leave Hildegard's monastery. She had been offered the post of abbess at Bassum, a celebrated Benedictine house far away to the north. This was a conspicuous promotion for the young Richardis, whose exact age is unknown but who (judging from genealogical tables) was probably around twenty years younger than her abbess. That her brother Hartwig was Archbishop of Bremen, the diocese in which Bassum abbey stood, requires no comment. Hildegard's account of events (continuing on from the quotation at the head of this chapter, after she describes the completion of *Scivias*) is terse, the writer showing her haughtiest colours, with an air of Emma Woodhouse about her. First she accuses Richardis of class arrogance. Then, worse still, she charges her with securing the job by irregular means:

> But after this, because of the high station of her family, she inclined after the dignity of a higher title, so that she was named the mother of a certain very eminent community. She did not seek this however, according to God, but according to this world's honour. After she withdrew from me, in a region far away from us, she soon lost this present life, and along with it the title of her new dignity.[2]

This short paragraph reveals nothing of the angry battle Hildegard waged to prevent Richardis' departure. Every avenue was explored, with pleas made to the highest authority in Christendom, the Pope himself. Richardis' niece Adelheid, another young nun, also wanted to leave the Rupertsberg and accept a job as abbess. In a letter to the marchioness, mother and grandmother of the deserting nuns, Hildegard makes her plea out of concern for the women rather than on her own account, though she admits to shedding bitter tears at the prospect of her imminent loss. Her strength of feeling brings to mind the soul-searching letter Bernard of Clairvaux wrote to his nephew Robert when the young monk wanted to leave his uncle's abbey at Clairvaux to return to the comforts of Cluny. Whereas Bernard at least considers that he might be at fault ('I was too severe with a sensitive youth . . . too hard on a tender stripling'[3]), Hildegard rushes to the attack. Her style is hectoring, her message plain, namely: take heed, these nuns are not ready for the high office proposed:

> *I see them now glowing in the dawn and graced with pearls of virtues. So take care lest by your will, your advice and connivance, their sense and their souls be moved away from the sublimity of that grace. For the position of abbess, that you desire for them, is surely, surely, surely not compatible with God* [certe, certe, certe non est cum deo] *or with the salvation of their souls.*[4]

Making no headway, she released Adelheid but fought on for Richardis. Ever one to go to the top, she wrote to Pope Eugene III, who had supported her at Trier and in effect established her reputation. Only his reply survives. As a rare example of a pope writing to a woman at this time, it deserves quoting at length. Reading between the lines of the Pope's grandiose rhetoric and conventional blandishments, this is a hard-hitting and slightly impatient three-part response; having given a helping hand to this unusual woman, he now regards her persistence as tiresome. Her attempt to bypass procedure and leapfrog up the hierarchy was unwise. First he praises her already widespread celebrity (the year is 1151, just three years after the Synod of Trier) and her good works. Then, in stern terms, he warns her not to succumb to the snare of intransigence and ambition. In a final snub, he washes his hands of the Richardis matter and passes the problem back, in the 'please deal; see copy attached' mode of modern office life, to the head of department concerned, namely her old ally Heinrich, Archbishop of Mainz. In his apocalyptic imagery, the Pope is every bit a match for the abbess:

Bishop Eugene, servant of the servants of God, to Hildegard, beloved daughter in Christ, mistress of Mount St Rupert, greetings and apostolic blessings.

We rejoice, my daughter, and we exult in the Lord because your honourable reputation has spread so far and wide that many people regard you as 'the odour of life unto life' [II Cor. 2:16], *and the multitudes of the faithful cry out, 'Who is she that goes up by the desert, as a pillar of smoke of aromatical spices?'* [Song of Songs 3:16] *Therefore . . . we consider it superfluous to exhort you further or with a prop of words attempt to support a spirit which already sufficiently rests on divine virtue.*

All the same, because a fire is increased by the bellows and a swift horse is impelled to greater speed by the spurs, we feel it incumbent upon us to remind you that the palm of glory belongs not to the one who begins but to the one who finishes the race, as the Lord says, 'To him, that overcometh, I will give to eat of the tree of life, which is in the middle of paradise [Apoc. 2:7]. *And so bear in mind, my daughter, that the ancient serpent who cast the first man out of Paradise longs to destroy the great (like Job) and, having consumed Judas, seeks power to shift the apostles. Moreover, as you know, many are called but few chosen* [Matt. 22:14] *so bring yourself in to that small number . . .*

Finally, we have delegated the matter you wished to consult us about to our brother Heinrich, Archbishop of Mainz. His task will be to make sure that the Rule is strictly observed in that monastery entrusted to that sister (the nun that you delivered up to him) – either that or to send her back to your supervision. The transcript of my letter to him will give you the details.[5]

In what was quickly turning into an unseemly tug of war, Heinrich, Archbishop of Mainz, a diligent if toadying bureaucrat, promptly wrote to Hildegard (the dates are uncertain; this letter could equally have preceded the Pope's). In a brief note, he praises her reputation for performing miracles and apologises for having been too busy to visit her of late. Then he goes straight to the point, commanding her by his authority as prelate to release Richardis immediately: 'If you accede to these requests, you will know our gratitude from now on in even greater measure than you have known so far; but if not we will issue the same command to you again in even stronger terms, and we will not leave off until you fulfil our commands in this matter.'[6]

By good fortune, Hildegard's furious reply survives. She refuses to cooperate. Accusing her opponents of simony and calling on God as her guide, she ends with a bellow of disgust in terms hardly suited to an abbess writing to her archbishop. In short, she is a woman scorned:

> The Bright Fountain, truthful and just, say these legal pretexts brought forward to establish authority over this girl have no weight in God's eyes, for I – high, deep, all-encompassing, a descending light – neither initiated nor wanted them. Rather they have been manufactured in the conniving audacity of ignorant hearts . . . The Spirit of God says earnestly: O shepherds, wail and mourn over the present time, because you do not know what you are doing when you sweep aside the duties established by God in favour of opportunities for money and the foolishness of wicked men who do not fear God. And so your malicious curses and threatening words are not to be obeyed. You have raised up your rods of punishment arrogantly, not to serve God, but to gratify your own perverted will.[7]

After this outburst, she tackles Richardis' brother Hartwig, Archbishop of Bremen, who was instrumental in securing the post for his sister. By now Hildegard is emotionally sapped but still determined, in more direct terms than ever, to defend her resistance on grounds of simony. She appeals to Hartwig, as a man of God, to put spiritual matters before those of the world. She makes a powerful and well-argued case. Anguish never quite gets the better of a shrewdness born of desperation. Her description of Richardis being 'dragged' from the cloister suggests abduction, though there is no evidence that the nun herself tried or wanted to stay. The abbot referred to is Cuno of Disibodenberg, who still held authority over Hildegard and her sisters:

> *You are a man worthy of great praise, as one must be who holds the episcopal office in direct succession from almighty God Himself. Therefore may your eye see God, your intellect grasp His justice . . . Be a bright star shining in the darkness of the night of wicked men . . . Be alert, for many shepherds are blind and halt nowadays, and they are seizing the lucre of death, choking out God's justice.*
>
> *O dear man, your soul is dearer to me than your family. Now hear me, cast down as I am, miserably weeping at your feet. My spirit is exceedingly sad, because a certain horrible man has trampled underfoot my desire and will (and not mine alone, but also my sisters' and friends') and has rashly dragged our beloved daughter Richardis out of her cloister. Since God knows all things, He knows where pastoral care is useful, and so let no person of faith canvass for such an office. Thus if anyone in his madness wilfully seeks to gain ecclesiastic office, he is a rapacious wolf seeking the delights of power more than the will of God. The soul of such a person, therefore, never seeks spiritual office with proper faith. Therein lies simony.*
>
> *It was therefore inappropriate for our abbot, in his blindness and ignorance, to involve this holy soul in his affair and, in the blindness of his spirit, to encourage such great temerity. If our daughter had remained content, God would have fulfilled his glorious purpose for her.*[8]

Here, as in all her letters on the subject, she protests that she has no objection to any selection God has made, but refuses to accept that Richardis' appointment falls into that category. 'Therefore,' she continues, 'I beseech you, you who hold episcopal office . . . to send my dearest daughter back to me.' She begs him not to refuse her 'as your mother [the Marchioness von Stade] and your sister, and Count Hermann [brother-in-law of the Emperor, Conrad III, and a supporter in the move to Rupertsberg] have all done'. For the second time in the letter she promises him, almost bribes him with, divine guidance and 'the blessing of the dew of heaven and may all the choirs of angels bless you' if he will only listen to her. Her implication is clear: you have been warned.

Once again, we must ask what dark, obsessive force had driven Hildegard to these extremes of behaviour. Nowhere else does her tongue run away with her quite so rashly, her heart reveal itself in all its nakedness. In later letters, when she assails the heretics threatening to undermine the foundations of the Church, her language is excessive and vivid, drawing freely on apocalyptic imagery. Yet nothing compares with the strength of feeling mixed with a palpable tone of panic and petulance in the correspondence concerning Richardis. The distinguished American Hildegard scholar Barbara Newman has gone so far as to suggest that Hildegard's vision of Virginitas in *Scivias* is a glittering pen-portrait of Richardis herself (though others have preferred to identify the figure as a self-portrait, which seems less likely). She stands in the capacious, calyx-like embrace of Ecclesia, in a scarlet gown, with long flowing hair and surrounded by a multitude of richly clothed virgins in jewels and crowns:

> *In this splendour there appeared a beautiful girl, bareheaded, with dark hair wearing a red tunic that flowed down about her feet. And I heard a voice from heaven saying: 'This is the flower that blooms in the Zion above: mother and rose and*

lily of the valley . . . you will marry the son of the most
mighty King' . . . And around this girl I saw standing a
great throng of people shining brighter than the sun, who
were all wonderfully arrayed in gold and jewels . . .[9]

When Hildegard saw her appeal to higher authorities had
failed to have any effect, she wrote to the source of her agony,
Richardis herself. Whatever gloss you choose to put on it, this
remarkable document is a love letter as painful and full of the
wounds of rejection, with a hint of bitterness, as any ever written.
As usual, Hildegard quotes from the Bible to embellish her words
of lamentation, yet for once she scarcely calls on God as a screen
to her own strong feelings. With a degree of effrontery close to
blasphemy, she compares her own situation to that of Christ
crying out to God from the cross. It follows in full:

Daughter, listen to me, your mother, speaking to you in the
spirit: my grief flies up to heaven. My sorrow is destroying
the great confidence and consolation that I once had in
mankind. From now on I will say: 'It is good to trust in
the Lord, rather than to trust in princes' [Ps. 117:9]. *The*
point of this Scripture is that a person ought to look to the
living height, with vision unobstructed by earthly love and
feeble faith, which the airy humour of earth renders
transient and short-lived. Thus a person looking at God
directs his sight to the sun like an eagle. And for this
reason one should not depend on a person of high birth,
for such a one inevitably withers like a flower. This was
the very transgression I myself committed because of my
love for a certain noble individual.

Now I say to you: As often as I sinned in this way, God
revealed that sin to me, either through some sort of difficulty
or some kind of grief, just as He has now done regarding
you, as you well know.

Now again I say: Woe is me, mother, woe is me, daughter.

Why have you forsaken me [Ps. 21:2, Matt. 27:46, Mark
15:34] *like an orphan? I so loved the nobility of your
character, your wisdom, your chastity, your spirit, and
indeed every aspect of your life that many people have said
to me: 'What are you doing?'*

*Now, let all who have grief like mine mourn with me,
all who, in the love of God, have had such great love in
their hearts and minds for a person – as I have had for
you – but who was snatched away from them in an
instant, as you were from me. But all the same, may the
angel of God go before you, may the Son of God protect
you, and may his mother watch over you. Be mindful of
your poor desolate mother, Hildegard, so that your
happiness may not fade.*[10]

By writing in this style, Hildegard was following in the
tradition of her contemporary Aelred of Rievaulx's *De Spirituali
Amicitia* (*On Spiritual Friendship*, 1150–65), or the letters of St
Anselm and Bernard of Clairvaux. Their passionate correspondence with other men has been misinterpreted as a sign of
their homosexuality, latent or overt, even though the language
is manifestly scriptural, the evidence scant. Aelred is known to
have lost his chastity and 'freely abandoned himself to all that is
base' (*On the Institution of Recluses*) while a youth in the court of
David I of Scotland, before embracing the Cistercian life,
following in the footsteps of and using similar language to
St Augustine. Despite assumptions, the exact nature of his
transgression is not specified and we should tread with extreme
caution. Nevertheless, a link between male friendship and
eroticism had long been identified, and found greater freedom
of expression in the twelfth century. That Benedict himself ruled
that monks (and by implication nuns too) should sleep in
separate beds indicates that he was alert to the possible
temptation of monastic life. For those in monastic institutions
then as now, again following St Benedict, close friendships, still

known as 'particular friendships', were discouraged, not only for implied sexual reasons but also because such intimacies ran counter to the life of the community and the individual's relationship to God. Inevitably, Hildegard's feelings for Richardis have been read in some quarters as a clear sign of a lesbian sympathy, even if those desires never found physical expression. Futile though such speculation is ultimately, since we can never know, we should ask whether any justification exists for such a line of enquiry. Due heed is required. Hildegard herself condemned homosexuality in ringing terms: 'A man who sins with another man as if with a woman sins bitterly against God and against the union with which God united male and female. Hence both in God's sight are polluted, black and wanton, horrible and harmful to God and humanity and guilty of death, for they go against their Creator and His creature.'[11] In a letter to an Abbot Conrad written at this time (1153), she warns him against 'that sin that is against his nature'.[12] Nor is she any less severe on the question of sexual activity between women:

> *And a woman who takes up devilish ways and plays a male role in coupling with another woman is most vile in My sight, and so is she who subjects herself to such a one in this evil deed. For they should have been ashamed of their passion, and instead they impudently usurped a right that was not theirs. And, having put themselves into alien ways, they are to Me transformed and contemptible.*[13]

Few reported cases of lesbianism survive from the twelfth century. One explanation is that those who laid down the law, that is to say men, considered women sexually passive and therefore less susceptible to vice. Lacking an easy way of monitoring the goings-on in all-female institutions, these lawmakers may have devoted their energies towards men, allowing women to get away with their transgressions, of whatever nature, more easily. Nevertheless, examples exist, such as that of the twelfth-century Bavarian nun who wrote to another: 'To G, her singular Rose, from A – the bonds of precious love . . . When I recall the kisses you gave me/ And how with tender words you caressed my little breasts/ I want to die'.[14] In the fourth century, St Augustine had warned a group of nuns that the love they shared 'ought not to be carnal but spiritual', and that 'those things which are practised by immodest women, even with other females . . . ought not be done even by married women . . . much less by widows or chaste virgins dedicated by a holy vow to be hand maids of Christ'.

Whatever Hildegard's true inclination, whatever the essence of her sentiments for Richardis, the crisis was short-lived and intense, with worse yet to come. In 1152, barely two years at most since Richardis' departure, her brother Hartwig, Archbishop of Bremen, wrote to Hildegard with news of Richardis' sudden death. Even in his grief Hartwig pointedly, and pettily, refers to his sister's superior title of abbess (*abbatisse*) while Hildegard, though usually addressed as abbess, remained, at fifty-four years old, officially only mistress of the sisters (*Hildegardi magistre sororum*). He writes in tones of stubbornness, sorrow and humility. The tacit understanding is that for all her antagonism, Hildegard may have been right to warn against Richardis' departure, and that, before her death, Richardis may have thought so too.

> Hartwig, archbishop of Bremen, brother of the abbess Richardis, sends that which is in the place of sister and more than a sister, obedience, to Hildegard, mistress of the sisters of St Rupert.
> *I write to inform you that our sister – my sister in body, but yours in spirit – has gone the way of all flesh, little esteeming that honour I bestowed upon her . . . I am happy to report that she made her last confession in a saintly and pious way, and that after her confession she was anointed with consecrated oil. Moreover, filled with her usual*

Christian spirit, she tearfully expressed longing for your cloister with her whole heart. She then committed herself to the Lord . . . and died on 29 October in perfect faith, hope and charity as we know for certain.

Thus I ask as earnestly as I can, if I have any right to ask, that you love her as much as she loved you, and if she appeared to have any fault – which indeed was mine, not hers – at least have regard for the tears that she shed for your cloister, which many witnessed. And if death had not prevented, she would have come to you as soon as she was able to get permission . . . May God, who repays all good deeds, recompense you fully in this world and in the future for all the good things you did for her, you alone, more even than relatives or friends; may He repay that benevolence of yours which she rejoiced in before God and me. Please convey my thanks to your sisters for all their kindness.[15]

What tears of bitterness and regret must Hildegard have shed when she received the news. Rising above the temptation to crow at her own foresight, she wrote a dignified and generous reply. This episode ends with her final words on the painful affair. Notice how she compares the world (herself, perhaps) and God as competing lovers:

O how great a miracle there is in the salvation of those souls so looked upon by God that His glory has no hint of shadow in them. But He works in them like a mighty warrior who takes care not to be defeated by anyone, so that this victory may be sure. Just so, dear man, was it with my daughter Richardis, whom I call both daughter and mother, because I cherished her with divine love, as indeed the Living Light had instructed me to do in a very vivid vision.

God favoured her so greatly that worldly desire had no power to embrace her. For she always fought against it, even though she was like a flower in her beauty and loveliness in the symphony of this world. While she was still living in the body, in fact, I heard the following words concerning her in a true vision: 'O virginity you are standing at the royal bridal chamber.' Now in the tender shoot of virginity, she has been made a part of that most holy order, and the daughters of Zion rejoice. But the ancient serpent had attempted to deprive her of that blessed honour by assaulting her through human nobility. Yet the mighty Judge drew this my daughter to Himself, cutting her off from all human glory.

Therefore, although the world loved her physical beauty and her worldly wisdom while she was still alive, my soul has the greatest confidence in her salvation. For God loves her more. Therefore, He was unwilling to give His beloved to a heartless lover, that is the world. Now you, dear Hartwig, you who sit as Christ's representative, fulfil the desire of your sister's soul, as obedience demands. And just as she always had your interests at heart, so you now take thought for her soul, and do good works as she wished. Now, as for me, I cast out in my heart that grief you caused me in the matter of this my daughter. May God grant you, through the prayers of saints, the dew of His grace and reward in the world to come.[16]

As an epilogue, an elegiac speech and chorus from the *Ordo Virtutum* (*Play of Virtues*), completed around the time of Richardis' death, are believed by Barbara Newman to have been Hildegard's memorial to her. There is no reason to disagree:

CASTITAS:
O Virginity, you stand in the royal bridal chamber.
O how tenderly you burn in the King's embraces
when the sun shines through you
so that your noble flower shall never wilt.
O noble virgin, no shade will ever find your flower drooping!

VIRTUTES:
The flower of the field falls before the wind,
The rain scatters its petals.
O Virginity, you abide forever
in the chorus of the company of heaven!
Hence you are a tender flower that shall never fade.[17]

CHAPTER EIGHT

IMPERIAL AND PAPAL UPHEAVAL

1152 Herman, the Count of Winzburg, and his wife were killed. During January there was an immense flood in the Rhineland region. King Conrad died on the fifteenth day before the Kalends of March [15 February]. Frederick, 99th emperor of the Romans, cousin of king Conrad, began to reign.

1153 A sign appeared in the sun on the seventh day before the Kalends of February [26 January]. Heinrich, Archbishop of Mainz, was deposed at Pentecost by order of Pope Eugene and Arnold the Chancellor was elected. Heinrich, archbishop of Mainz died on the Kalends of September [1 September].

1155 Frederick was made Emperor at Rome by Pope Hadrian.

1156 . . . a very serious schism arose in the Church.
(CHRONICLES OF DISIBODENBERG)

Beyond the cloistered walls of the Rupertsberg, Germany was changing. On 15 February 1152, while Hildegard was busy establishing a way of life in the new monastery as well as coming to terms with the personal loss of Richardis, Emperor Conrad III died. His successor was his famous nephew, Frederick Barbarossa, named after his striking strawberry-blond beard. His appointment as German king marked the start of one of the most illustrious reigns of the Middle Ages. Indeed, Germany regarded him as a hero right up until the mid-nineteenth century, a torch-bearer for imperial Germany and a role model for the Prussian Kaiser Wilhelm I seven centuries later. Legend had it that the sky would fill with ravens as a sign from Frederick that a new German empire was dawning. Whereas the ineffectual Conrad had made little impact, Frederick was a charismatic idealist, a persuasive realist and, at least at the start of his reign, a willing negotiator. His high ambitions were threefold: to subjugate the papacy to imperial power, to re-establish the Holy Roman Empire in its ancient glory and to end the civil unrest which had split his country asunder for nearly seventy-five years. The principal feud was between two noble families, the papalist Welfs and the imperialist Weiblingens (thanks to Dante better known by their later, Italianised names of Guelphs and Ghibellines). That Frederick was related to both these ancient and warring lines was regarded as a hopeful sign at home that peace might at last be possible.

Rome, meanwhile, was weakened in the 1150s by a quick succession of different pontiffs. Shortly after Frederick's coronation, the brief papacy of Pope Anastasius came to an end. He died in 1153, only a year after replacing Bernard of Clairvaux's great follower, the Cistercian Eugene III. Already in his eighties when he was elected, Anastasius was feeble in the face of heresy and ecclesiastical corruption. Hildegard, no great fan, wrote to him in intemperate tones: 'You O man, who are too tired . . . to rein in the pomposity of arrogance among those placed in your bosom, why do you not call back the shipwrecked who cannot rise from the depths without help? . . . Why do you put up with depraved people who are blinded by foolishness and who delight in harmful things, like a hen which cackles in the night and terrifies herself. Such people are completely useless.'[1] No reply survives.

This letter is significant because it contains one of Hildegard's few direct references to her *lingua ignota* and *litterae ignotae*, her secret language and alphabet which still puzzle scholars, saying that God had inspired her 'to form unknown letters and utter an unknown language'. No one has been able satisfactorily to explain why Hildegard felt moved to invent her own enigmatic code, or to ascertain whether her nuns, or anyone else, shared her secret with her. Frustratingly little is known about it. About one-third of the total nine hundred words invented relate to medicine and botany. Many of the remainder, or at least those which have been deciphered, are of liturgical origin. Some derive directly from Latin or Low German; others remain a mystery. (Her *düveliz*, for example, is close to the medieval German *düwel*, meaning 'devil'. Her *muzimia* connects loosely with the Latin *nuzmuscata*, in English 'nutmeg'. But *malskir*, meaning 'tooth', is far from the Latin *dens* and has not yet been equated with any German word. See Appendix I).

The new Pope was Nicholas Breakspear from St Albans, the only Englishman ever to succeed to the see of Rome. He took the name Hadrian IV. Seizing a chance to break the deadlock with Rome, Frederick forged an alliance with Hadrian – short-lived, as it turned out – who, after much wrangling, crowned him Holy Roman Emperor in 1155. Hildegard, too, grasped the moment and issued welcoming pronouncements to both new king and new pope alike. Her letter to Hadrian IV, short, peppery and obscure, utters darkly prophetic warnings against shipwreck, booty, careering horses and falling into traps. A letter to Hildegard from Frederick, written around 1152, confirms that the monarch had immediately invited the abbess to the newly fortified and lavishly rebuilt imperial palace at Ingelheim (no longer extant but close by, conveniently placed between Bingen and Mainz). Characteristically, she advised Frederick on his new role and warned him of the pitfalls ('We now have in hand the things you predicted to us when we asked you to come before our presence at Ingelheim,'[2] he later wrote obediently to her). Frederick was just thirty, Hildegard in her mid-fifties; his aims were imperial and grandiose, hers reactionary and papal. Yet initially she held him in esteem. Within a few years, however, their friendship would cool and eventually turn sour. With the death of Hadrian IV in 1159 and the start of the papal schism, he became caught in the very snares of anti-papal greed and ambition against which she had warned.

Hildegard had other concerns at this time. In 1153 her old ally and champion, the pro-monastic Heinrich, Archbishop of Mainz, had been deposed by Frederick Barbarossa, whose election Heinrich had been almost alone in contending. (The Disibodenberg chronicles, confusingly, say his departure was ordered by Pope Eugene III). He was replaced by Arnold, who was soon to meet a worse fate. Hildegard petitioned the Pope on Heinrich's behalf, but the once august prelate, now living in reduced circumstances as a Cistercian monk, died the same year. Moreover, the shadow of her abrupt departure from Disibodenberg hung over Hildegard through the first half of the decade. After her initial efforts to secure the dowries of her nuns at the time of the move to Rupertsberg, she still fought for independence from Abbot Cuno. Their bitter administrative wrangle lasted several years and caused her severe physical and mental stress. The aftermath of her desertion from her old abbey and its depleting effect on the monks is evident in a letter written to her some time between 1150 and 1155 by Adelbert, a Disibodenberg prior. His tone is petulant and emotionally pressurising. Why, he asks, have you abandoned your old friends who nurtured you from childhood and still need you? The meaning is unmistakable: success has cut her off from her roots, like a celebrity grown too grand to support her old school or college. The document is of particular value for its description of her education with Jutta so many decades earlier – confirming its narrowness by the phrase 'appropriate only to a woman':

> *Since you send the words of your admonition into foreign regions and cause large numbers of people to desire the paths of righteousness, we (who have known you almost from the cradle and with whom you lived for many years) wonder why you have withdrawn the words of your celestial visions from us who thirst for them.*
>
> *We remember how you were educated among us, how you were taught, how you were established in the religious life. For your instruction was that appropriate only to a woman, and a simple psalter was your only schoolbook. Yet without complaint you embraced the good and holy religious life. But the will of God filled you with celestial dew and opened up to you the magnitude of its secrets. And just as we were set to rejoice in these thing with you, God took you away from us against our will, and gave you to other people. We cannot fathom why God did this, but, willy-nilly, we are suffering great distress from the deed. For we had hoped that the salvation of our monastery rested with you . . .*[3]

The *Vita* for this period reports, in Hildegard's own voice, attacks from many quarters, 'just like Joshua whose enemies tried to bring him to confusion because he was to conquer others. But just as God helped him so he freed both myself and my daughters.'[4] The ever irksome Abbot Cuno, meanwhile, stung by the sudden loss of income, was still trying to ensure that the finances of the Rupertsberg remained in his control. The legal quarrels limped on in a protracted fashion until Hildegard was eventually forced to make an unavoidable return visit to Disibodenberg. The prospect, according to the *Vita*, was not one she relished. Hanging back in alarm 'like the prophet Jonah', she fell sick and 'was struck by the whip of divine reproof . . . almost to the point of death'. In order to find release from this divine retribution, she vowed to go where God bade her and, intrepid as ever, prepared for her journey:

> She then asked to be placed on a horse and supported by hands be led off. As soon as she had been led a very little way along the road she recovered her strength and went gladly on her way. When she reached Disibodenberg, she explained why she was compelled to come and while there, separated the place of her new monastery along with some other properties belonging to her community, from the brother of that monastery, but left to them the larger portion of possessions, which had been given to it when the sisters had been first received and in addition left them a not inconsiderable sum of money so that there might remain no just cause for complaint.[5]

Her instinct was right. Despite her generosity in settling the property issue, she received short shrift from the monks. In a savage letter from her to 'the abbot', probably still Cuno, shortly before his death in June 1155, but perhaps addressed to his successor, Abbot Helenger, she gives a crisp account of the turbulent occasion:

> I returned to the place where God has bequeathed to you

> *the rod of his authority* [i.e. Disibodenberg]. *But a mob*
> *of some of your monks rose up and gnashed their teeth at*
> *me, as if I were a bird of gloom or a horrid beast, and they*
> *bent their bows against me in order to drive me away. But*
> *I know for a fact that God moved me from that place for*
> *his own inscrutable purposes, for my soul was so agitated*
> *by His words and miracles that I believe I would have died*
> *before my time if I had remained there . . . Alas, O my*
> *mother, with what sorrow and grief you have received me'.*[6]

Around the same time as this letter, she received a request from Cuno, simpering in tone and apologising for not having visited her because he is getting old and has 'been impeded by the various things I have to do'. He asks whether she could spare him a few visionary insights into 'our patron, the blessed Disibod'.[7] Her acerbic reply (nevertheless complete with three songs in honour of St Disibod) suggests an uneasy truce. His desire to make peace with his celebrated former abbess before his imminent death is understandable. She graciously complied. Towards the end of her life, in a retrospective letter to her nuns recalling the move to Rupertsberg, she described her release from the monks' jurisdiction in bland terms, without bitterness: 'they granted me this freedom and even promised me a written charter'. The *Vita* states more baldly that 'the community of St Disibod was precluded from usurping a right over the estates of St Rupert, or to put it more accurately, was forbidden to do so by the Divine power on high'. You would never guess how hard-won this liberty was for Hildegard.

Finally, in a charter dated 22 May 1158 Arnold, the newly appointed Archbishop of Mainz, confirmed the economic independence of the nuns, including freehold possession of Rupertsberg, as a gift of Hermann, Count Palatine of the Rhine, and his wife Gertrude. A second charter of the same date orders Disibodenberg to remain as the mother house, so that 'these sisters might not suffer neglect through uncertainty about priests', providing essential male clerics as needed to celebrate Mass and hear confession and so forth, but allowing the sisters free election of a new abbess after Hildegard's death. The breathtaking catalogue (even allowing for a degree of documentary inaccuracy) of properties given over to the Rupertsberg in 1158 shows how powerful the monastery had become since the nuns' arrival. In addition to the extensive lands in and around Bingen bequeathed by the late Hermann (d. 1156) 'as a righteous oblation for all time at the altar of the above mentioned church', donations had come from numerous noble well-wishers, including Hildegard's brothers Hugo and Drutwin. This incomplete list gives a picture:

A house in Bergen
A vineyard in Budesheim
A half-share of a house in Bermersheim
Five houses and a half-share in Bermersheim
Four houses in Weitersheim
A house in Harwesheim
A sixth part of a tithe in Roxheim and twenty servants
Vineyards next to Bingen (for the sum of 20 marks)
Three houses in Bermersheim (for 15 marks)
Five houses in Appenheim[8]

By whatever fruitful combination of heavenly guidance and earthly gamble, a mere decade after arriving at the Rupertsberg Hildegard had become a woman of property. Helenger, Cuno's replacement as Abbot of Disibodenberg, was one of the forty-five named witnesses of these two charters issued by the Archbishop of Mainz in 1158. We might surely permit ourselves a moment's speculation on the thoughts that may have entered Helenger's head as he stood among a throng of fellow abbots, provosts, deans, cantors, canons, counts, freemen, ministers 'and many others', all jostling to sign away his authority over one 'poor little woman' and her daughters in Christ.

CHAPTER NINE

CORRESPONDENCE AND FRIENDSHIP

Yet on a Sunday, when I was, as usual, in a state of
ecstasy, the angel of the Lord stood before me and said
'Why are you hiding gold in the mud?'

(LETTER FROM ELISABETH OF SCHÖNAU
TO HILDEGARD, *c.* 1152/6)

After her return to the newly independent Rupertsberg, the exact chronology of Hildegard's life for a time becomes uncertain. Her correspondence from the 1150s gives a good indication of her preoccupations in this period, the full diversity of which will be examined in the following chapters, before returning to the chronological account of her life. Hildegard was a keen correspondent. Nearly 400 letters exist to and from emperors, popes, bishops and others in holy orders from all over Europe seeking her advice on spiritual issues and solace for their transgressions. Most simply want her to pray for them. Her range of epistolary activity compares directly with Aelred of Rievaulx. Surprisingly, despite the overlap of illustrious recipients, they appear not to have written to each other: '[He] was sending letters to the lord pope, to the king of France, the king of England, the king of Scotland, the archbishops of Canterbury and York and nearly every bishop in England and especially to the Earl of Leicester, letters written with a noble pen to every grade of the ecclesiastical order, in which he left a living image of himself.'[1]

We should add here a note of caution concerning Hildegard's correspondence. The culture of the Middle Ages was still predominantly oral. The written word, not only because of the laboriousness of producing a manuscript and the level of education required to do so, still had a degree of novelty. Furthermore, letters were a literary genre, public pieces of writing bound by their own rules and forms, drawing heavily on Scripture and subject to the formulas of spiritual friendship. Personal messages would usually be delivered by the messenger himself, and secret correspondence was forbidden. Together with sermons, they rank as the great literary genre of the period. Collecting letters, especially by spiritual leaders whose words could be reused for religious and moral purposes, was accepted practice; 550 survive from Bernard of Clairvaux, ranging from lengthy treatise to brief, stinging riposte. Hildegard's letters, still in the early stages of scholarly investigation, remain an area of dispute and, in some quarters, scepticism and even dismay. The key issue concerns the degree to which Hildegard approved the rewriting of her correspondence at a later date with a view to enhancing her reputation for posterity. Since they were to act as an exemplar, it can be argued, corrections and rewritings were a necessary form of spiritual contrivance for the good of all, rather than worldly falsification in the interests of one. The tone of Hildegard's letters is rarely domestic, or personal, or concerning the monastic household of writer or recipient. Instead they offer homilies and theology, usually spiked with apocalyptic imagery. This may be a result of editing. Removing the personal or newsy and emphasising the pious and eternal was part of the honing process. At what point, however, does enhancement turn to falsification? Herein lies the controversy.

The assumption that Hildegard's letters were grouped and corrected by the admiring and industrious Guibert, at the time of her death or shortly after, has since been usurped by knowledge of an older manuscript. From this we can deduce that Volmar amended the letters according to Hildegard's instructions (nothing we know of Volmar suggests he would have wanted or dared to make changes of his own accord). The implication, examined exhaustively by the German editor of the letters, Lieven van Acker, is that a degree of fabrication resulted not from a later hagiographic effort to emphasise her saintliness but at the instigation of Hildegard herself. Why do this if not to make her reputation shine still brighter? The pairing of letters in the surviving Riesencodex (as the name implies, a giant manuscript of her *opera omnia* dating from during her lifetime or just after) suggests she was bombarded by requests for solace and advice, to which she graciously replied. Yet all the evidence now points to her having initiated many more exchanges than this convenient construction would indicate. The alacrity with which she dispatched vehement directives to those on high, not least popes and emperors as well as royalty (including Queen Eleanor of Aquitaine and King Henry II of England), tends to confirm that view. In addition, the smudging of historical facts and the unseemly grouping of letters according to the correspondents' social standing, with a certain amount of upgrading, offers further opportunity to elevate Hildegard's own position. This lurking spectre of manipulation has caused distress among her more ingenuous supporters. They prefer to believe that all the adjustments occurred after her death, arguing, reasonably enough, that anyone as busy as Hildegard, always moving forward, would scarcely have had time to tinker with past letters.

In this light, it is quite justified to read her entire correspondence as strictly generic and impersonal, to interpret her searing attacks on sin and evil as prophetic condemnations, within a recognised tradition, of the condition of mankind as a result of the Fall. How dull that would be. No amount of scholarship will ever disentangle entirely the layers of meaning and countermeaning, self and self-image, interference and manipulation, fact and fiction contained in them. Yet that they exist at all is a marvellous bonus. Compare the elaborate and far more extensive scholarly investigations over the celebrated love letters of Abélard and Héloïse, alleged in the 1970s and 1980s, to be forgeries. Héloïse's letters were assumed to have been written by Abélard, not least because male historians seemed unable to imagine that a woman might have produced anything quite so interesting. Fresh light cast by the discovery of 113 more letters has switched opinion once more in favour of their authenticity and their direct expressions of love.[2] The doors of scholarship should never be considered shut. The glory of Hildegard's writing is that, despite the tamperings and attempted smoothings by her secretaries or anyone else, the personal impulse still drives powerfully through convention. Her autocratic voice rings out loud and clear. The literary routines she observes are neither more peculiar nor more obtrusive than our own less ornate habit of starting all letters 'Dear' even to those who are anything but. The important fact, whatever artifice has occurred, is that men in high office from all over Europe were consulting a woman, a mere abbess, about matters of spiritual and doctrinal magnitude. Were Hildegard to have achieved nothing else in her life, she could justifiably be singled out by history for that fact alone.

Many of the correspondents write as if to a father (or mother) confessor seeking penance. The Archbishop of Trier, having succumbed to some unnamed temptation, begs consolation for 'a poor sinner', also adding as a sharp aside that her support will help quell rumours that her divine inspiration may not live up to her reputation. Her prophetic response, describing the times in which they live as 'squalid' and 'womanish', advises him to battle on in the high office to which he has been entrusted, even if the 'city' all about him is reduced to rubble. To the monks of the celebrated Cluniac monastery of Hirsau she writes in terse fury at their spiritual indigence, accusing them of 'foetid iniquity', 'self-imposed blindness', succumbing to the 'savage spears of lust of the flesh and the spittle of the devil'. The monks' sheepish response elicits a marginally softer reply from Hildegard, allowing that with due effort they might redeem themselves if they 'reach out and grasp mercy'. She issues brief, bland platitudes to an abbot worried about transubstantiation, which are unlikely to have allayed his doubts. She might have been wiser to refer him to *Scivias*, which explores the mystery of the sacrament at length, comparing it with a chick springing from an egg, or a butterfly from a chrysalis. (The belief in the Real Presence in the eucharistic bread and wine, though widespread, only received official notice in the Lateran Council of 1215.)

Odo of Paris begs her to help him, a 'broken reed', crawl

back out of 'the depths and slime of my sin'. He, too, consults her on a point of theology. His letter, referring to her music, offers useful evidence that her songs may already have been well known. The Bishop of Liège is 'plagued by instability of mind and body', while the Bishop of Prague is frustrated at living too far away to visit her but knows of her good works 'as we have heard tell about you even in these far-flung places'. An abbot writes of problems in his once illustrious monastery which 'through our own sins [has] been besmirched by the vilest kind of rumour'. She writes back describing her vision of his doomed monastery shaken by a whirlwind, 'a hurricane, as it were, filled with lightning, all black and murky', then stingingly points the finger of blame at the poor abbot himself, accusing him of malice, an 'appetite for perverse things' and lethargy. He may have wished he had never written. The likelihood, too, is that he would have had to endure his letter being read aloud to his fellow monks, since the epistolary art was not the private affair it was to become once the vernacular, rather than Latin, became common for written documents. Moreover, receiving a pronouncement from a public figure such as Hildegard excited interest.

Her letters to or concerning women frequently shed light on personal rather than spiritual matters. Significantly, she usually (but not always) refers to a vision, or what she 'saw and heard', combined with the 'poor little woman' formula when writing to men, as if needing to establish her authority, a tool she does not tend to employ so assiduously with her female correspondents. A common theme, whether from monks or nuns, is requests for advice about staying in administrative office, which Hildegard always recommends they should. The Abbess Sophia of Kitzingen enjoyed a close friendship with Hildegard; she writes about a proposed visit, promising to bring with her 'a well-born peer of mine, a praiseworthy nun' (of whom she can guarantee Hildegard will approve). A wife suffering from infertility travelled on foot to Rupertsberg, bringing a letter from five abbots who pleaded on her behalf for Hildegard to exert her healing powers. Its tenderness is touching, its subject matter a reminder that even in the Middle Ages, when birth control was haphazard and forbidden, when giving birth was both the main preoccupation and principal cause of death among women, failure to conceive was as much a cause of sorrow as it is now:

> *The woman who brings this letter to you is a noble lady, the wife of a man who loves her very much. With great devotion she comes to you, humble and afoot, although she could have come on horseback with a large company. And she has come to you for the following reason: although she bore children early in her marriage, for a long time now she has been sterile. Those first children died and she has been able to bear no others, for which she and her husband are consumed with grief. That is the reason she has flown to you, the handmaiden and friend of Christ, in the firm belief that through your merits with God, and your prayers, she may become fertile and, having borne a child, present the blessed fruit of her womb to Christ. Therefore, because we have been petitioned by both her and her husband, we ask that you stand in prayer for them before God. May God grant them the desire of their hearts.[3]*

Hildegard struck up a singular companionship with her younger contemporary, Elisabeth of Schönau, whom Hildegard scholars have awarded the doubtful accolade of 'second most famous female visionary of the twelfth century'.[4] Following in Hildegard's footsteps and, like her, struggling to deal with powerful visions and their consequences, Elisabeth sought advice from the older woman. She, too, had been confined since childhood, in a double monastery not far from Bingen. She visited Hildegard and corresponded with her following a vision in which an angel led her to a tent in a meadow in which there was a pile of books, with Hildegard's *Scivias* on the top. Their relationship demonstrates the concerns and anxieties of two religious women of the twelfth century fighting for recognition from their fellow monks and nuns. Elisabeth, too, kept her visions secret, confessing openly only in 1152. She was twenty-three years old and, like Hildegard, had endured years of illness and anxiety, which she understood as the hand of the Lord upon her.

Sharing her mystical experiences with others, however, did little to relieve Elisabeth of this deep physical and mental melancholy, and at one time she contemplated suicide. Her extant letters all twenty-two of which were written within the Rhineland locality and nearly all addressed to those in monastic establishments, show that she, too, sought the wisdom of someone older whom she could trust, much as Hildegard had appealed to Bernard of Clairvaux. Between 1152 and 1156 she wrote at length to the Rupertsberg abbess. The tone is confessional, providing a narrative of events in a candid and conversational vein quite absent in Hildegard's writings. Elisabeth's main concern is the scorn, censure and malicious gossip she had endured as a result of her apocalyptic perceptions (which, unlike Hildegard, she describes as 'ecstatic'), not to mention the physical suffering which accompanied them. Furthermore, her name had been taken in vain in false prophecies:

> To the Lady Hildegard, venerable mistress of the brides of Christ in Bingen . . .
> *I have been disturbed, I confess, by a cloud of troubles lately because of the unseemly talk of the people, who are saying many things about me that are simply not true. Still, I could easily endure the talk of the common people, if it were not for the fact that those who are clothed in the garment of religion cause my spirit even greater sorrow. For stirred by I don't know what spirit, they ridicule the grace of the Lord in me, and they have no fear of making hasty judgements about things that they have no understanding of. I hear, too, that some people are circulating a letter under*

my name about the Spirit of God. They have slandered me by claiming that I have prophesied about the day of judgement – which certainly I have never presumed to do, since such knowledge is beyond the ken of any human being.

But let me inform you of the cause of this talk, so that you may judge for yourself whether I have said or done anything presumptuously in this matter. As you have heard from others, the Lord has poured out His mercy to me beyond what I deserve ... Through His angel, He has frequently disclosed to me what sort of things are about to befall ... Seeking to avoid arrogance and not wishing to spread novelties, I sought, to the best of my ability, to keep all this hidden. Yet on a Sunday when I was, as usual, in a state of ecstasy, the angel of the Lord stood before me and said, 'Why are you hiding gold in the mud? This is the word of God that has been sent to the world to be spoken by you, because they have turned their faces away ...' And after He had said this, he lifted a scourge up over me, and as if in great wrath he struck me harshly five times, so that for three days thereafter I suffered from that beating in my whole body ...

Elisabeth then describes subsequent encounters with the angel of the Lord, the slander she suffers, and the support of her abbot, concluding:

It happened that on the fourth day before Easter I had endured great bodily suffering and then entered a state of ecstasy. Then the angel of the Lord appeared to me, and I said to him, 'Lord, what will be the outcome of the message that you spoke to me?' And he answered, 'Do not be grieved or disturbed if the things I predicted to you do not occur on the day that I had set, because the Lord has been appeased by the repentance of many.' After this, on the sixth day at about the third hour, I went with great pain into a state of ecstasy, and again the angel stood before me and said, 'The

Lord has seen the affliction of His people and has turned from them the wrath of His indignation.' I said to him, 'What then, my Lord? Will I not be an object of derision . . . ?' And he replied, 'Whatever happens to you on this occasion, endure it all with patience and kindness. Diligently heed Him Who, although He created the whole world, endured the derision of men. Now, the Lord is putting your patience to the test.'

My lady, I have explained the whole sequence of events to you so that you may know my innocence – and my abbot's – and thus may make it clear to others. I beseech you to make me a participant in your prayers and to write back to me some words of consolation as the Spirit of the Lord guides you.[5]

Hildegard's reply, while attentive, has the detached wisdom of experience rather than the hands-on advice for which Elisabeth might have hoped. She addresses Elisabeth as her 'daughter'. After a conventional apology for her own feminine inadequacy, she offers a brief résumé of the story of Creation, to show that those who are chosen by God are also vulnerable to the devil. Accordingly, they must learn to be especially humble:

I, a poor little form of a woman and a fragile vessel, say these things not from myself but from the Serene Light: People are vessels which God has fashioned for Himself, and which He has imbued with His inspiration so that He might complete all His works in them. For God does not work as man does, but all things are brought to perfection by His command. Vegetation, forests and trees appeared, the sun, moon and stars came forth, in order to serve mankind. The waters brought forth fish and birds. Herds and beasts also arose, all to serve human beings as God commanded. Of all Creation, however, human beings alone did not acknowledge Him . . . Ach! Woe! Then all the elements became entangled in the alternation between light and darkness, just as mankind did by transgressing against God's commands . . .

So, O daughter Elisabeth, the world is in flux . . . Listen now, O my anxious daughter. The arrogant deception of the ancient serpent sometimes wearies those persons inspired by God. For whenever that serpent sees a fine jewel he hisses and says, What is this? And he wearies that jewel with the many afflictions that distress a blazing mind longing to soar above the clouds, as if they were gods, just as he himself once did.

Listen again, Those who long to complete God's works must always bear in mind that they are fragile vessels, for they are only human . . . They can only sing the mysteries of God like a trumpet, which only returns a sound but does not function unassisted, for it is Another who breathes in to it that it might give forth a sound . . .

O my daughter, may God make you a mirror of life. I too cower in the puniness of my mind, and am greatly wearied by anxiety and fear. Yet from time to time I resound a little, like the dim sound of a trumpet from the Living Light. May God help me, therefore, to remain in His service.[6]

Despite these initial anxieties, Elisabeth's visions were written down and eventually circulated in Provençal and Icelandic as well as German. She was fortunate to have had a brother, Ekbert, who saw his sister's potential and sacrificed his own clerical career to be a humble monk at her service. Her biographer, Anne Clark, paints him as a medieval spin doctor (not a role which could be attributed to Hildegard's Volmar), calling him 'scribe, translator, editor, censor, publicist and publisher'. At times he appears to have suppressed those of her writings he considered too contentious. He was obviously skilful, though on occasion Elisabeth truculently withheld visions from him. The survival of 145 different manuscripts of her works, compared with the handful of Hildegard's, reflects well on his industry. Moreover, whereas Hildegard's writings were lengthy and not easily assimilated, Elisabeth of Schönau's visionary *Liber varium dei* might be described as a snappier affair, quicker to read and, crucially, less of a mammoth undertaking for copyists and thus more likely to find its way into monastery libraries.

Elisabeth's reputation reached England ahead of Hildegard's, thanks to Roger of Ford, an English Cistercian travelling in France. He sent a copy back to his abbot, with a disclaimer: 'And indeed I do not know how this work will be appreciated where you are, but I do know how that in these parts it is eagerly copied and read and heard not only by the unlearned but by bishops and abbots.'[7] He advised his abbot to initiate further copies, of which one could be sent to the women's religious foundation where his mother lived. This seemingly insignificant deed of an English monk is unexpectedly germane to several aspects of medieval life: the transmission of manuscripts between monasteries and between countries; the cautious acceptance of religious writings by women; the distinction between the uneducated and the clerics, both groups of whom had read the work in question; and finally, incidentally, the fact that his mother lived among nuns, common practice for widows, single mothers and the elderly.

CHAPTER TEN

PHYSICIAN AND HEALER

These remedies come from God and will either heal people or they must die, or God does not wish them to be healed.

(CAUSAE ET CURAE, 165.21)

The Middle Ages was a time of taxonomy. Europe was beset with a desire to classify, to make lists of things and group them in the world, and to order them like an index of the book of Creation. Bestiaries and herbals, cosmographic diagrams and maps had started appearing during the previous century. One of the earliest illustrated herbals, a version of the fifth-century *De herbarum virtutibus* of Apuleius Platonicus, was written at Bury St Edmunds around 1120. Advances in agriculture prompted numerous studies of husbandry. Animals, birds, fish, trees, stones, plants and stars all had to be listed and described, not only for the quixotic pleasure of their existence, but also for their medicinal or spiritual purpose. This was not empirical science but the necessary gathering of data which precedes it. Hildegard was as assiduous as any in her desire to catalogue, to comprehend, to control. From 1152 until 1158, in addition to an outpouring of letters and her ongoing negotiations with the monks of Disibodenberg, she was engaged in compiling two substantial scientific works. By their typological nature they must have been easier to compose in such hectic and unsettled times than a visionary work, which would have necessitated prolonged and quiet contemplation. In addition to all her other laurels, these writings have led her to be called the first woman doctor and the first woman scientist. If you insert the qualification 'one of the first' or 'one of the first by whom we have surviving works', the assertion retains a degree of accuracy. It is even possible that in her lifetime and shortly after these were the achievements by which she was popularly known, not least because they were more readily understood by the uneducated than her visionary and theological works. Yet they should not be classed entirely separately. To Hildegard, a study of the bounties of earthly Creation would have constituted an act of praise no less valid than her examination of the universe and salvation in *Scivias*. The physical world, too, has its own litany.

Until recently the two works, *Physica* and *Causae et Curae* (known by several titles but here referred to by those most commonly used; see Appendix I), have been dismissed by scholars, their authenticity doubted not least because the original manuscripts are lost and they fell from public attention for so many centuries after Hildegard's death. Charles Singer, the early twentieth-century historian of science and one of the first English commentators on Hildegard, with eloquent con-descension called the *Causae et Curae* 'an interesting relic of the Dark Ages'. Even her finest champion, Barbara Newman, only allows it as a 'series of haphazardly compiled jottings'. Others have been even less polite. Feminist scholars, however, in tones of immoderate evangelism, have leapt on the neglect of the works as a sign that their vigorous content was too strong for men to stomach. In addition, the fact that the Latin, debased with a generous smattering of German words, contrasted sharply in style with the often obscure but more elevated usage of her visionary works added further doubt to the authorship. Since these books are manuals, digests of detailed factual information, compendiums of local herbs and plants whose Latin names are unlikely to have been formulated, such arguments seem irrelevant.

The most recent investigations tend to confirm that while interpolations have been added by others, the work is essentially Hildegard's. In this respect, the books fall within the tradition of most medieval texts which have evolved in the process of being copied by many hands. That neither work has been easily available to a modern reader except through questionable and incomplete Latin editions has not helped, and this area of Hildegard studies lags way behind in the recent rush of scholarship, with much yet to be learnt. A new English edition of *Physica* (1998) and an abridged translation of *Causae et Curae* (1999, under the title *On Natural Philosophy and Medicine*) may redress this. Should we be surprised that one who showed such determination to communicate the secrets of the heavens should also want to reveal the workings of the earth?

In keeping with other anthologists of the time, Hildegard does not name her sources. Much scholarly energy has been spent trying to determine which newly translated texts from antiquity or Arabic she might have known. The most practical, if unprovable, conclusion is that she was familiar with the findings of many works in their translated or abridged versions – Pliny, pseudo-Apuleius, Isidore of Seville, Galen, Soranus and the like – combining that magpie knowledge with observation and popular tradition. Her outlook extends some of the theories propounded in the early Church penitentials. Thus the duty of the physician, wrote Alexander of Tralles in the sixth century, was 'to cool what is hot, to warm what is cold, to dry what is moist, and to moisten what is dry'. Similarly, the pseudo-Roman Penitential, written *c.* 830, argued that no physician could treat the sick 'unless he familiarises himself with their foulness'.

Hildegard was not alone of her sex to deal with such matters. Around 1175/85, another German nun, Herrad of Hohenbourg, compiled a celebrated encyclopedia on astronomy, geography and natural history entitled *Hortus deliciarum* (*Garden of Delights*), most important for its 636 drawings. Even less is known of Herrad's life than Hildegard's, though she appears not to have shared her senior contemporary's polymathic turn of mind. Had the two women lived in any later century they might not have embarked on such grand projects. The shift of learning, whether theological or scientific, from the monasteries to the universities proved a retrogressive step for women by excluding them from learned discourse. When the enthusiasm for a religious life declined, so too did women's opportunities. Moreover, medicine became a separate discipline, with the monastic *medicus* replaced by the university *physicus*. In this respect, as in so many others, Hildegard might be said to have been born at the right time.

The *Physica*, consisting of nine books listing almost a thousand plants and animals in German, is a study of botany, zoology, stones, metals and elements, describing their physical and medicinal properties. *Causae et Curae*, as its title indicates, examines the causes and cures of diseases, relating them to what has been clumsily called an 'allegorical microcosmic physiology' and offering remedies, mainly using plants. The scope of this book allows only a glance at the range of material covered: even to précis the categories and inventories of which they consist would extend beyond a chapter's reasonable length. If the latter years of her life were consumed by public activity, the first forty were spent in the quiet of Disibodenberg, with ample chance to list and observe the human and natural life around her. How, otherwise, could she have identified in such extraordinary detail the thirty-seven species of fish named in Book V of *Physica*, many common to the rivers Glan, Nahe and Rhine, on whose banks she lived all her life?

Presumably calling on the lore of local fishermen, she describes their habitat, whether they prefer to be near the surface or in the depths of the river, whether they flourish in mud or near rocks and where and how they breed and lay their eggs. Not all her knowledge came from first-hand experience. She includes, for example, the whale – listed as a fish rather than a mammal – with a hearty recommendation to eat the flesh as a panacea for most ills, from fevers and ague to scrofula, just as using a knife handle made from whale bone will cure a painful arm, and wearing shoes or a belt made from the skin will banish infirmities. Bladder of sturgeon soothes dropsy, liver of turbot rubbed on the eyes is recommended for clouded sight, powdered salmon bones are a remedy for rotting gums. Shellfish, however, are considered unclean and of no value, while lampreys have 'the nature of serpents', live in caverns and swamps, eat unclean foods, are bad for the stomach and incite lust.

Other sections of *Physica* are equally encyclopedic. The first contains 230 individual entries on plants, with many herbal remedies, love potions and lust quenchers. Hildegard does not share our modern enthusiasm for St John's Wort (which she dismisses as good for animal fodder but otherwise 'small, uncultivated and neglected'), preferring the antidepressant properties of primrose, rue or fennel. Arnica, today used liberally by middle-class mothers as a cure-all for children's bumps and bruises, was considered as potent an aphrodisiac as that given by Isolde to Tristan. Anyone touched with it 'will burn lustily with love for the person who is afterward touched by the same herb. He or she will be so incensed with love, almost infatuated, and will become a fool.' She celebrates the soothing and healing properties, still recognised today, of calendula, camomile and aloe. Her grasp of diet is often borne out by modern theory and practice. Butter should be eaten in moderation by those who are fat 'lest his weak flesh becomes fatter',[1] salt (like eggs, listed as a plant) is good but not to excess, spearmint aids digestion. In essence this type of catalogue as the standard household herbal still survives, albeit now with Linnaean refinements. Present fashions for natural remedies have rehabilitated many nostrums long dismissed as old wives' tales.

In the second book she describes the elements, including seas and rivers; the third lists trees, the fourth stones and gems. Book VI is devoted to birds, listing seventy-two different kinds, mostly familiar to us today (though precise identification is sometimes hampered by Hildegard's Latin and German names), but including the mythical griffin as well as flying insects such as the honeybee, grasshopper, gnat, firefly and glow-worm. With only a few exceptions, most of the data again concerns edibility or medicinal purpose. A bat, knocked senseless, tied to the loins of a human and left to die, is guaranteed to cure that person's jaundice. The pulverised bladder of a capercaillie will help anyone suffering from maggots or worms. The head of a lark fed to a mad dog will restore it to sanity. An unguent of sparrowhawk and fat cools ardour if rubbed on the 'privy member and loins' of a man or (following the medieval belief that the navel is the source of female desire) 'around the umbilicus, and in the opening of the belly button' of a woman. Peacock and falcon are bad to eat, seagull, cock and hen good. The pelican, however, knows whether a person is sad or happy, and reflects their mood by singing or staying silent. It also has the prophetic power to know when a person is about to die, which it indicates 'with a few sounds and is then quiet'.[2]

Hildegard's classification of animals (Book VII) follows an apparently random grouping. On closer inspection it has a logic of its own, according to whether the animal in question has fur or is hoofed, is clean or unclean, and whether its value to humans is medicinal or for food or clothing. Following the tradition of bestiaries dating from this period, superstition and magic play as important a role as observation. Because animals live on the earth, they have closer links with humans.

> *Tame animals that walk on land show the gentleness of the human being, which he has through his correct ways. And so human rationality says to each person, 'You are this or that animal,' since animals have in them qualities similar to the nature of humans. Animals which eat each other, are nourished on bad foods, and bear multiple offspring (as the wolf, dog and the pig) are, like weeds, harmful to the nature of a human being, since he does not do those things. However, herd animals that eat clean foods like hay and similar fodder, and bear no more than one offspring at a time are – like good and useful plants – beneficial for people to eat. In both kinds of animals certain medicines are found.[3]*

The more like man animals are, the better. Thus the donkey, though stupid enough to make its flesh stink, nearly blind and crazed with lust, has the incomparable advantage of being obedient and subservient. 'It is willingly with people because some part of its nature nears that of humans.' Hildegard's portrayal of the dog is especially touching: 'It senses and understands man, loves him, willingly dwells with him and is faithful. The devil hates and abhors the dog because of its loyalty to humans. A dog, recognising hatred, wrath and perfidy in a person, often howls at him . . . If there is a thief in the house, or someone who wants to steal, it growls and gnashes its teeth.'[4] It also has powers of divination, wagging at a happy prospect, howling when sadness is a certain outcome. The heat in its tongue can heal ulcers, and shoes made from its skin ease painful feet. Its flesh should not be eaten, nevertheless, since it is unclean, its intestines and liver poisonous, its brain soft and weak. Boiled hedgehog with wine, cinnamon and pimpernel is recommended for a good health-giving supper, likewise the meat of sheep and goats. Most other flesh is considered unclean or unhealthy, that of the horse heavy and indigestible, that of the pig and bear liable to arouse lustful thoughts. A little cake made from a good helping of mole's blood, duck beak, the feet of a female goose and wheat flour, eaten for five days, should cure epilepsy (though the sufferer should omit pork, beef, eel, cheese, eggs and raw fruits and vegetables from his diet), as should drinking water in which the body of a dead mouse has been steeped. A broth made from pounded hamster liver and eaten with bread relieves scrofula and swellings, and the pelt is good for clothing. No indication is given as to where a sufficient number of hamsters might be found to make even a modest human garment.

Of reptiles, which include man-hating and devilish dragons, Hildegard can find scarcely a kind word to say. Their over-whelming affinity with the serpent and the Fall gets the better of her reason:

> *When human beings were wiped out in a flood of waters,*
> *in divine vengeance, these vermin, unable to live in water,*

were suffocated by it. The flood scattered their cadavers,
full of poison, putrefied. From the putrefaction, other worms
of the same kind were born and were spread throughout
the world. Certain vermin kill people or animals with their
poisons, others kill only humans. Vermin that are a bit like
diabolic arts in their nature kill other animals, as well as
humans, with their poisons. Those that do not . . . have in
them poisons which are a bit weak. Through their poisons,
they bring humans many diseases and dangers along with
death, but they are unable to kill other animals.[5]

An exception is the earthworm, which has the advantage of
having grown in the same greenness (*viriditas*) in which grass
sprouts. A paste-like concoction made up of wine, vinegar,
wheat flour and several mashed-up earthworms provides yet
another remedy for the all-too-common complaint of scrofula
(mentioned thirty-five times in *Physica*). If no worms are
available, slugs can be used instead. The detail, as precise as
any recipe, with which each salve is offered suggests a practical understanding of how these medicines should be made
and applied.

How did Hildegard acquire such knowledge? The likelihood
is that as a young woman she would have served a form of
apprenticeship in the infirmary at Disibodenberg, helping to
treat not only the sick but also the deaf, blind, lame, old
and infirm with a range of common applications of the time,
including baths, taking the pulse and examining urine. *Causae*
et Curae has an extensive account of the appropriate use of
bloodletting, the various methods, the illnesses the practice can
treat and the suitable age or condition of patients on whom it is
to be enacted. An architectural plan, rare in its survival and
its detail, from the ninth-century monastery of St Gall in
Switzerland, shows a separate bloodletting house (as well as a
physician's house, a medicine store, in effect a pharmacy, and
a medicinal herb garden, all common to monasteries built

subsequently). Nuns would have been accustomed to acting as midwives to local women and even, in the absence of a priest, hearing their confessions before labour because of the high risk of mortality, or baptising babies in cases of stillbirth. Oil of thyme, lily or musk, rubbed on the midwife's hands, was used to ease the turning of a baby in the womb or the enlarging of the mother's cervix. Strange cases of surrogate births are recorded, as in the instance of the woman who used a pillow to feign pregnancy, then adopted a peasant woman's child. Hildegard's biographers record no comparable event but list several miracles concerning labour, childbirth and infertility (later cited as evidence of her sanctity), in which Hildegard's hair, or a fragment of clothing, brought about a cure. Sexually transmitted diseases commonly required medical treatment. Often referred to as leprosy and thus adding to the shame of that illness, they were thought to be carried only by women, especially whores. A work from the thirteenth century entitled *On the Secrets of Women*, attributed to Albert Magnus, accused prostitutes of using iron or other metals in their vaginas in order to hurt men. More likely to have been intended as contraceptives, their corrosive properties nevertheless caused women severe internal damage.

Hildegard's knowledge, of women's health especially but of men's too, was wide-ranging and must have become more extensively known as her celebrity grew. Many of her letters and miracles (described in conventional hagiographic terms in the *Vita*) suggest she had healing powers, not entirely reliant on visionary wisdom, but involving practical application of tinctures, herbs and precious stones. None the less, whatever her methods – and she tended not to recommend the more invasive kind – she considered the Heavenly Father as the single true doctor of man. As God states in *Scivias*: 'I am the great Physician of all diseases and act like a doctor who sees a sick man who longs to be cured.' St Benedict, six centuries before, had expressly forbidden the study of medicine – at that time almost entirely derived from pagan texts – insisting that prayer be applied as the only remedy. Gradually the Rule was disregarded and monasteries became centres of healing and medical expertise, with their own elaborate herb gardens in which to grow their remedies. Gathering, pounding and pulverising herbs, animals and stones, reducing them to a powder to mix with oils, wine or vinegar, must have been a time-consuming and exacting process. Little evidence of women doctors survives from the period. What there is tends to relate to women in holy orders, notably abbesses or prioresses, usually spoken of as midwives (today still called *sages-femmes* in French) concerned largely with gynaecological matters. The most frequently cited female medical writer from the time is Trotula of Salerno, information on whose life is scant and much debated. Her treatise on women's health (*The Diseases of Women*) survives in nearly one hundred manuscripts, with further corrupt versions in French and German.

Hildegard's view of the natural world, shared by most early Christian writers, was that the perpetual truths of the spiritual life found everyday expression in temporal objects. In broadest terms, this meant seeing the divine patterns of the world deranged by the sinful behaviour of man. Thus when Lucifer was cast out of glory because of his pride, the fallen angels became a galaxy of stars. The four temperaments, in harmony before the Fall, turned into raging elements. The tears of man derive from the overexcited humours of the lungs and breast which spring to the eyes in liquid form, just as the waxing and the waning of the moon disturbs the winds and causes fogs from the waters of the world. Illness, likewise, is caused by an imbalance of these humours. An excess of *livores* leads to profound physical disorders such as gout, paralysis and cancer, and mental afflictions such as melancholy, anger and suicidal tendencies. Bad nutrition and bad attitudes can affect this balance. Disorders of the bowel are related directly to lack of harmony in the world, and to

Adam eating at the wrong time, 'like a glutton'.

Her notion that all illness stems from a single cause rather than an array of different ones has been compared with the holistic approach of alternative medicine today. That *Hildegardmedezin* has been so enthusiastically embraced by alternative practitioners is hardly surprising. Two German doctors recently constructed an entire pseudo-scientific curative theory based on Hildegard's teachings,[6] with treatments in the form of syrups, oils, salves, powders and teas for a range of conditions from breast cancer, AIDS and heart disease to halitosis and morning sickness. Her favourite grain, spelt (a form of wheat), makes frequent appearances. They argue that her account of cancer, including the pre-cancerous stages of the disease, is wholly in keeping with modern scientific knowledge. Swallowing Hildegard's outlook wholesale, they claim that although the German Food and Drug Administration has recognised more than one hundred herbal drugs, many used by Hildegard, such scientific recognition is not necessary for the 'believing Hildegard friend' since her knowledge comes from 'God's wisdom'. However, they draw the line at her divinely sanctioned advocacy of whale meat (or even pounded hamsters?), 'which the editors felt ethically best to delete from the body of the book'. To their credit, they list the omitted references in a footnote.

Yet even the most briskly sceptical, among whom the present writer might be included, must surely marvel at the fact that Hildegard's theories and therapies have such a close affinity with homeopaths and others outside conventional medicine today. The white coat may not be all that different from the black habit. In language close to the terms Hildegard herself might have used, the late Poet Laureate Ted Hughes, interviewed by a British newspaper shortly before his death in 1999, explained his cancer of the bowel as the direct result of his own black thoughts affecting his immune system. This example is given not to suggest the validity of such views, merely to show the surprising modernity of medieval thinking or, conversely, the crude level of guesswork we continue to apply to the cause of disease today, in many respects little more understood now than in the twelfth century. After a similar lapse of time as that which separates us from Hildegard, one might guess that a large proportion of what we think and believe will seem 'medieval'. The idea of needing works of reference does not seem extraordinary today. That each monastery should make such compilations and that word would get about that a particular person in a particular abbey had made a useful list which could be copied should not surprise us. Somewhere in the human psyche, great works of reference are still revered and thought of as acts of celebration.

The distinguishing feature throughout Hildegard's scientific and medical writings is her insatiable appetite for offering practical advice. Spiritual matters, though always present, take second place. Let us take, as a final example, her detailed account of water and its suitability for drinking,[7] a matter of no less interest then than now, and certainly no less of a minefield. She may have known the works of Bartholomew of Salerno (a centre of medical thinking in the eleventh and twelfth centuries), whose treatises on pathology and therapeutics were in wide circulation at the time but who also wrote a study on distilled water. Her prime concern is the well-being of the drinker: swamp water should be boiled, well water is better than spring-water, spring-water an improvement on river water, which should be boiled and allowed to cool before drinking, while snow-water is, quite simply, dangerous. The salt waters of the west are too turbid, the fresh waters of the west not sufficiently warmed by the sun; the salt waters of the south are venomous because of the worms and small animals found therein; southern waters, though naturally warm, make the drinker's flesh fatty and black in colour. Finally, as an aid to digestion, Hildegard advises drinking water in which the dried liver of a lion has been left, counsel which seems certain, if not to have relieved the crisis in question, at least to have prompted a different one.

CHAPTER ELEVEN

ON SEXUALITY

And the Lord God said to the woman: Why hast thou done this? And she answered: The serpent deceived me, and I did eat.

And the Lord God said to the serpent, Because thou hast done this thing, thou art cursed among all cattle, and beasts of the earth. Upon thy breast shalt thou go, and earth shalt thou eat all the days of thy life...

To the woman also he said: I will multiply thy sorrows, and thy conceptions. In sorrow shalt thou bring forth children, and thou shalt be under thy husband's power, and he shall have dominion over thee.

(GENESIS 3:13–16)

A woman conceives a child not by herself but through a man, as the ground is ploughed not by itself but by a farmer.

(SCIVIAS, II, VI)

Perpetual virginity, in Hildegard's view, was supreme among virtues. Holy maidenhood was God's unique gift to womanhood, and to nuns in particular. Christ had been born of flesh 'which had never secreted filth' or known sin. Virginity is 'the most beautiful fruit of all the fruits of the valleys, and the greatest of all the persons in the palace of the unfailing King'.[1] Yet considering her lifetime's confinement in monastic institutions, Hildegard of Bingen had an impressive grasp of the heterosexual, sexually active life. It is not impertinent to wonder how she acquired such knowledge, nor on consideration surprising that she did. Her communication with the outside world would have been more direct than that of an enclosed nun today. As we saw in the last chapter, she encountered married women, widows, prostitutes and midwives in what was in effect the abbey clinic. From frank illustrations and contemporary accounts, it is evident that the people of the Middle Ages were less prudish than we are today over sexual issues. Even had she not read the work firsthand, Hildegard would have been familiar with *De Coitu* by the eleventh-century monk and translator Constantine the African, a wide-ranging treatise on the pleasures and penalties of intercourse which manages to avoid all mention of women. (Chaucer later named him in *The Merchant's Tale* as that 'accursed monk' whose numerous aphrodisiac recipes the sexually incompetent January tried in order to satisfy his nubile May: 'He drank them all, not one did he eschew.')

Though she saw Creation as the gift of God, Hildegard's understanding of mankind is surprisingly functional and detailed. She gave practical, rather than specifically Christian advice, by letter and in person, on an extensive range of medical and physiological problems. Her works, including the visionary texts as well as the non-theological writings, offer opinions on an array of matters physical and biological. By any standard this description of sexual intercourse, taken from *Causae et Curae*, is realistic, technically graphic and, intentionally or not, erotic. Twelfth-century accounts of sex are not in themselves rare, but the absence of moral judgement here is exceptional:

> *When a woman is making love with a man, a sense of heat in her brain, which brings forth with it sensual delight, communicates the taste of that delight during the act and summons forth the emission of the man's seed. And when the seed has fallen into its place, that vehement heat descending from her brain draws the seed to itself and holds it, and soon the woman's sexual organs contract and all the parts that are ready to open up during the time of menstruation now close, in the same way as a strong man can hold something enclosed in his fist.[2]*

In the Middle Ages the sexual act was of as much concern to the theologian as to the physician. The sole purpose of intercourse, in the eyes of the Church, was reproduction. The relationship between pleasure and sin was necessarily complex. Gnosticism and Manichaeism held that flesh was essentially evil, that the nether regions of men and women in their entirety were works of the devil. The early Church Fathers described sex variously as unclean and shameful. The imminent second coming of Christ, together with the fact that The Child had already been born, rendered sexual intercourse unnecessary. Behind their teaching was the more practical view that unbridled lust, within or outside marriage, was degrading. St Paul held that celibacy was superior to marriage, but that it was 'better to marry than to burn' (Paul 1, Cor. 7:9). The Revelation of St John called sex an experiment of the serpent, marriage a 'foul and polluted' way of life.

Indeed, marriage, for several centuries, was considered an indulgence of the weak rather than an honourable institution. Only in the twelfth and thirteenth centuries did it become a sacrament, theoretically at least permanent in the eyes of God and indissoluble. St Jerome considered it useful only to those feeble men who could not sleep alone at night. Indeed, he could find little good about it, arguing that a faithful slave is better than a wife who 'thinks she proves herself mistress if she acts in opposition to her husband'. Furthermore, a wife was an untried commodity (unlike 'horses, asses, cattle, clothes, kettles, wooden seats, cups and earthenware pitchers'). You had to take what you got even if she had a bad temper 'or was proud or had bad breath'. Clerical celibacy, though made obligatory by the Second Lateran Council of 1139, was still not enforced with complete success. Hildegard considered a priest incapable of having 'two marriages', of the spirit and of the flesh. 'The priest is the pastor and father of the people who have physical marriages; so if he has one to the same extent, who will be his priest?'[3] Muslims had a low opinion of Christian priests. As the twelfth-century writer Ibn'Abdun sardonically observed, they were 'evil doers, fornicators and sodomites'. Writing from a position of prejudice though he was, his rebukes are merciless: '[among the Christian priests] there is not one who has not two or more women with whom he sleeps. This has become a custom among them, for they have permitted what is forbidden and forbidden what is permitted. The priests should be ordered to marry, as they do in the eastern lands.' Some monks may have had wives or concubines. It was not at all unknown for a nun to become pregnant.

Famously Héloïse, on retreat (but not yet a nun) at Argenteuil, succumbed to carnal passion with Abélard in a corner of a cloister. Later, writing from her convent to the now castrated husband from whom she was separated, she recalled that hot encounter in literal and specific terms. She cannot have been the only nun to have found it difficult keeping her mind on the Mass:

> *Even during the celebration of Mass, when our prayers should be purer, lewd thoughts are on their wantonness instead of on prayers. I should be groaning over the sins I have committed, but I can only sigh for what is lost. Everything we did, with all the times and places are stamped on my heart, along with your image, so that I live through it all again. Even in sleep I know no respite. Sometimes my thoughts are betrayed in a movement of my body, or they break out in an unguarded word.*[4]

Beyond the natural curiosity about her own body, and possible frustrations on occasion during her long life, Hildegard prized virginity above all else. Had she known Héloïse, she might have found it hard to square the Frenchwoman's known loss of virginity with her position as abbess of the Paraclete. She would, however, have shared Abélard's view that nature had made women's genitals with the express purpose of pleasing men. That she should advise many straying monks and abbots on the matter of concupiscence suggests she was forced to think hard and often about the matter. In common with other theologians of the time, Hildegard believed that a version of innocent sexual pleasure, neither erotic nor ecstatic, was possible before the Fall. Quite what kind of endeavour this implies is not easy to say; perhaps a kind of agreeable toil with an intended outcome, in this case conception. With the Fall came lust and darkness. Sex became vice. A range of carnal sins was identified, from sodomy to adultery, abortion, contraception, castration, nudity and sexual relations while a woman was menstruating or weaning a child. Peter Lombard (d. 1160), the influential theologian who taught at the school of Notre-Dame in Paris, explored the time of pre-Lapsarian innocence with some vividness of imagination: 'If the first humans had not sinned there would have been carnal union in Paradise without any sin or stain and there would have been an "undefiled bed" [Heb. 13:4] there and union without concupiscence . . . Just as we move some bodily members towards others, such as the hand to the mouth, without ardour of lust, likewise they would have used genital organs without any itching of the flesh.'

Hildegard's account is equally potent. In the sweet day of the Beginning, when Adam gazed at Eve,

> he was entirely filled with wisdom, for he saw in her the mother through whom he would procreate children. And when Eve looked at Adam, it was as if she were gazing in to heaven . . . But man's love, with its blazing heat, compared with woman's love is like the fire of blazing mountains, that is difficult to extinguish compared with a wood fire that is easily quenched. Woman's love, compared with man's love, is like sweet warmth proceeding from the sun, which brings forth fruits.[5]

Her Adam seems to be depicted in the sexless creature at the centre of the widely reproduced image of the Trinity and the Macrocosm in the Lucca Codex of *Liber divinorum operum* (made in the early thirteenth century; see Appendix I). After the Fall, however, a new, uncontrollable desire is awakened. In the moment of Adam's sin, his natural powers of procreation were transformed to another organ. 'And so, because a man still feels this great sweetness in himself, and is like a stag thirsting for the fountain, he races swiftly to the woman and she to him – she like a threshing floor pounded by his many strokes and brought to heat when the grains are threshed inside her.'[6] The ploughing and tilling image, hardly sustainable in today's language of political correctness, follows the tradition of Plato, Virgil and St Augustine. Man, Hildegard observed, had changed from a state of perfection to one of bitterness. 'For man's blood, burning in the ardour and heat of lust, ejects a spume from itself that we call semen, as a pot placed on the fire brings up foam from the water because of the flame's heat.'

Sexual desire, for men and women alike, originates in the very core of the being, the bone marrow (*medulla*, literally pith, kernel, marrow, quintessence), which, pulsating with fire and desire, sends out a 'blazing sexual wind', like a storm. As in the recurring image of the boiling pot, the result is ejaculation in women and men. During orgasm both secrete a frothy fluid 'identical to milk', which in the case of the man contains seed. This seed derives from the blood of Adam, of which women's menstrual blood is the counterpart. This 'foam' reaches the cavities of the genital organs 'accompanied by a sweet sensation'. With a particularly lively image, Hildegard graphically explains the strength of male desire by man's physiology: because of the narrowness of the loins and its tight musculature, his craving is confined, with nowhere to spread. The wind of desire blows like bellows into two tents (*tabernacula*) and inflates them. These two organs (testicles) defend the penis 'like bastions fortifying a tower', causing an erection. Thus his passion grows uncontrollable and 'he can no longer abstain from spilling his foamy seed'. Woman, on the other hand, is more temperate because the wide space of the womb and pudenda allow the sexual wind to gust freely. Her pleasure, essentially passive, must be aroused by a man. Female desire is like the sun, bringing ripeness rather than violence, thus women can refrain from sexual pleasure more easily than men.[7]

> *When the storm of lust surges in a male, it turns around in him like a mill. For his loins are like a forge which the marrow provides with fire. This forge then pours the fire into the male's genital area and lets it strongly burn. But when the wind of pleasure comes forth from the female's arrow it falls into her uterus, which is joined to the navel, and it stirs her blood toward pleasure. This wind spreads out in her abdomen because in the area around a woman's*

navel the uterus has a wide and, as it were, open space.
Consequently she will burn there more gently with pleasure,
albeit more frequently because of her moisture.

Therefore out of shame woman is able to refrain from
pleasure more easily than man, so that she emits the foam
of semen more seldom than man; it is sparse and scanty
compared to man's foam, like a piece of bread compared to
a whole loaf. Yet when the said foam is not expelled from a
woman after she has experienced pleasure, it happens
frequently that it mingles in the blood vessels of the uterus
which are white and fatty, so that it then flows off through
menstruation. Any residue is discharged from the uterus.
Sometimes it is also dispersed, broken up and reduced to
nothing in the uterus when a woman experiences pleasure
without being touched by a man.[8]

Intercourse in marriage was essential for procreation, but
what restraints could be imposed on all other sexual activity?
The Church laid down various restrictions as to when intercourse might be allowed, with most days of the ecclesiastical
calendar offering opportunity for denial (in addition to Lent
and Easter, Thursdays recalled Christ's arrest, Fridays His
death, and so on). Only the conventional sexual position was
allowed; others were regarded as bestial, likely to inhibit
conception and therefore sinful. For the same reason oral
intercourse (*semine in ore*) was punished by years of penance,
while *coitus interruptus* required fasting and abstention for
anything up to ten years; one penance instructed whipping by
the parish priest as well as singing penitential psalms. Menstruating women, according to Pliny and to the Old Testament,
were out of bounds sexually. This was the time when they were
at their guiltiest, dirtiest and most dangerously alluring. As Pliny
famously opined, not only could menstrual blood turn red wine
sour and crops barren, cause fruit to fall from trees and give
dogs rabies; worse still, any child conceived during

menstruation would have red hair and leprosy. Hildegard shared the view that intercourse with a menstruating woman was illicit, apparently as much as anything out of sympathy for the woman. At the same time, women's periods were one of the penalties of Eve's digression. Urging man to follow his desires only 'in the right way with his wife' and out of desire for children, Hildegard writes (speaking in the voice of a vision):

> But I do not want this work done during the wife's menses, when she is already suffering the flow of her blood, the opening of the hidden parts of her womb, lest the flow of her blood carry with it mature seed after its reception, and the seed, thus carried forth, perish; at this time the woman is in pain and in prison, suffering a small portion of the pain of childbirth. I do not remit this time of pain for women, because I gave it to Eve when she conceived sin in the taste of the fruit; but therefore the woman should be cherished in this time with a great and healing tenderness.[9]

Restrictions for menstruating women extended beyond the bed to the church. Whereas in Augustine's day the Pope allowed 'polluted' women to take communion according to choice, by the seventh century they were forbidden. The Penitential of Theodore ruled that 'neither nuns nor laywomen' could enter a church or take communion while menstruating. If they did, three weeks of penitential fasting ensued. The segregation of women while menstruating is of course an ancient and continuing tradition in diverse civilisations. The Dogon of Mali still maintain the custom of building adobe huts, furnished with little more than trestles, to one side of the village where women sleep in the days in which they bleed, returning to their families in the morning. In *Scivias*, a woman who has recently given birth or lost her virginity is likewise instructed not to enter God's temple, 'because her hidden members have been broken'. She should wait 'while injured by the bruise of her corruption' until fully healed. A worse sin, however, is for a man to have sex with a pregnant woman, not only because the foetus will be polluted but because of the 'wasted semen': 'Therefore O humans, weep and howl to your God. Whom you so often despise in your sinning, when you sow your seed in the worst fornication and thereby become not only fornicators but murderers; for you cast aside the mirror of God and sate your lust at will.'

Paradoxically, physical union was nevertheless considered health-giving. St Paul (Cor. 7:3–6) allowed that husband and wife must not 'refuse each other except by consent for a time'. One strong ground for divorce was the failure of a man to perform sexually. Wise women, of whom Hildegard would have been one, were entitled to inspect women for their virginity or otherwise. Legal cases from the thirteenth century describe witnesses gathering round the bed of newly married couples to examine the man's potency, and 'if the member is always found useless' the marriage is annulled, though in Hildegard's practice he might first have had to try a dose of the rue, wormwood and honey infusion she recommends as an antidote to any failure to ejaculate. Hildegard denounces the notion of divorce unless either side breaks the law by fornication, in which case they may part 'not so that the husband or wife can seek another marriage; either they shall stay together in righteous union or they shall both abstain from such unions, as the discipline of church practice shows'.[10]

The reason women escaped so lightly on the grounds of their husband's impotence was the widely held belief that sexual activity was essential for female well-being, denial a physical danger to all. Hildegard, like others at the time following the theories of the Greek physician Galen (recently translated and becoming widely dispersed), believed that both men and women had seed. This was emitted during ejaculation and led to conception. To retain it was detrimental to health.[11] Women, especially, should rid themselves of bodily excess through intercourse, menstruation and, if necessary, masturbation to prevent a condition described as 'uterine suffocation'. Descriptions of this condition, to which nuns themselves must have been especially prone, sound uncannily close to Hildegard's own unexplained and regular illnesses. The symptoms include fainting, breathing difficulties, hysteria and, at worst, madness.

A modern physician or psychiatrist might identify a combination of sexual and psychological repression. Hildegard herself, describing women of a 'sanguine' temperament, warned that those who have to live their lives without a man and cannot bear children are prone to an array of physical ailments, whereas when they have a man, they are healthy. In *Causae et Curae* she draws attention to the dangers of early menopause (which she states should occur with a cessation of periods at the fiftieth year), attributing subsequent gout, melancholia, kidney pain and general swelling to the congestion of 'waste matter and foulness' from which 'menstruation should have purged their bodies'.[12] So dangerous was the build-up of women's seed or menstrual blood considered in the Middle Ages that urgent remedies were required. While male masturbation incurred moderate penance (a thirty-day fast for a monk, fifty for a bishop; mild punishment since the sin was considered a solitary one), for women it was on occasion deemed an essential form of purging, sometimes requiring the assistance of a doctor or midwife to enact. This is within the tradition of medieval theories of purgation, which held that sweating, sneezing, tears, nose-bleed, vomiting, excretion and urination, as well as menstruation and bloodletting, helped rid the body of damaging waste material. Still following this line of thought, a central belief of modern homeopathy is that all discharge is healthy.

Hildegard herself took a stern view on masturbation, or the emission of seed in any form except in quest of conception. She castigates those who 'cast out their semen like asses' as liable to suffer red eyes and bad sight, while sexual excess of any kind in

The child Hildegard being presented by her parents to Jutta at Disibodenberg
– but who are the other two nuns? (*Polychrome bas-relief at the Rochus
Chapel, Bingen, 1895*)

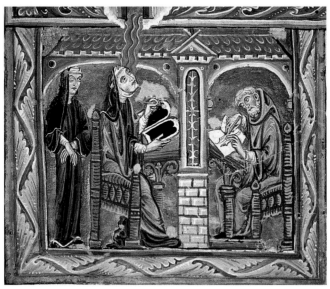

In the Scriptorium. Hildegard, with wax tablet and stylus, receives the divine
message watched by a figure thought to be the nun Richardis; Volmar
inscribes Hildegard's vision on vellum. (*Liber divinorum operum, Lucca
MS1942 c. 1230–40*)

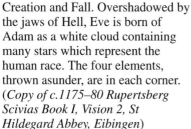

Creation and Fall. Overshadowed by the jaws of Hell, Eve is born of Adam as a white cloud containing many stars which represent the human race. The four elements, thrown asunder, are in each corner. (*Copy of c.1175–80 Rupertsberg Scivias Book I, Vision 2, St Hildegard Abbey, Eibingen*)

The Fallen Stars. Lucifer, the great dark star, and his followers are turned to cinders and tossed in a whirlwind towards the abyss. (*Copy of the c.1175–80 Rupertsberg Scivias Book III Vision 1, St Hildegard Abbey, Eibingen*)

The Day of the Great Revelation. Mother Church, once pure, is sullied with scaly blemishes and a monstrous head of Antichrist at her genitals. Hildegard describes how the head, 'covered in excrement', is released from the woman then struck dead by a thunderbolt, seen to the right of the picture. *(Copy of the c.1175–80 Rupertsberg Scivias, Book III, Vision 11, St Hildegard Abbey, Eibingen)*

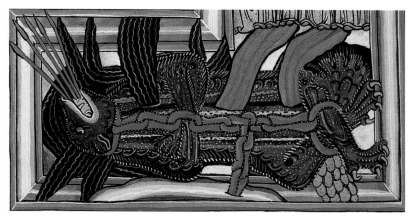

The Devil in Chains. The serpent, covered in ulcers and pustules and spewing forth flames, is fastened to a rock in the abyss. Its headbone has been crushed, its jaw dislocated. *(Copy of the c.1175–80 Rupertsberg Scivias, Book II, Vision 7, St Hildegard Abbey, Eibingen)*

The Tower of Salvation, showing God seated on a throne, the three-winged Head of God and a four-walled city pointing north, south, east and west. The building is at an angle, representing man's struggle against the devil. Oliver Sacks cites this as a manifestation of Hildegard's possible migraines (see also The Fallen Stars on page 2 of this picture section). (*Copy of the c.1175–80 Rupertsberg Scivias Book III, Vision 2, St Hildegard Abbey, Eibingen*)

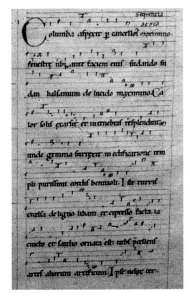

Columba Aspexit, a hymn from Hildegard's *Symphonia*. (*From Lieder Facsimile Riesencodex c. 1180–90, Hessische Landesbibliothek M32*)

God, ruler of the universe, regards mankind from his mountain summit. His divine light dazzles the headless 'Poverty of Spirit' (bottom right), who with 'Fear of the Lord' are seen against the starry cosmos. *(Copy of the c.1175–80 Rupertsberg Scivias, Book I, Vision 1, St Hildegard Abbey, Eibingen)*

Body and Soul. A child in the womb receives its soul from God. The many eyes in the golden kite depict divine presence. Men on earth carry cheeses of differing quality, representing procreation and gifts to the child. *(Copy of the c.1175–80 Rupertsberg Scivias Book I, Vision 4, St Hildegard Abbey, Eibingen)*

The Trinity and the Macrocosm in relation to Man. God embraces the wheel of Creation, surrounded by flames, ocean, winds and animals which force the world into motion. Hildegard is seen (bottom left) recording her vision. (*Liber divinorum operum, Vision I, 2, Lucca MS1942, c. 1230–40*)

The Mystical Body. The powerful female figure of the incorrupt Bride of the Church emerges from white mountain peaks and golden calyxes. The figure in red (Mary) might also be Richardis, or Hildegard herself, surrounded by virgins crowned and with flowing hair. (*Copy of the c.1175–80 Rupertserg Scivias Book II, Vision 5, St Hildegard Abbey, Eibingen*)

The Cosmic Egg. The universe is shown with the earth, in four elements, at the centre. In allegorical terms, the sun is Christ, the moon is the Church, the stars are acts of piety, the waters, baptism. God's love embraces all in a circle of fire. (*Copy of the c.1175–80 Rupertsberg Scivias, Book I, Vision 3, St Hildegard Abbey, Eibingen*)

The Hildegard Abbey, Eibingen, built in 1900–04 in the German Beuron style, situated on the hill above the site of Hildegard's second monastery.

Hildegard's skull on the altar of the old Eibingen Parish Church, 1928. The church burnt down in 1932 but by then Hildegard's relics had already been placed in a newly made reliquary.

A procession in 1929 through pre-war Bingen to mark the 750th anniversary of Hildegard's death. According to one account, 25,000 people took part.

men causes genital swelling and sores. Even those men who experience 'pollution that occurs in sleep' do not escape censure: 'For if the semen of a man who sleeps and dreams is stirred up unawares, I do not want him to approach the sacramental office of My Altar in that condition of ardent heat.'[13] Her thundering attack (in visionary mode) on those, men or women alike, who engage in such activities when awake shows a thorough grasp of the power and effects of sexual desire, while pointing a finger of blame directly at men for having initiated the practice:

> And men who touch their own genital organ and emit their semen seriously imperil their souls, for they excite themselves to distraction; they appear to Me as impure animals devouring their own whelps, for they wickedly produce their semen only for abusive pollution. And women who imitate them in this unchaste touching, and excite themselves to bodily convulsions by provoking their burning lust, are extremely guilty, for they pollute themselves with uncleanness when they should be keeping themselves in chastity. Hence both women and men who elicit their own seed by touching themselves in the body do a filthy deed and inflict ulcers and wounds on their souls.[14]

In *Causae et Curae*, primarily a handbook to the body and soul rather than a narrowly theological volume, her tone is less hectoring, more domestic, the meaning plain. A male must pour forth his semen into a woman (in the right conditions of marriage and so forth), like someone putting cooked food on a plate to be eaten. 'If, however, he is not with a woman, but with a being that is contrary to him in nature, he sordidly ejaculates his semen into the wrong place, similar to someone taking cooked food from a pot and pouring it on to the floor.'[15]

Hildegard offers many remedies for gynaecological problems and hysteria, including the rubbing of the genitals with various oils and potions. Spikenard, camomile and fennel were commonly cited to bring on menstruation. The *Physica* recommends bathing in boiled tansy and feverfew to soothe the pain of 'obstructed menses', as well as taking a porridge of camomile and wheat flour or drinking a malodorous-sounding cocktail of yarrow, bearberries, cloves, pepper, honey and various herbs. Young girls whose periods do not arrive, however, should rub oil of white dock and roses on their groin, hips and navel. Dill, mint and poppy are good lust quenchers, as is betony as long as you put it up your nose and under each foot. Man's ardour can be cooled by infusing a steam-bath with lettuce and placing the cooked leaves around his genitals. Methods of contraception, though condemned by the Church, were commonly known, whether from folk practice or from gynaecological tracts, of which a few are notable, dating back to antiquity and often appearing under a pseudonym to protect the identity of the writer.

Many late Roman physicians referred freely to plants which brought on periods (emmenagogues), had anti-fertile properties or the power to cause an embryo to abort (abortifacients).[16] Abortion was advised in the first or third month, but even the eighth month was not unknown. Pliny named thirteen anti-fertility plants, including dittany, thought to be so powerful that a woman only had to be in the same room for it to be effective. Galen cited rue as a means of drying up semen, but the intention seems more to have been to quell desire rather than to prevent conception, for which he had other recipes; Cleopatra the Gynaecologist, about whom little is known, least of all whether she was a man or a woman, listed several potions for abortion, as did the widely known herbalist pseudo-Apuleius. Trotula listed several recipes to prevent conception. Vaginal suppositories were used to obstruct the mouth of the cervix, possibly altering the acidity or alkalinity of the vagina as would a spermicide. Placing hemlock on the testicles before coitus was common folkloric practice.

Although the applications were specific, the treatments were often interchangeable. Bringing on a period and stopping conception, in an anxious woman's eyes, amounted to the same end. Inasmuch as most were to be taken by the woman rather than the man, little has changed. These methods which must have been known to Hildegard and her fellow clinicians, though not necessarily condoned, appear to have enjoyed a degree of success; the falling birth rate around this period cannot be explained entirely by plague or famine. Modern experiments on rats with a number of named anti-fertility plants (including *Urtica dioica* L. and *Adiantum capillus* L.) have demonstrated, in some cases, a high degree of effectiveness. Generally, however, this was an approximate science, not least because of the debasement of meaning through translation and retranslation of medical texts, from Greek, to Latin, to Old English or German.

With each passing century, moral and ecclesiastical attitudes towards contraception and abortion hardened, though the laws were by no means clear-cut. Hildegard offers her recipes with surprisingly little comment, identifying rather than encouraging their use (and generally preferring German to Latin plant names, suggesting an absence of reliance on existing texts, even if she knew of them by repute). In *Physica* she names seven plants with anti-fertile properties, including tansy, recognised today as an abortifacient. Hildegard's reference is thought to be the first known mention in the West of this particular property of tansy.[17] The seventeenth-century botanist Nicholas Culpeper similarly described the plant's power to 'promote the menses', which suggests at least a degree of continuity in folk herbals. That Hildegard the scientist and taxonomist should, in effect, have extended without excess of censure our knowledge of abortion will not chime with everyone's views of a theologian and saint.

Throughout the Middle Ages, the difference between men and women and the varying personality of individuals was explained in accordance with the Hippocratic theory of the four temperaments, identified as sanguine, choleric, phlegmatic and melancholic. These temperaments, it was thought, shaped and determined human nature. For good physical and mental health, a balance had to be achieved between heat and cold, dryness and moisture, blood, bile and phlegm. Men, since Adam was made of earth, were thought to be hotter, hairier and drier than women, made of God's flesh. Women's coolness accounted for their physical weakness and their volatile, perfidious natures. Their voracious sexual appetites were the physical result of having cold uteruses, which needed heating with hot semen. Because of Satan's special wrath, they were easily seduced, as the serpent had proved in Eden. These distinctions had been in common circulation since Hippocrates and Galen.

Hildegard's views of women remain within the tradition of the time, and are firmly conservative. As we know, in a literal sense she did not entirely practise what she preached, but she always took a traditional line regarding women's subservient role. Women, she argues poetically (in *Causae et Curae*), are airier, their bodies like the frame joining the strings of a lyre, full of wind and susceptible to raging elements. Nevertheless, they are also earthbound, like reptiles living in the ground; they should sit more than they walk on account of their weakness. Passivity and limited movement was a woman's lot. Their role should be servile, like the moon to the sun, the soil to the sower's seed. Many of her attitudes, in *Causae et Curae* and elsewhere throughout her writings, tally with widespread views of the day. Though she defied many of her own prescripts and set an example of militancy, in no sense could she be recognised (as many would like to regard her today) as a pioneering feminist.

Where Hildegard shows her individuality, however, is in the colourful and graphic descriptions of physical types and in her purposeful association of bodily temperament and sexual behaviour. Her distinctions compare with the personality and physical types identified in women's magazines, newspapers' health pages and diet books today (endomorph, ectomorph extrovert, introvert, moody, neurotic), where the desire is to recognise yourself and treat yourself accordingly. We know Hildegard's women as well as we know Chaucer's. Here are her specifications in *Causae et Curae*:[18]

> **Sanguine:** *Some women are inclined to plumpness, and have soft and delectable flesh and slender veins, and well-constituted blood free of impurities . . . And these have a clear and light colouring, and in love's embraces are themselves lovable; they are subtle in arts, and show self-restraint in their disposition. At menstruation they suffer only a moderate loss of blood and their womb is well-developed for child-bearing, so they are fertile and can take in the man's seed. Yet they do not bear many children, and if they are without husbands so that they remain childless, they easily have physical pains; but if they have husbands, they are well.*

In comparison, sanguine men share similar characteristics but sound well suited to the monastic life: they too are fleshly, with hot brains, rich, red blood and delightful characters. Sexually they tend to be windy rather than fiery and thus more easily satisfied or content to abstain. They belong with men but blossom with women. Their semen has the appearance of watery, uncooked foam. They are usually fertile, their children happy and good.

> **Phlegmatic:** *There are other women whose flesh does not develop as much, because they have thick veins and healthy, whitish blood (though it does contain a little impurity which is the source of its light colour). They have severe features, and are darkish in colouring; they are vigorous and practical, and have a somewhat mannish disposition. At menstruation their menstrual blood flows neither too little nor too abundantly. And because they have thick veins they are very fertile and conceive easily . . . They attract men and make men*

pursue them, so men love them well. If they want to stay away from men, they can do so without being affected by it badly, though they are slightly affected. However, if they do avoid making love with men they will become difficult and unpleasant in their behaviour. But if they go with men and do not wish to avoid men's love-making they will be unbridled and over-lascivious according to men's report. And because they are to some extent mannish on account of their vital force [viriditas, literally greenness] *within them, a little down sometimes grows on their chin . . .*

In contrast to these strongly drawn women, the phlegmatic man has fewer traits to commend him. His brain is thick, white and dry, his blood soft and foamy; he has full, womanly flesh, a flawed complexion and little beard growth. By character he is lively in thought rather than action, regarded as easy-going but weak and childlike; he has little sexual appetite, and lacks sufficient fire easily to have an erect penis. His semen is thin, like uncooked foam, and tends to be sterile.

Choleric: *There are other women who have slender flesh but big bones, moderately sized veins and dense red blood. They are pallid in colouring, prudent and benevolent, and men show them reverence and are afraid of them. They suffer much loss of menstruation; their womb is well-developed and they are fertile. And men like their conduct, yet they flee from them and avoid them to some extent, for they can interest men but not make men desire them. If they do get married, they are chaste, they remain loyal wives and live healthily with their husbands; and if they are unmarried they tend to be ailing – as much because they do not know to what man they might pledge their womanly loyalty because they lack a husband . . .*

Beware the choleric man. A lover of sex and women,

he would find monastic life onerous. His brain is strong and thick, his veins red and visible, his blood strong, burning and wax-coloured, his complexion ruddy. His chest is firm, his limbs strong and muscular rather than fat. His sexual desire is unquenchable, more fiery than windy. So incapable is he of restraint that he is likely to resort to inanimate objects and perversion to satisfy himself. If by necessity celibate, he must avoid women like poison, though he craves to embrace them. With women he is healthy and happy, without dried up and sombre. He is highly fertile, his testicles able to hold a strong erection. His children tend to be cruel and incontinent.

> **Melancholic:** *But there are other women who have gaunt flesh and thick veins and moderately sized bones. Their blood is more lead-coloured than sanguine, and their colouring is as it were blended with grey and black. They are changeable and free-roaming in their thoughts and wearisomely wasted away in affliction; they also have little power of resistance so that at times they are worn out by melancholy. They suffer much loss of blood in menstruation and they are sterile because they have a weak and fragile womb. So they cannot lodge or retain or warm a man's seed, and thus they are also healthier, stronger and happier without husbands than with them – especially because if they lie with their husbands, they will tend to feel weak afterwards. But men turn away from them and shun them, because they do not speak to men affectionately, and love them only a little. If for some hours they experience sexual joy, it quickly passes in them. Yet some such women, if they unite with robust and sanguine husbands, can at times, when they reach a fair age, such as fifty, bear at least one child . . . If their menopause comes before the just age, they will sometimes suffer gout or swelling of the legs, or will incur an insanity which their melancholy arouses, or else*

> *back ache or a kidney-ailment . . . If they are not helped*
> *with their illness, so that they are not freed from it either by*
> *God's help or by medicine, they will quickly die.*

Melancholy men, dark, violent and impulsive, hold little charm. They are large, strong and muscular, with high colour and fiery, snaky eyes. By nature they are bitter, greedy, stupid and violent, though they work hard and carefully. Their sexual appetite is greedy, driven by a mixture of wind and fire. They want quick gratification rather than love; they want women but hate them enough to kill them. Their penises are capable of powerful erection, inspired by bitterness rather than sensuous passion. Their children tend to suffer insanity and perversion.

There seems no reason to disagree with Peter Dronke's proposition that *melancolica*, highly strung, neurotic and prone to illness, describes Hildegard herself. We know little of what she looked like, but we have a strong sense of her complexion, or humour. The *Vita* gives no physical account, and the depictions of her in the manuscripts are generic (but then so is the typology of *melancolica* and the other temperaments).

Since the only purpose of sexual intercourse is to conceive, it followed that in order not to be sinful, it should only take place at certain times. A combination of factors, including the position of the moon and a woman's fertile days (generally misapprehended), must be taken into account. Moreover, conception, and the child that would result, was conditioned entirely by these variables. Just as the woman has times of greater fecundity, so too does the man, the strength and nature of whose semen is affected by the moon. The degree of love between husband and wife directly affects the unborn child: great mutual love will produce a boy of prudence and virtue; if only the man is truly loving, the result is a feeble boy of limited virtue. A loving man with thin semen and an affectionate wife can expect a virtuous girl to be born. A child born out of mere lust is likely to be a boy, 'but he will be bitter with this parents' bitterness; and if the man's semen is thin and there is no cherishing love on either side in that hour, a girl of bitter temperament is born'. Worse still, depravity may be punished by the birth of a stunted or deformed child: 'And often, as you see, when male and female unite in forgetfulness of Me and in the mockery of the Devil, those who are born are found to be stunted so that their parents, who transgressed My precepts, may feel anguish and having these children so return to Me in penitence.'[19]

In *Causae et Curae* Hildegard enumerates the character types to which children will be predisposed according to which day of the lunar cycle they were conceived. The predictions can have offered parents little comfort. Was her purpose to dissuade couples from transgressing, and from conceiving unwanted children, by effectively restricting the days on which coitus and its fruits might be joyful? Given the endless variables of fertility, potency, the moon and the Church calendar, engaging in sexual activity required exact planning. No longer does the notion that a couple might need to consult their diaries in order to conceive seem an idiosyncrasy of our own times. According to Hildegard, a child engendered on the first day after a new moon will be proud, vengeful and healthy but will die young. A boy conceived on the eighteenth day will be a thief, while a girl will be healthy but evil and libidinous. Wait another two days and matters are worse still: the boy will be a murderer and a bandit, the girl a poisoner and a man-eater 'who will easily become a lunatic'. Let's call the whole thing off.

Having gone so far as to conceive, man and woman become one flesh, as foreshadowed by Eve being born of Adam. Man's blood is boiled by woman's fire and foam, sweat and fluid, and 'whirled around like water in a mill' until semen and blood join as one and the embryo develops. For the first four weeks, that embryo is inanimate (a view commonly held at the time). In the second month, the fleshy, fatty mixture comes to life, heated like a dish in a pot. At this point, God endows the embryo with soul and breath. The limbs now form and develop, the baby moves. A skin, like a little sac (presumably the amniotic fluid), grows out of the woman's menstrual blood, surrounding the child and nourishing it until the time of its birth. Here it remains until it is fully grown and endowed with reason, when it desires to break out. Leaving the darkness of the womb after the Fall, it emits a loud scream:

> When birth is approaching, the vessel in which the child is enclosed is torn, and then comes the eternal energy that took Eve from Adam's side, and is present and turns upside down all the corners of the shelter in the woman's body. All the structures of the woman's body rush toward this energy, receive it and open up to it. They do so until the child emerges. Afterwards, they return to their previous state. As the child emerges, its soul too feels the eternal energy that sent it, and meanwhile it rejoices.[20]

Hildegard offers many remedies for painful labour, from the general application of boiled herbs (fennel, galingale) to rubbing a poultice of dried crane's blood on the vulva or placing a lion's heart on the umbilicus. Equally effective in that same place (though surely even harder to obtain) are stones eaten and ejected by a pregnant mouse. Not all the antidotes are physical. The rate of infant and maternal mortality being so high at the time, birth was the moment at which the devil stalked the world. Thus in *Physica*, in her catalogue of the properties of stones, she writes:

> When a woman brings forth an infant from the time she gives birth through all the days of its infancy, she should keep a jasper on her hand. Malign spirits of the air will be much less able to harm her or the child. The tongue of the ancient serpent stretches out toward the sweat of the infant as it emerges from its mother's vulva. At that time he is trying to ensnare the child as well as the mother. Also, if a

serpent sends out its breath in any spot, place a jasper there. The breath will be weakened, so that it will be less harmful, and the serpent will stop breathing in that place.[21]

Hildegard's pragmatism, whether steeped in science and biology or not, can never be divorced entirely from her theology. In her mind, they sprang from the same visionary and prophetic source.

CHAPTER TWELVE

HARP OF GOD

Then in the above mentioned vision I also composed and sang chant with melody, to the praise of God and his saints, though I had never studied human chant and I did not know how to tell the neumes [notes] by myself.

(HILDEGARD, IN GUIBERT'S REVISIONS TO THE *VITA*)

Unless you believe in divine revelations, what I'm saying will sound like nonsense, but I believe that when God created the world, he created everything, so music is something that already exists. You just have to be very still and hear it. Plato believed that was the case. I'm not being over-pious if I say to God 'Guide me, help me.' It's a kind of prayer, so therefore writing music is a kind of prayer.

(SIR JOHN TAVENER, COMPOSER, INTERVIEWED 2000)

The Bible, in Genesis, names Jubal as the first musician, 'the father of all such as handle the harp and organ' [Gen. 4:12]. He was a descendant of Cain, eight generations after Adam. Recent musicologists, equally keen to nominate a pioneer, have designated Hildegard of Bingen the earliest named composer. This is as yet her chief claim to modern celebrity. Awarding this accolade to a woman has pleased those who wish to recast the male-dominated history of music in more equal terms. Isolated exceptions notwithstanding, women may be absent from the annals until the late twentieth century, but at least, it might be argued, they were in at the start. Sticklers, and those with a less narrowly millenarian viewpoint, will cite the seventh-century Greek lyric poet Sappho and others as nameable avatars, if only by reputation.[1]

How, then, is it possible to proceed thus far with an account of Hildegard's life with so little mention of the activity that has catapulted her to fame in our own times? Why, too, until a quarter of a century ago, did most music history books not mention her at all? Instead they bestowed the honour of first identifiable composers on the French monks Adam of St Victor and Leonin, of the Notre-Dame school in Paris, always cited as a crucible of musical innovation. Leonin and his contemporary Perotin are usually dubbed the fathers of polyphony, as if the 'real' history of Western music only began once music started moving in several parts. We now know (though most popular histories of music have not yet caught up with scholarship on this matter) that an extensive amount of polyphony already existed, notably via the Winchester Troper, an important British source dating from c. 1000. The Notre-Dame school was adapting and extending existing practices in the music of the liturgy, perhaps known to Hildegard herself, and in that of the Provençal troubadours, some of whose decorated monodies derived from plainchant.

Hildegard is absent from the 1927 *Grove Dictionary of Music and Musicians* as well as the *Larousse Encyclopedia of Music*, 1971. She is even omitted from the *New Oxford History of Music* Vol. 2 (1954), a standard reference work on music of the medieval period. She finally makes an appearance, still only a paragraph, in the revised version of 1990. Similarly Donald J. Grout's *A History of Western Music*, that essential tool-kit for generations of music students, slips her in somewhere between the first edition in 1960 and the fifth edition nearly forty years later (though even the eight-and-a-half-line entry she is awarded lacks a certain conviction).

It might seem then that the composer Hildegard is a modern invention. She owes her musical rehabilitation, however, to a happy combination of circumstances, not least the lucky survival of copies of her music. In addition, the appetite for early music and period instrument performance, growing throughout the twentieth century, reached a peak around the time of the 800th anniversary of her death in 1979. It has remained insatiable ever since. A review in the *Musical Times* in June of that year notes that the British musician Philip Pickett and his New London Consort gave what were said to be the first English performances of four of Hildegard's songs to mark her octocentenary, together with music by Peter Abélard, that other more famous twelfth-century theologian skilled at composition, though scarcely any of his music has survived. An irresistible target for feminist musicologists, Hildegard's gender has worked in her favour, especially considering the period in which she lived, which until a quarter of a century ago was chronicled largely by male historians basing their insights on material written by monks, with all the inevitable limitations that implies. The Middle Ages, we now know, gave monastic women a chance to sing, perform and arrange their own music. This realisation, together with a thirst for musicological dis- covery, has sparked much vigorous excavation into manuscripts of the past, leading to the first modern performances of many works dating from early in the last millennium, a few by women. Without doubt there were others, but their works are lost, their names unknown.

The surprise Hildegard breakthrough, as it might be called, came in 1983 when *A Feather on the Breath of God*[2] – the title borrowed from *Scivias* – won a coveted *Gramophone* Award. This collection of sequences and hymns, edited[3] and directed by Christopher Page and sung by members of Gothic Voices, unexpectedly made the classical best-seller charts and spawned a batch of further recordings by other groups (notably Barbara Thornton's Sequentia). Some have been sung by men, some by women; some in pristine church acoustics, others in studios. Instruments and backing tracks have been added, anachronistic liberties taken. The Gothic Voices disc, austere and undecorated (despite the use of a whispered drone beneath the voices) continues to sell steadily. At the time of writing, nearly half a million of these CDs have been sold (irrespective of the opinion of the sound engineer, who predicted at the time of the record- ing, for which Page was paid a princely £45, 'Lovely music. Shame no one will buy it'). In the light of new knowledge, Page has further refined his views on performance, preferring a single voice per part, and no form of instrumental accompaniment at all. His virtuosic singers are well able to meet the demands of *a cappella* singing. We should perhaps be grateful that the less skilled ensembles do not generally follow suit, believing that a less chaste interpretation is permissible. By contrast, the nuns' choir of the St Hildegard Abbey, Eibingen, more than a dozen strong, sound decidedly hearty, singing several voices to a part in their 1998 recording. Who can say which is the more authentic?

In a sober programme note, as if foreseeing the fate to which his successful CD might expose this little-known but fascinating woman, Page warned against romanticising Hildegard's creative personality, observing that she writes with 'a quiet mastery that controls ecstasy and shuns delirium, always working within the mainstream of Christian tradition'. By 'Christian' Page presumably meant only the ecclesiastical tradition of the West, rather than Eastern Orthodoxy, to which Hildegard's music owes no obvious relation or debt. He also pointed out that medieval Latin has no exact match for the verb 'to perform', with its intimations of self-conscious, extrovert activity. Instead, in a monastic context, chant was a meditative, almost internalised activity, an extension of speech, of prayer sung in the course of observing the daily office, the weekly cycle and the annual pattern of church seasons and feast days.[4] This is a crucial point. Almost without exceptions, the music surviving from this period is monastic and liturgical in origin. Secular music, though widely performed, was hardly written down until some two centuries later, or has simply not survived in any quantity. One of the first significant collections to have been preserved is the *Carmina Burana* (familiar from Carl Orff's 1935–6 reworking), songs on love, drinking, gambling and other profane matters, which dates from *c.* 1200.

Following ancient Jewish rite, music had been central to the liturgy from early Christian times onwards. In the Middle Ages a sharp distinction existed between one who theorised about music (the *musicus*) and the lowlier being who executed it (the *cantor*). Observing the wisdom of the sixth-century theoretician Boethius, music was judged an aspect of mathematics. In the theory of the ordered universe, declared in turn and variously by Pythagoras, Plato, Boethius and Isidore of Seville, the ratios of harmony evident in the cosmos match those which unite body and soul. Music was the mirror of divine order. Hildegard, in keeping with others before and after, saw the world as a hymn of praise to God. The invisible and unheard music of the heavens (which Boethius called *musica mundana*), or the Music of the Spheres, parallels the physical and emotional make-up of human beings who in turn make their own music (*musica humana*). Before the Fall, Adam's voice was in tune with the choirs of angels and he could hear the Music of the Spheres, a point to which Hildegard returns repeatedly in her letters and elsewhere. In a long exposition to her superiors at the See of Mainz (written *c.* 1178–9), she expresses her theory of music as an allegory of the body and soul and a way of understanding history. She wrote this letter under bitter protest when, near the end of her life, the prelates forbade her to hear Mass or sing the Divine Office (for reasons we shall learn). For the first time ever, she and her nuns were deprived of music, the performance of which she considered a natural right and divine duty of mankind. She concluded by warning the men that they issued the interdict at their own peril:

> *Men of zeal and wisdom have imitated the holy prophets and have themselves, with human skill, invented several kinds of musical instruments, so that they might be able to sing for the delight of their souls, and they accompanied their singing with instruments played with the flexing of the fingers, recalling, in this way, Adam, who was formed by God's fingers, which is the Holy Spirit. For, before he sinned, his voice had the sweetness of all musical harmony. Indeed, if he had remained in his original state, the weakness of mortal man would not have been able to endure the power and the resonance of his voice... Therefore those who, without just cause, impose silence on a church and prohibit the singing of God's praises... will lose their place among the chorus of angels, unless they have amended their lives through true penitence and humble restitution.[5]*

In order to understand the tradition in which Hildegard's music may have been written, we need a grasp of context. The history of plainchant, with its conflicting strands of oral and written, Roman, Milanese, French and Mozarabic traditions, is complex and much disputed. To sum up in a few sentences is foolhardy but essential.[6] Known widely today as Gregorian chant (despite the non-existent connection with the sixth-century Pope in question, Gregory the Great, whose name was only attached to it three hundred years after his death), plain-song is monophonic, or a single line of music sung in unison or octaves and probably unaccompanied, though Hildegard herself mentions accompanied singing. It was almost certainly (though this, too, is a matter of continuing debate) sung in unmeasured time. Its rhythmic shape is thought to have grown out of the groupings of words rather than from an externally imposed pattern. The chant melodies were written in medieval modes (as if using only the white keys of a piano), each mode having its own distinct flavour and in no sense comparable to our modern system of keys. Indeed, the idea of a fixed pitch system as we understand it, of a note called C which always sounds the same, was not yet known. The tuning fork, a means by which instruments could adjust to a universally accepted note and thus be in tune with one another, was not invented until 1711, though bells were presumably used as a guide. The adjustment of tuning known as equal temperament, to which all pianos today are tuned (and which we tend narrowly to assume presents the authoritative yardstick of music), also only came into being in the eighteenth century. This simplification of music into tones and semitones may indeed provide the ingredients of Western music for the last two centuries, but it bears little relation to what went before or beyond. Contemporary music, which admits microtones and quarter-tones, has thrown off the harness and returned to earlier freedoms shared by much non-Western music.

None of this mattered in the twelfth century. Since sacred music was largely dependent on the voice, that most flexible of all instruments, the only rule required was that everyone start on the same note, whether or not it matched the note which initiated the same piece the day before. Then, as now, anyone possessing the aural attribute known as perfect pitch could hold yesterday's note in his head and lead his colleagues, but otherwise tuning was an approximate business. Some singing was accompanied by instruments, but even these could not be guaranteed to hold a constant pitch. Monks and nuns would have had to commit the music of the liturgy to memory, not least because most could not read music even when a copy existed; until then, with notation in its infancy, that skill had not been required. One reason why music began to be written down was the Church's desire to curb stylistic excess and ensure conformity to Roman models. Nevertheless, information about performance practice, how the chant might sound or the words be pronounced and how many sang it is negligible. Performers today, whatever authenticity they claim, have to rely on a combination of intelligent guesswork, stylistic intuition and imaginative good sense. A handful of manuscripts has survived from the ninth and tenth centuries, from the famous library of the Benedictine abbey of St Gall in Switzerland and elsewhere. By the mid-twelfth century, more strenuous attempts were made to bring order to the sprawling practice of chant, in an effort to streamline the Christian rite. In 1147, Bernard of Clairvaux, ever present with a view on all matters political and liturgical, wrote a prologue about the origins of Cistercian chant and supervised a treatise by a fellow monk (Guy d'Eu) in which new principles were decreed according to 'natural laws': melodies should lie within an octave, textual repetitions should be avoided, ornamentation kept to a minimum and so on. Simplicity, in keeping with the Cistercian ideal of austerity, was the dictum. Laying down such a particularised aesthetic manifesto was itself, of course, akin to composition.

About the same time Hildegard, as it would appear, was beginning to compose in her own style. She paid little heed to Bernard's guidelines (even supposing she knew them). Let us consider the little we know about Hildegard the composer.

References in the *Vita* are scant. The principal evidence is a body of nearly eighty songs attributed to her, collectively known as *Symphonia armonie celestium revelationum* (or *Symphonia*) and a morality play with music, one of the first known of its kind, the *Ordo Virtutum*. This *Play of Virtues*, in which the Devil alone shouts rather than sings his utterances, depicts the journey of the soul and the temptations of the flesh encountered *en route*. Some writers have speculated that the work was performed at the consecration of the Rupertsberg monastery, sung by the nuns in unison. Others note that the Virtues' loss of Anima (the soul) mirrors Hildegard's separation from Richardis, which occurred during or just before the period in which the piece was written (the early 1150s). The music itself is generally simpler in style than Hildegard's other compositions.

The songs of *Symphonia*, set to Hildegard's own texts, range from antiphons (a type of refrain sung as a response to psalms) to hymns (a strophic form), sequences (in which melodic phrases are paired) and responsories for feasts of the Virgin Mary and others, notably the German Rhineland saints Ursula, Rupert and Disibod. Providing music for special feast days as required was normal monastic practice. The songs may be grouped to form a cycle under such headings as Mary, Virgins, Martyrs, Confessors and Angels. *O virga ac diadema* and *Columba aspexit per cancellos fenestre*, today among her most frequently performed works,[7] relate to the Virgin Mary and to the Confessors. However, we can only surmise the *Symphonia*'s order, which differs in the only two existing manuscripts. It is impossible, too, to be certain whether they were intended to be sung within the liturgy, and if so whether on a particular feast day, but it seems plausible that they were.

The language of the texts overflows with exuberant and sensual imagery. Greenness, gardens, growth, fecundity, flowers and jewels recur, as do towers and cities, fire, purity and womanhood. Christ is frequently addressed as husband and lover, with attendant erotic imagery echoing the Song of Songs.

In O *ecclesia*, which celebrates Saint Ursula and the 11,000 virgin martyrs of legend, Ursula rejects earthly marriage for the love of God, whom she awaits with 'great desire' (*multo desiderio*). Peter Dronke and Barbara Newman have applied the scholarly tenets of practical criticism to these texts, analysing wordplay, metre and symbolism to argue, convincingly, that the author's highly individual literary style is attributable to Hildegard.[8] The general reader may readily find examples of these free verses in the sleeve notes of commercial recordings, which usually reproduce the original Latin with modern translations alongside. It would be an oversight, however, not to quote one example in full. The dazzling imagery of *Columba aspexit* shows Hildegard at her fluent best. St Maximin (patron saint of the Benedictine abbey at nearby Trier, for whose monks the work may have been written) is depicted celebrating Mass in the presence of the Holy Ghost, symbolised as the dove at the latticed window. Drawing on scriptural language, Hildegard represents God's love as the sun's rays shining into the shadowy gloom. Her favourite images shape each verse: perfume (symbolising Divine Grace), greenness, jacinth and diamonds, the balm which oozes from St Maximin ('*sudando sudavit balsamum*') like sweet, steamy gum from a tree, the tower of Lebanon wood and the high building, the swift stag and the pure spring-water. A reader with only an elementary grasp of Latin will nevertheless sense the poetic richness of the language. Barbara Newman's literal translation appears below, better used to gain the flavour of the original than to attempt to analyse its sometimes elusive meaning.

> Columba aspexit
> per cancellos fenestre,
> sudando sudavit balsamum
> de lucido Maximino.

Calor solis exarsit
et in tenebras resplenduit,
unde gemma surrexit
in edificatione templi
purissimi cordis benivoli.

Iste, turris excelsa
de ligno Libani et cipresso facta,
iacincto et sardio ornata est,
urbs precellens artes
aliorum artificum.

Ipse, velox cervus,
cucurrit ad fontem purissime aque
fluentis de fortissimo lapide,
qui dulcia aromata irrigavit.

O pigmentarii!
qui estis in suavissima viriditate
hortorum regis,
ascendentes in altum
quando sanctum sacrificium
in arietibus perfecistis:

Inter vos fulget hic artifex,
paries templi,
qui desideravit alas aquile,
osculando nutricem Sapientiam
in gloriosa fecunditate
Ecclesie.

O Maximine,
mons et vallis es,
et in utroque alta
edificatio appares,

ubi capricornus
cum elephante exivit,
et Sapientia
in deliciis fuit.

Tu es fortis et suavis
in cerimoniis
et in choruscatione altaris,
ascendens ut fumus aromatum
ad columpnam laudis:

Ubi intercedis pro populo
qui tendit ad speculum lucis,
cui laus est in altis.

A dove gazed in/ through the lattice of a window,/ where before her face a dripping balm dripped down/ from lucent Maximin.

The heat of the sun blazed out/ and shone in the darkness,/ so that a gem arose/ in the building of the temple/ of the most pure, benevolent heart.

He, a lofty tower/ built from the wood of Lebanon and cypress,/ is adorned with jacinth and ruby,/ a city surpassing the arts/ of other artisans.

He, a swift stag,/ ran to the spring of the purest water/ flowing from the mighty stone,/ the spring that watered sweet spices.

O spice-dealers!/ you who dwell in the sweetest foliage/ of the King's gardens,/ mountains on high/ when you have accomplished/ the holy sacrifice with rams:

Among you shines this architect,/ a wall of the temple,/ he who longed for an eagle's wings,/ as he kissed his foster-mother Wisdom/ amid the glorious fruitfulness/ of the Church.

O Maximin,/ you are a mountain and a valley,/ and in both you appear/ as a lofty structure,/ where the mountain goat/ walked with the elephant,/ and Wisdom/ was in rapture.

You are strong and sweet/ in the rites/ and in the shimmer of the altar,/ rising like the smoke of incense/ to the pillar of praise:

Where you intercede for the people/ who strive towards the mirror of light./ Praise to him in the highest![9]

Hildegard's music, here and elsewhere, is characterised by a free, often irregular metre and ornate, melismatic style (one in which several notes are set to one syllable). It is monophonic or written in the single line of chant, without harmony or polyphony, though, as has been noted, the absence of a second written part is in no sense proof that doubling or harmonising did not occur (this remains a contentious issue among musicologists). The upward leaps, often of a rising fifth followed by a scalic pattern extending over two or more octaves, characterise the vocal line. In its almost rhapsodic style, it comes close to sounding like improvisation, developing organically rather than systematically. Neither easy to sing nor to remember, this music falls into no convenient category, though similar models can be found in the monodies of the troubadours. Hildegard may have been spiritually and physically remote from the travelling Provençal musicians, but we should be wary of suggesting that in some way she inaugurated a wholly new style. Some proportion of her music's exotic individuality may well spring from geographic isolation rather than aesthetic originality alone. As is the case with schools of illumination, carving and so on, the two cannot be entirely separated.

The *Symphonia* compositions are thought to date back to the 1140s and were collected in the early 1150s, soon after Hildegard arrived at the Rupertsberg. A letter from Odo of Soissons to Hildegard dated *c.* 1148 acknowledges her songwriting, though there is the usual speculation as to whether this comment was added at a later date to augment her reputation. Two chief manuscript sources for the music exist, written on staves in early German neumes (graphic signs representing pitch, predating modern notation), dating from the 1170s and the 1180s.[10] Additions and changes, some only now coming to light, make assumptions about the works' precise origins all the more difficult. One manuscript (the Dendermonde) is thought to have been sent to the monks of Villers, indicating that the music could as appropriately be sung by men as women. The greatest difficulty today, however, is in determining the precise metre in which these pitches should be sung. As we have seen, scholars and performers alike have celebrated the intimate relationship between text and music, and their jointly expressive nature. One feminist theoretician, June Boyce-Tillyard, has gone so far as to put Hildegard in the tradition of woman singer and songwriter 'that includes figures such as Joan Baez and Joni Mitchell'. This view, far-fetched though it may be, indicates one reason why Hildegard has attracted such a popular modern following.[11] Her subject matter, too, with its fondness for greenness (*viriditas*) and nature chimes with a modern pre-occupation with matters environmental and ecological, and a belief, anachronistic or not, that her chant represents a simplicity to which later Western music has only recently (and exceptionally) returned.

Should we be surprised that a woman who wanted to build her own monastery and place herself in the forefront of political and religious activity also wanted to invent, originate or adapt music for her nuns to sing? As abbess, one of her duties would have been to lead her nuns in chants. Unless she appointed a cantrix to fulfil the task, she also needed to choose versicles, soloists and liturgy. Yet musicology is a quixotic and inexact discipline. No sooner is a fact categorically proven than some radical fresh discovery renders it insecure. We scarcely know, despite the voluminous documentary evidence, how Bach's music was performed a mere 250 years ago. Beethoven,

Schumann, Berlioz, too, are constantly being subjected to revised interpretations: a different-sized orchestra, new ways with vibrato or bowing, rethinking of phrasing or tempo. Anyone daring to commit himself to a definitive point of view on the music of Hildegard, so much further back in time with mere morsels of evidence to go on, lays himself open to scepticism. The question, however, which must always be asked, is can Hildegard really be identified as the composer of these works at all?

In 1998, in a bracing if inconclusive article in the journal *Early Music*, Richard Witts proposed that we have only the flimsiest evidence on which to call Hildegard a composer and her iconic status as he judges it should be considered dubious. He wrote:

> *There is not a scrap of evidence that [Hildegard] actually composed any of the 77 songs in her name, or wrote them for her nuns to sing at daily service. Attributions from the period can be construed in different ways, and her own testimonial is unclear. Just as Walt Disney put his signature to films quietly made by others, or Coco Chanel lent her nickname to laboratory-produced scent, it is possible that Hildegard supplied nothing more artistic than a title for some of the remarkable cultural treasures associated with her Rupertsberg convent. Possible, but unprovable.[12]*

With a clever and provocative analogy, Witts might seem to have pinpointed a fundamental weakness in the assumptions generally drawn about Hildegard. Setting aside the specious analogy with Coco Chanel, the comparison with Walt Disney (before he became an industry which grew into a corporation) is highly relevant. At twenty-four frames a second, no one would expect a Disney colour short to be entirely from Disney's hand. Take Disney away, however, and you take away a created world, an aesthetic vision, a narrative style that characterises all his earlier cartoon films, even those in which he never drew a line.

The doubter's case was voiced still more plainly at an international conference held in Bingen in September 1998 to mark the 900th anniversary of her birth, attended by theologians, musicologists and academics. A short report of the findings, also in *Early Music*, concluded (with a degree of confused logic) that the 'extremely overdrawn image of Hildegard' can no longer be deemed valid:[13]

> In recent years Hildegard has been accorded the status of a modern composer, with a presumption that she expected her works to last and would have liked to be regarded as the originator of a specially individual corpus. The problems already begin here. Our contemporary approach fails to see that the term 'composer' as it came to be used in the 19th century and has continued to be used in the 20th lays a stress on the qualities of 'genius' that cannot conscientiously be applied to her. The 'stunning presence and effect' (Wulf Arlt) which builds upon an image of Hildegard as the first female composer of Western music sees in her 'our woman' in the 12th century presenting the missing link to a politically correct view of Western music . . .
>
> Both parts [of the conference] reversed the legends about Hildegard, for the first time in the history of research into her and her work. Untenable – that is, historically not provable – is the image of a composer writing music for the liturgy in her own convent. Untenable that around 1151, with the completion of her first important visionary text, Scivias, the main chunk of the music was already composed as well. Untenable the legend about the fame of her music during her lifetime; untenable the story of other abbots commissioning music from her. Untenable, finally – and this seems to be the most important result of the congress – that her music can be read as symptomatic of

> *the new and – in terms of music history – revolutionary 12th century, which has rightly been labelled the 'origin of modernity'. Her music is by no means symptomatic; in the creative complexity of that century her songs stand as isolated, local manifestations, which are only transmitted in sources from the Rupertsberg. And in regard to the questions of reception of her music or possible uses of it outside her own cloister, nothing has remained – just as nothing entered the musical mainstream of her own time.*[14]

What is the impact of these findings? Should we feel shocked or cheated and cast aside our Hildegard discs in dismay? Should those who perform her works with loving conviction chastise themselves as gullible fools, or is the aesthetic beauty of the music enough? The article quoted above begs several questions, the first of which is the equation of 'composer' with 'genius'. There always have been and always will be humdrum or workaday composers, performing a task with no higher ambitions. Moreover, musical history is littered with instances of works found not to have been composed, as it were, by their composers: tunes are borrowed, incomplete works finished by other hands. The relatively recent example of Mozart's *Requiem* is only the best known. Many compositional styles demand that the singer or player improvise a cadenza or supply an ornament to a line. Our post-nineteenth-century, individualistic perspective on the genius of the artist makes it hard to accept that our 'favourite bit' was in fact written by another hand.

The great bonus with the music said to be by Hildegard is that a body of work, full of novelty and invention, is attached to a recognised person and is therefore performed today. Popular songs aside, works by 'anon', however good, struggle to make a lasting impression. In commercial terms, they don't sell. Thanks to a surviving fourteenth-century manuscript, the Spanish nuns of Las Huelgas, near Burgos and on the pilgrim route to Compostela, provide a critical link in the history of chant and polyphony. Yet who – beyond the specialists who perform their motets, sequences and organa, often alongside Hildegard's – has any firm grasp of their identity?

It is plain that someone at the Rupertsberg produced a number of songs dating from this period which have survived. Surely their very status as 'isolated, local manifestations', if such they are, is what separates them from their background. The isolation of their source is what gives them part of their originality, leading us to suppose that that originality has its centre in the energies of one place and its leader. We must remain vigilant, however, in any supposition we make; in scholarly terms, we are on shaky ground, since we necessarily know only what has survived and can make comparisons only in that severely limited context. To that extent, even if we speak of novelty in her music, the degree to which Hildegard represented the end of an old world order of monody, which the new Notre-Dame school would challenge, must be a matter of conjecture. Whether the author and/or composer was another monk or nun acting on Hildegard's guidance and setting her poems, or working on their own initiative, or whether the abbess herself did the whole job matters little. There is no sculptor of the *Leaves of Southwell*, that medieval rhapsody in stone to be found in the chapter house of the Nottinghamshire minster (so beloved of Pevsner), no architect of Chartres, because no name hovers about their making. Nor do we even have a name of influence to attach to them. All this, of course, only goes to prove that in that dim and distant period nothing was by anyone, a very unlikely premise. Tautological 'names' of artists exist in many cultures, a fact that bedevils ethnographic research. The identity of the artist who made a type of bronze head in Benin might be given to the eagerly enquiring fieldworker as 'the maker of the fine bronze heads'.

The same questions arise with the illuminated illustrations which accompany the Rupertsberg *Scivias*. Determining how her own texts should be sung seems to tally with dictating how her visions were to be pictured. Was Hildegard, therefore, in addition to all her other attributes, an artist? And what precisely does that question mean? Are the pictures of the nun-scribe which recur like leitmotifs on each page of the Rupertsberg manuscript portraits, self-portraits or merely generic representations? Did she design the images, or order others to draw at her behest or elaborate her jottings (adding a critique as they went along)? If she instigated them in some way, does that make her the originator?

The more rigorous the critique, the more Hildegard becomes the creative will that controls the final image. The Walt Disney analogy can be taken a step further by comparing the teamwork required to make an illuminated manuscript with the complex industry of producing an American comic strip. In the case of comic books (Superman, etc.), usually two main authors are credited, those responsible for the colouring and the lettering, rather than the single creative spirit who originated the characters and their actions. Signatures may be found on medieval manuscripts, but their meanings are manifold and ambiguous. As the perspective of history has broadened, so the roles of women, particularly nuns, as artists, creative anthologists and patrons has had to be reassessed, or in many cases considered for the first time. Until a decade ago, Hildegard's name would not be found in a dictionary of artists. Now, as attitudes are revised, so her name begins to appear, but art historians have taken longer to catch up with musicologists in relation to Hildegard, and still lag way behind.

Research has identified various medieval women scribes who also drew, such as the twelfth-century nun Guda, and Claricia (c. 1200), who wittily depicts herself, apparently naked (she appears not to have been a nun), astride an initial letter Q. These women were, nevertheless, exceptions. The norm was for men to perform these tasks. Another German nun, Diemud (d. 1130), was famous for her illuminations and calligraphy, her work praised by her contemporary biographer as having 'exceeded what could be done by several men'. Yet there could indeed have been not one but several of her: the name, meaning 'Humility', was often taken by nuns, which may explain why her name appears so frequently. Two centuries earlier, in 975, a Spanish woman known as Ende (*Ende pintrix et dei aiutrix* or 'Ende, woman painter and servant of God') contributed illustrations to an Apocalypse manuscript, with wonderfully vivid depictions of the Great Whore and the Battle of the Dragon with the Child of the Woman. In this respect, she shared the preoccupation with salvation and damnation common to the Middle Ages. Angels and demons, dragons, serpents, mythical beasts and horrific scenes of death, destruction and deliverance seethe and jostle in the pages of Romanesque manuscripts. Hildegard's visions (in image as well as words) are thus firmly rooted in the iconographic convention of the time, and for this reason, perversely, have attracted little interest from art historians. Their learned searches may have been otherwise directed towards the influence of French Gothic which was in the ascendant in Europe by this time, but not much in evidence in the Rhineland. Otto Pächt, the veteran authority on illuminated manuscripts, gives a formidable analysis of the multiple allegories in the 'Cosmic Egg' (from *Scivias*), then rather myopically demotes it in artistic status by explaining that its chief value is as theological commentary. The *Scivias* illustrator, assumed by Pächt to be male, has interpreted Hildegard's visions, but in so doing it was inevitable that 'their allegorical–didactic character would be foremost'. In short, he concludes, 'the miniatures remain for the most part mere curiosities'.[15]

This seems an oversight, to say the least. The first thing to be said is that the illustrations are works of exceptional skill and visual organisation. Like the music, they have (to use the words of the *Early Music* report) an 'isolated, local' flavour. Their bold directness, saturated colour and unequivocal detail have a stark graphic certainty that scarcely reappears in German art until the woodcuts of the twentieth-century Expressionists. Independently of the question of authorship, their quality should be asserted. To dismiss the possibility of Hildegard having had direct input in these potent images merely on the grounds of lack of hard evidence suggests a visual bleariness and literal-mindedness on the part of the commentator. It is a lazy assumption that they were not in some way her work, and that she was not in some sense their author.[16] (The design world has a more positive view. On both occasions when Hildegard has been commemorated on German stamps, pictures from *Scivias* have been selected as being clearly unequivocal – and graphically potent – images.)

Several factors indicate her direct involvement. First, the pictures relate precisely to the descriptions of her visions in *Scivias*, while almost imperceptibly enlarging their meaning rather than simply illustrating them. In effect, they provide a new layer of meaning beyond word or image alone. Considering the degree to which Hildegard controlled matters in which she was engaged, the suggestion that another artist blithely added inappropriate iconographic elements, or, more to the point, dared without due authority to be as grotesque or shocking as these pictures sometimes are, does not ring true. Whether or not Hildegard ever held a paintbrush or measured up a column is of little consequence. She may have directed an atelier of half a dozen artists (as one scholar has suggested) in the execution of the work. She may have made her own rough sketches (it does not need an artist to say where a battlement should appear and how many windows or crenellations it should have). The more conventional Lucca manuscript of the *Liber divinorum operum* was certainly produced some half a century after Hildegard's death, and may serve to show what dilution with time and absence of an authorial figure produces. The exact date of the extraordinary *Scivias* manuscript known as the Rupertsberg Codex is unknown. It was produced some time between 1150 and the end of Hildegard's life (or, some argue, soon after). This manuscript was lost from storage in Dresden in 1945. Luckily, a black-and-white photographic copy survives. When the thirty-five pictures are compared with the twentieth-century facsimile made by nuns at the Hildegard Abbey between 1927 and 1933, it is clear that their work is in all ascertainable respects completely faithful and thus trustworthy. Even the shapes of the faces and their expressions, especially the great androgynous figures Sapientia, Ecclesia and Synagoga, are indistinguishable from those in the original. The triangulated drapes and flat, compartmentalised bodies link them to other twelfth-century Romanesque illuminations of the period in the Rhineland, strongly echoing Byzantine styles. Similarly, the fondness for architecture, towers, pilasters and columns is a common feature, with nuns or monks regularly depicted standing in front of their newly built monasteries.

Yet the *Scivias* illustrations, conservative though they are in theology and content, burst out of the boundaries of time and place. Their powerful unity and self-confidence must strike even those already familiar with twelfth-century imagery. They may lack the dramatic intensity of the Winchester Bible (*c.* 1150–80), one of the masterpieces of the period, known to have been the work of six distinct artists (as well as involving the vellum made from the skin of 250 sheep), but they have a defiant, almost confrontational power. Majestic, staring women encompass entire worlds full of people in their outstretched arms, in their breasts or in their bellies, each image defined by its own geometric unity. Buildings tilt, feet extend beyond distinctively shaped frames (by our own terms, how singularly modern). The 'Day of Revelation', which portrays the crowned figure of Mother Church with a monster in place of her genitals, remains the most lurid depiction I have encountered of a subject competitive in its capacity for horror. While steeped in the fixations of the time, they could have been conceived yesterday. At first glance the 'Cosmic Egg', vast, round and shadowy, or the cascading stars, might as well have been a product of the hallucinatory, psychedelic art of the 1960s or more pertinently the metaphorical images of Bosch or his later fellow artist/writer/visionary William Blake (also long treated by art historians as mere curiosities).

Madeline H. Caviness has pinned an entire thesis of Hildegard being the primary author of the illustrations – though a rash comparison with the work of Leonardo da Vinci does not help her case – on her empathetic belief that only a migraine sufferer could have produced such work. Following the line of Oliver Sacks, she argues that the bright colours and tiny shimmering dots, not to mention the strange castellations and dark contours, blazing lights and lashing flames, correspond to the effect of scintillating scotomas suffered at the onset of a headache. 'This confirms Hildegard's hand in the first stage of design,' she writes, 'since autobiographical and biographical accounts of her sickness and pain accord well with a migraine disorder of early onset (at three or four) that was particularly severe in her forties, presumably around the menopause, at the time she was composing the *Scivias*.'[17] Writing as a fellow sufferer, which few of us can, and despite the absence of proof of Hildegard's exact medical condition, Caviness puts her case passionately. This can go too far, almost denying artistry itself (where is the migraine in the music?). Stylistic innovation in art is often ascribed to madness or eye defects ('they saw funny'), as if vision and invention need some doctor's or optician's certificate as an alibi: think of El Greco or Monet – or Picasso, who has recently been added (by a Dutch doctor in Leiden) to the catalogue of hypothetical migraine patients. Thus, in the case of the pictures, which have a physical existence and do not need to be resurrected from fragmentary sources, as is the case with the music, Hildegard's presence is clear as the presiding genius unifying their worlds. Her reputation as an artist may one day equal her hazy eminence as a composer.

But all these arguments about someone not being the author of x or y are like an Agatha Christie novel missing the final pages where Hercule Poirot assembles the suspects. 'Anon did it' is no more satisfactory than the classic ending of the first detective story, Edgar Allan Poe's *The Murders in the rue Morgue* (in which the gorilla is revealed to be the assassin). We are left with one name to which either truth or a concatenation of circumstances has attached these musical, literary and visionary offerings. As the old classical scholarly chestnut has it, the *Iliad* was written by Homer or someone else of that name. Through anonymity, Hildegard gathers power as the person without whom none of these things would have occurred and is in an ancient and proper sense their author. As the figure who by not existing would have caused their non-existence, she must be their one true begetter.

To be properly up to date and in tune with revisionist scholarship, Hildegard's works should now perhaps be ascribed on CD covers, following the example of the rock star Prince, to the Artist formerly known as Hildegard of Bingen.[18] But revisionism has a habit of succumbing to revisionism. By strange fate, on the day the final words of this chapter were written, the Artist formerly known as Prince announced his intention to revert to his old name, Prince. (Some, quite reasonably, may now insist on calling him the Artist formerly known as the Artist formerly known as Prince.)[18] No supersensory powers are needed to grasp the timely relevance of this dance of names. With Hildegard, the negative information has been adduced, but even when accepted it leaves us with a corpus unattributable to anyone else. Art, like crime, has to be committed by someone, though history too often seems to forget the fact. The Middle Ages does not offer us many names of the figures responsible for its magnificent artistic achievements and tends not to promote the reputation of its women. Thus, on two counts alone, the tradition of ascribing the musical works to Hildegard is more than merely persuasive.

CHAPTER THIRTEEN

RHINE TRAVELS

Amidst all this it is remarkable that she, not so much led as driven by the Divine Spirit, came to Cologne, Trier, Metz, Würzburg and Bamberg to announce to the clergy and the people what God wanted of them.

(VITA, III, XVII)

I also made haste to travel to communities in other places, and reveal there the words which God ordered me. Through all this time the vessel of my body was being baked as it were in an oven . . .

(VITA, II, X)

A man should never put on feminine dress or a woman use male attire so that their roles may remain distinct, the man displaying manly strength and the woman womanly weakness . . . But as a woman should not wear a man's clothes, she should also not approach the office of My altar, for she should not take on a masculine role in her hair or in her attire.

(SCIVIAS, II, VI)

One essential tenet of the Benedictine Rule, as we have seen, was that those committed to the cloister for life should remain within its walls, for their own safety as well as for their spiritual well-being. In the words of St Matthew, 'Narrow is the way which leadeth to life.' Nuns, even more than monks, were expected to keep their thoughts, prayer and industry within the confines of their enclosure. In addition, following the teachings of St Paul, canon law forbade women to preach. None the less, at some time between 1158 and 1171, Hildegard embarked on no fewer than four preaching tours. That she was sixty years old and famous may have helped her to overcome, or simply to ignore, these obstacles. Yet her health, as ever, was frail, which makes her extensive expeditions all the more remarkable and hazardous. At the start of this period she endured another bout of acute, unexplained illness in which 'even the marrow in my bones dried up so much it was as if my soul must be released from my body'. She remained 'in that strife' for thirty days, 'such that my abdomen burned with the heat of a fiery air'. So concerned were her nuns that they took the precaution of preparing her for death, laying her inert body on the ground on haircloth just as they had the dying Jutta so many years before. 'My superiors, my daughters and my neighbours came in great mourning to watch my passing', an autobiographical passage in the *Vita* reports.

It proved a false alarm. The month-long crisis passed. Hildegard endured the after-effects of her malady for another three years, at which point she had a vision in which a sword-brandishing cherub chased away the evil will-o'-the-wisps which were torturing her, triggering anguished cries from these retreating spirits: 'Ach, ach! Woe, woe! Surely that woman is not escaping us? That means we shall not be able to carry her off!' Having banished the spirits and cheated death, Hildegard once again promptly made a full recovery: 'And soon my spirit within me fully revived and my body was renewed in its veins and marrow, so that I completely recovered my health.'[1] What are we to make of these frequent near-death encounters? In part hagiographers exploited any chance to emphasise their subject's holiness. What could be more miraculous than escaping the jaws of death? Bernard, too, like Hildegard a sickly being, was saved several times at the last minute visions, with the Virgin Mary, whose cult was only now beginning in earnest, quick to lend a helping hand. (Later depictions of the saint show him drinking milk as it spurts from the Virgin's breast.)

In the midst of this illness, Hildegard wrote her second major theological work, the *Liber vitae meritorum* (*Book of Life's Merits*, 1158–63), six visions with a discourse between the virtues and their corresponding vices, the first depicted in feminine perfection, the latter as monsters and grotesques. In language and imagery prefiguring Dante, she describes the punishments imparted to each sin, exploring the still embryonic notion of purgatory (also discernible in her accounts of volcanic fires and boiling springs in *Causae et Curae*). Avarice has the beard of a goat since it loves foulness; robbers are thrown in a pit so deep you cannot see the bottom and lashed by flames; the vain-glorious wallow in a foul-smelling marsh filled with filth and vermin; the envious are punished variously by ice, flames and scorpions. The central figure is a winged man, a cosmic giant clad in shining cloud, his feet in the oceans, his calves in the earth, his thighs in the air. Cosmological though its trappings are, the book's main purpose is to examine the struggle of man within the Christian ethical world order. Hildegard may have drawn as much on the Heavenly Light in its visionary in-carnation as on experiences inside her own cloister at that time, of which she writes feelingly, and with frank self-awareness, in the *Vita*. Some of her nuns were beginning to resent her autocratic style, which Hildegard considered an essential part of fulfilling her role as abbess. In her own words, she saw that some of her noble-born daughters had become caught 'in a net with an array of vain thoughts'. She disciplined them with the Rule, but 'several of them darting at me with glowering eyes, tore me to pieces with words behind my back, saying they could not endure it, this insufferable hammering way of mine and the discipline of the Rule by which I wanted to curb them. But God also comforted me with other good and wise sisters, who stood by me in all my sufferings.'[2]

Shortly after, perhaps willingly given the fraught circumstances at the Rupertsberg, she embarked on her first journey. In practical respects we know little about her travels or her exact itinerary. Her detailed knowledge of so many monastic foundations beyond her own locality indicates that she enjoyed the privilege, as well as the discomfort, of travel on a regular basis. No description of her mode of transport survives. Since most of her destinations were on or near the course of the rivers Rhine, Mosel and Main, she must have travelled, at least in part, by boat, going on foot or by horse or litter the rest of the time. In 1158, she journeyed east along the river Main towards Bamberg, where the new Romanesque cathedral was under construction; in 1160 she went south via Trier to Lorraine. On the day of Pentecost, she preached publicly in the great cathedral of Trier. Fittingly, that building had been consecrated in 1147 by Pope Eugene III in the presence of Bernard of Clairvaux (at the time of the Synod where *Scivias* had been read aloud and sanctioned). One question raised again by these public discourses is to what extent and to what degree of fluency did Hildegard speak Latin? Had she mastered it, or did she speak in the vernacular leaving Volmar to translate her words for circulation at a later date? Between 1161 and 1163 she travelled down the Rhine to the nearby monasteries of Siegburg, Boppard and Andernach, then to Cologne and

Werden/Ruhr. Finally, in her seventies, she visited the Swabian monasteries of Maulbronn, Hirsau and Zweifalten.

Extensive though her travels were throughout Germany, the speculation that she journeyed as far as Paris and Tours has no foundation. We can be sure, however, that her work was known in France, thanks to a letter written in *c.* 1166 by John of Salisbury (later Bishop of Chartres) in exile in Rheims, mentioning her name. In his loving correspondence with Gerard Pucelle, formerly clerk of Thomas Becket, he writes of the 'visions and prophecies of the blessed and most famous Hildegard', whom he holds in reverence 'since Pope Eugene III cherished her with an intimate bond of affection'. Naturally, her visits to these monasteries and cities prompted new correspondence. Around 1160–1 she exchanged extensive letters with the Abbess Hazzecha at Krauftal who, weary of the trials of high office, wanted to renounce her post. Typically, Hildegard exhorts her to concentrate on the matter in hand, give up gossip and follow the Rule of St Benedict rather than be destroyed by the 'noisome stench' of the ancient serpent. Some of Hildegard's own prophetic sermons from this time are known, thanks to those correspondents who had heard of them by repute and now wished to read them to their own communities. Thus copies or reworkings were sent, suggesting that Hildegard read them to the assembled crowds in cathedrals, monasteries or churches. Two, from Trier and Cologne, survive.

As ever her chief concern in these orations was to denounce the evil and felony sweeping through the Church. While her tone is apocalyptic and provocative, her attitude is hardline, reactionary rather than revolutionary. Her principal target is not Mankind but the clergy, who in her eyes had neglected their duties and sought temporal power and wealth over and above spiritual humility. Her other targets of scorn were the various heretical sects sweeping through the newly articulate urban populations of France, western Germany and Italy. In the Catholic Church, as taught by St Paul, heresy signalled the end of the world. In the words of commentators such as Bernard of Clairvaux, quoting the Song of Songs, heretics were the little foxes destroying God's tender vines. Since early in the eleventh century, various forms of heresy, associated in popular belief with magic, excrement, possession by the devil, sodomy, orgies and debauchery, had been stirring. Chroniclers reported their practices with alarmed and alarming relish. In 1160, when Hildegard was on her first preaching journey, a group of German heretics were said to have prepared a feast for those Christians they wished to convert. After laying out the food, they made the sign of the cross, whereupon the food turned to excrement, the wine to urine. Only now did these devilish sects, as they were perceived, gather momentum.

The most famous were the Cathars, who flourished in the Rhineland in the twelfth century and towards whom Hildegard, and Elisabeth of Schönau and her brother too, directed their most trenchant sermons. Confusingly, given their louche reputation, the Cathars took their name from the Greek for 'pure' (*katharos*). The sect's exact origins remain unclear and controversial. Their dualist beliefs in good and evil link them with the earlier Bogomils or Bougres of Bulgaria (hence 'bugger', originally meaning 'Bulgar') and the later Albigensians in Languedoc. Their name has also been associated with the Manichaeans of the third century, though their doctrines share few common features. They regarded the Catholic Church and the state as equally satanic, being part of the material world and thus evil. In addition to rejecting belief in hell, the resurrection, purgatory, meat, milk and eggs, they also denounced marriage, forbade sexual intercourse and held that suicide was both lawful and commendable. These extremist views, for all their undeniable purity, left few options open for the survival of the human race.[3]

In 1159, fearing persecution, a group of thirty German Cathars left to seek refuge in England, where they were condemned by Henry II and bishops at the Council of Oxford, scourged, branded on the forehead and left as vagrants. A worse fate faced those who were burnt in 1163 in Cologne shortly after Hildegard's preaching tour there. In that year she recorded her apocalyptic vision of the Cathars in which, following the devil's release from the bottomless pit, four angels set in motion four winds which roar destructively across the four corners of the earth. She gave the date 'twenty-three years and four months' ago (i.e. 1140) as the starting point of their activities in the Rhineland. By the thirteenth century, the threat of Catharism, above all other heresies, prompted Innocent III to launch the Albigensian Crusade in 1209 and Pope Gregory IX to appoint a full-time Papal Inquisition in 1233. Hildegard's role in condemning the early Cathars is more than a footnote in their history.

Remarkable though it is to picture this elderly woman breaking all the rules and preaching, in physically demanding and treacherous circumstances, yet more was at stake. The continuing rivalry between Rome and Empire had reached a critical juncture following the death of the English Pope, Hadrian IV, in 1159. In Rome, the college of cardinals was split over who should replace him. Two names emerged in the contest: the aristocratic Octavian of Monticelli, an imperialist, and the bourgeois Roland Bandinelli from Siena. Octavian was elected by a minority and called himself Victor IV. Roland, meanwhile, announced himself Alexander III. An unseemly and quasi-operatic brawl took place in St Peter's, with Victor IV tearing the purple cloak, symbol of papal power, from Alexander's back 'with his own hands', uttering loud shouts as he did so. A complicated farce of mutual excommunication then ensued, with neither giving in and both exercising a degree of power. Alexander was forced into exile in France, from where he had close involvement with Henry II of England and the Thomas Becket affair, insisting the King observe penance following his archbishop's murder. Intriguingly, the chronicles of Disibodenberg for the year 1156 give another reason for the schism, namely Barbarossa's second marriage to a sixteen-year-old heiress two years earlier: 'This year the Emperor Frederick took as wife Agnes daughter of the Duke of Burgundy, having previously repudiated his lawful wife at Constance. Out of this there arose a very serious schism in the Church.'

Events of the next eighteen years, the period which history has named the 'Papal Schism', were far darker and bloodier than a mere administrative tiff between cardinals over who should be pope might indicate. Hildegard, in her pivotal role, had reason to fear for her life. Most Hildegard biographers, understandably, place their subject alone centre stage with political events at one remove, spinning slowly round on a cyclorama behind her, from time to time catching her in its light. In the generic, allusive and symbolic style of her writings, she encourages us in that viewpoint. Her task, inspired by God, is to contemplate mankind against the grand canvas of apocalypse, from which we may or may not find redemption. The petty specifics of temporal current events are not her concern. They are, however, ours, for Hildegard was at the geographical and emotional centre of the imperial turmoil – a crisis in which her own diocesan archbishop, Arnold of Mainz, was murdered in 1160, the monastery in which he was killed razed to the ground at the instruction of her friend Frederick Barbarossa. This same Arnold had signed the Rupertsberg charter of 1158 confirming the monastery's independence and properties. The Disibodenberg chronicle of 1160 reports events without comment:

> In 1160 the Emperor ordered a council to be held after the Octave of Easter at Pavia at which Pope Victor was present, but Alexander was absent. Hence Victor was confirmed while Alexander was rejected. After these events, Bishop Arnold returned to Mainz, and on the Nativity of St John the Baptist [24 June] was killed in the monastery of St James. That monastery was set fire and all its fields laid waste.

Despite Hildegard's growing uneasiness about the Emperor, in 1163 Frederick Barbarossa granted the Rupertsberg monastery an edict guaranteeing imperial protection. This was not a matter merely of granting his one-time adviser further recognition and independence, but a safeguard against the civil strife going on all around. The Emperor's charter, we should observe, whether for reasons of flattery, politics or inattention, makes the only contemporary reference in a formal document to Hildegard as 'abbess'. That same year, in addition to shorter volumes on St Rupert and St Disibod, Hildegard began work on her third and last visionary book, which would take ten years to complete. The *Liber divinorum operum* (*Book of Divine Works*), still only available in English in an abridged edition translated from a version in German, was her most complex undertaking (see Appendix I). This ambitious history of salvation, from Genesis to the Apocalypse, mixes prophetic speculation and medicine, macrocosm and microcosm, geometry and astronomy, all conceived as a theory of cosmology which, it has been argued, provided a model for works such as Alain de Lille's allegorical poem (1182–3) *Anticlaudianus*, and more remotely but directly, Dante's *Divina commedia* more than a century later. The ten visions illustrated in ten miniatures of the Lucca Codex from the thirteenth century provide the best route to the heart of this difficult work. (We may take consolation from one of Hildegard's later supporters, the thirteenth-century Cistercian abbot Gebeno of Eberbach, who confessed that most people had difficulty reading her works because she 'speaks obscurely and in an unfamiliar manner', though this complexity was also considered a mark of holiness.) In her own words: 'I then wrote *Liber divinorum operum* in which, as almighty God inspired me, I saw the height and the depth and the breadth of the vault, and how the sun and the moon and the stars, and the other objects were arranged in it.'[4]

In 1164, Victor IV died and another antipope, Paschal III, was appointed by Frederick, prompting a furious outburst from

Hildegard who, until that point, had been relatively restrained on the matter of the schism. Now she railed at him, condemning him as a 'juvenile fool'. Two years later, in 1165, in circumstances which are tantalisingly little documented, Hildegard established a sister house across the river at Eibingen, near Rüdesheim, at a former Augustinian monastery founded in 1148 by a local noble woman but destroyed by Frederick's troops (this earlier establishment not having enjoyed the benefit of imperial protection) seventeen years later. Little is known about Eibingen except that it was almost certainly intended for women of more humble birth for whom the Rupertsberg was thought unsuitable. By now the number of Rupertsberg nuns had more than doubled to fifty. Eibingen could house thirty. This increase in numbers should be seen in the context of both Hildegard's fame and the general growth in numbers of religious women, which reached a peak at this time. The abbess visited her second monastery twice a week, but never lived there. More out of the way and with no outstanding architectural features, it had none of the Rupertsberg's established glamour.

Hildegard's arrival by boat each week attracted crowds of local pilgrims in need of her spiritual counsel and healing powers. One of the miracles described in the third book of the *Vita*, in which she cures a blind child with the unlikely therapy of Rhine water, paints a striking picture:

> *At one time, close to the town of Rüdesheim, where she used to ford the currents of the Rhine and put in at a spot near the nuns' monastery, a certain woman approached her boat carrying a little child in the crook of her arms. She besought Hildegard in tears to lay her holy hands on the child. Being deeply moved, and remembering him who said: Go to the pool of Siloe, and wash* [John 9:7], *she drew water from the river with her left hand, and blessed it with her right. When she sprinkled it into the child's eyes, through the favour of God's grace it gained its sight.*[5]

Eibingen monastery and church in the seventeenth century.

Later this child, by then an elderly woman, described her experience as told to her by her mother as evidence for the attempt to have Hildegard canonised after her death. Like all saints' lives, Hildegard's abounds with accounts of miraculous healings and exorcisms to exemplify her sanctity. Charms, amulets, stones and gems are used to enact cures, as well as, in Hildegard's case, her hair and clothing. The wife of the mayor of Bingen, troubled by a prolonged labour, came swiftly to term thanks to a plait of Hildegard's hair wrapped round her naked body. Other miracles listed in the *Vita*, all fairly conventional and later also quoted in the unsuccessful petition for Hildegard's canonisation, include: a domestic in the monastery who was cured of a tumour in her neck and chest; a seven-week-old baby from Rüdesheim whose convulsions subsided; a young noble woman from Trier whose uncontrollable lust for a handsome young man was quenched thanks to bread blessed by Hildegard; and a man whose epilepsy was banished for ever.

The mentally tortured, variously classified as possessed by the devil, vessels of Satan, demoniac, had to be dealt with in the same way as the physically sick, in need of healing rather than blame. Their symptoms, ranging from violent convulsions and screaming to depression and insanity, were all seen as the work of Satan. Bernard of Clairvaux's miracles (related in Arnold of Bonneval's *Vita prima Bernardi*) include soothing the possessed soul of an old woman so disturbed that she 'ground her teeth while her tongue protruded from her mouth like an elephant's trunk, so that she appeared not a woman but a monster'. Variations on these straightforward cases of possession (to which women were considered especially prone) were the demon preachers, usually laypeople who gabbled sermons while possessed by the devil. Puzzlingly, they preached orthodox creeds and accordingly were taken to shrines as what might be called anti-celebrities.

One of the earliest recorded was a young woman of noble birth named Sigewize, perhaps herself once a Cathar and preacher, who may have been present when Hildegard chastised that sect in the woman's home city of Cologne in 1163. The evil spirit which had inhabited Sigewize for seven years reportedly announced that only 'a little old hag' named Schrumpilgard (roughly translatable as 'Wrinkleface') could banish the incubus. Bravely recognising this as a reference to Hildegard, Abbot Gedolphus of Brauweiler wrote to her in about 1169 asking for assistance. The episode is recounted in full in the *Vita*. At first Hildegard responded by offering a ritual of exorcism to be carried out on Sigewize, pleading another of her own illnesses as an excuse not to come in person (an affliction which, according to the *Vita*, lasted a whole year and caused a burning agony and sickness so great it was 'as if my soul were about to quit the life of the body'). In this proposed ceremony she ordered, among other detailed instructions, that a priest and six others should strike Sigewize lightly with rods on her head, back, breast, navel, knees and feet, while chanting 'Now, you, O satanic and evil spirit, you who oppress and torment this person, this form of a woman, depart!' Several more blows must then be administered, with cries of 'Flee, therefore, flee, flee from her devil, fell with all the evil, airy spirits' and so forth, to be repeated until the said devil departs.

The exorcism was duly carried out. In Sigewize's case all this beating and shooing had some impact on the foul spirit, who 'gave out an almighty roar, and with an extraordinary caterwauling and a frightful din he came out of her screeching to the utter fright of bystanders. For the space of about half an hour he had kept up this frenzy, until when it pleased God the demon forsook the vessel he had so long occupied.' The onlooking hordes cried out in praise with loud clapping and stomping. Guibert adds the detail that the monks were chanting the *Te Deum laudamus*. Unfortunately, the relief was temporary and the blight soon returned. Hildegard agreed to see the woman herself. She and her nuns devoted many precious hours to fasting, prayer and self-mortification on Sigewize's behalf. One of the autobiographical passages from the *Vita* gives an extensive account, the whole interlude lasting several pages:

> In the meantime it was reported to me that far from us in the regions of the lower Rhine a certain noble woman had been possessed by a devil. Indeed, messengers came to me about this woman again and again. But I, in a true vision, saw that God had permitted her to be obsessed and over-shadowed by a kind of blackness and smoke of a diabolical fog, which oppressed all the senses of her rational soul and did not allow her to hope by raising her intellect on high. It was as when the shadow of a person or some other object, or a smoke covers and envelops whatever is in its path. So this woman lost the right use of her senses and actions and was constantly shouting and doing unseemly things.[6]

Hildegard speculates that the devil cannot enter human

beings in his own form, for that person's limbs would disintegrate 'more quickly than chaff scattered by the wind'. Instead, he 'envelops his victim and warps him into insanity and unseemly ways, and snarls through him as through a window, and moves his limbs outwardly. Yet the demon is not within him in his own form, rather it is as if the soul of a person is in a stupefied sleep and does not know what the flesh of the body is doing.' She then goes on to offer an explanation as to how an all-seeing God can allow such evils and terrors in the world, a theme to which she returns repeatedly in her theological writings. This form of possession she regards as an essential process of purification. In this respect the devil is there to serve God:

> But since God wants His people to be purified by means of these demons, by His permission and mandate they stir up a stupor in the air and by means of a foam of the air they vomit up plague and cause floods and dangers in the waters, provoke wars and spawn adversities and evils. God allows these things to happen, because in their arrogance human beings wallow in crimes and murders. But when God has purified His people in this way, He reduces the same spirits to confusion, as happened to the woman mentioned above.[7]

Eventually, after Sigewize had spent several days during Lent at the Rupertsberg, pronouncing in her possessed state on a range of topics from baptism to the sacrament of the Body of Christ and the ruin of the Cathars, a crisis occurred in the middle of the Easter Vigil with, as Guibert would have us believe, about three thousand people present. Suddenly the woman was 'seized by a great fear and began to tremble'. Stamping the ground, hyperventilating and emitting great belches of air (from which end is not clear), Sigewize's acute suffering must have caused terror to those witnessing it. The lurid exorcism scenes in Ken Russell's version of *The Devils* seem mild in comparison. Hildegard, with timely providence, was guided by a sudden vision:

> *Immediately I saw and heard in true vision that the power of the Most High which once overshadowed and ever overshadows Holy Baptism spoke to the diabolical fog by which the woman was being worn out: 'Go forth Satan from the tabernacle of this woman's body; yield place in her to the Holy Spirit!' Then the unclean spirit withdrew from her in a horrible way with a discharge from the woman's private parts, and she was set free. From then on she continued in her right senses, both of soul and body as long as she lived. 'Glory to you O Lord.'*[8]

Sigewize lived on as a nun at the Rupertsberg until her death, which Hildegard's account would seem to indicate took place soon after this traumatic event.

CHAPTER FOURTEEN

LAST JOURNEY

Soon after this encounter with the possessed Sigewize, Hildegard herself succumbed to another illness. The symptoms, as ever, were acute, prolonged and alarming, but in their vagueness difficult to attach to any one medical condition, unless we accept as valid the theory that she suffered from migraine (see Chapters 4 and 12). She describes the malaise as 'withering the very blood in my veins and the very marrow in my bones and setting all my entrails below in turmoil', reducing her to a winter plant whose greenness has gone. This attack lasted a symbolic forty days and forty nights. Once again she escaped death and cast out all the wicked spirits greedy for her soul. While still sick, she had a vision in which she was 'to visit certain communities of spiritual people, both of men and women, and candidly lay before them the words that God would show me'.[1] Accordingly, in 1170, still in poor health and by now seventy-two years old, she embarked on her last preaching journey. During her absence, her secretary Volmar wrote a moving, loving letter, the only one of his to have survived in Hildegard's correspondence, anxious about her health and dreading the prospect, one day to be faced, of her death. After nearly thirty years in her service, his loyalty is undimmed:

> Even if, O sweetest mother, we should see you daily with our eyes of flesh, hear you daily with our ears of flesh and, as is just, daily cleave devotedly to you, understanding that the Holy Spirit speaks to us through you, we still do not doubt that your absence, which we cannot mention without tears, shall one day really weigh upon us when, as it pleases God, we shall not see you henceforth . . . for there

is no man who shall live who does not see death. For then
our lamentation and wretchedness shall be greater than
our present gladness.[2]

Hildegard's travels on this final excursion from the
Rupertsberg took her across land through Swabia to the Cluniac
foundation of Hirsau (of which a handsome Romanesque
tower still survives today) and other monasteries in the region
of Strasbourg. Once again she urged faith, humility, zeal and
duty and an end to simony and corruption. One of the houses
she visited was at Kircheim. A letter of 1170 from Werner, the
abbot there, refers to her visit and asks for a copy of her sermon
on priestly negligence, 'so that we may keep it ever before our
eyes, lest we forget'.[3] Her reply is among her most potent
and readily comprehended statements and a fine example of
the vibrancy of her writing. Even in her own time, few
people would have grasped all her scriptural references or
implications, but the gist is blazingly clear: the Church is soiled
by depravity, like a beautiful woman whose cloak is spattered
and ripped, her face besmirched. Hildegard's rhetoric has a
searing, apocalyptic intensity, her imagery embodies all her
visionary depictions of Synagoga and Ecclesia, Mother of the
Incarnation and Virgin Bride of Christ, first encountered in
Scivias three decades earlier:

> *In the year 1170, lying for a long time in my sickbed,*
> *fully awake in body and soul, I saw an exceedingly beauti-*
> *ful image of a woman. She was so delightful and so*
> *beautiful that the mind of man could never comprehend it*
> *and in stature she reached from the earth to the heavens.*
> *Her face shone with great brightness, and with her eyes*
> *she looked into the heaven. She was clothed in a garment*
> *of dazzling white silk, over which was a cloak set with*
> *precious stones – with emeralds, sapphires and pearls –*
> *and on her feet were shoes of onyx. But her face was*

smudged with dirt, and her dress was torn on the right side. Moreover her cloak had lost its exquisite beauty, and the tops of her shoes were soiled.

She cried out in a loud, mournful voice to the heights of heaven: Give heed, O heavens, because my face has been smudged, and mourn, O earth, because my garment has been torn, and tremble, O abyss, because my shoes have been soiled. 'The foxes have holes, and the birds of the air nests' [Matt. 8.20] but I have no one to help or console me, and no staff to lean on for support . . .

Those who nurtured me – the priests, that is to say – were supposed to make my face glow like the dawn, my clothes flash like lightning, my cloak gleam like precious stones and my shoes to shine brightly. Instead they have smeared my face with dirt, they have torn my garment, they have blackened my cloak and they have soiled my shoes. The very ones who were supposed to beautify me . . . have all failed miserably. This is the way they soil my face: they take up and handle the body and blood of my Bridegroom while defiled by the uncleanliness of their lustful morals, poisoned by the deadly venom of fornication and adultery, and corrupted by the avaricious rapine of buying and selling improper things. They encompass His body and blood with filth, like someone putting a child in the mud among swine . . .

And so let heaven rain down all kinds of calamities upon mankind in the vengeance of God, and let a cloud cover the whole earth, so that its greenness withers and its beauty fades. And let the abyss tremble . . . O you priests! you who have neglected me thus far, the princes of the earth and rash mob will rise up against you . . . They will take your riches away from you because you have not attended to your priestly office. And they will say about you: 'Let us cast these adulterers and robbers out of the Church, for they are full of every kind of wickedness' . . .

> *And again I, a poor little feminine form, saw an un-*
> *sheathed sword hanging in the air, one edge of which was*
> *turned towards the heavens, the other towards the earth . . .*
> *And I saw that that sword was cutting off certain mon-*
> *asteries of spiritual men, just as Jerusalem was cut off after*
> *the Passion of the Lord . . . Now may the unquenchable*
> *fire of the Holy Spirit so infuse you that you will turn to the*
> *better part.*[4]

As this sermon so vividly demonstrates, the catastrophe tearing at the heart of the Church was uppermost in Hildegard's mind. The chasm between Rome and Empire was deepening. In 1168, Paschal III had died and Barbarossa had appointed yet another antipope. Hildegard could hold back no longer. She at once fired off a furious epistolary missile at the Emperor, in Latin, consisting of just thirty-three words: 'He who is, says: I destroy disobedience, and I crush the opposition of those who scorn me. Woe, woe to the malice of evil men who despise me! Hear this, king, if you wish to live; otherwise my sword shall smite you.'[5]

Frederick Barbarossa took no heed. In 1168 Calixtus III was appointed pope. Two years later, Thomas Becket was murdered at Canterbury, word of which spread rapidly throughout Europe, underlining the deepening discord between Church and state. At home, Hildegard faced private grief, matched only by the loss of Richardis twenty years earlier. In 1173, as she was completing her mighty *Liber divinorum operum*, Volmar died. The 'certain monk', her 'only beloved son', attached to her like a shadow and so obscure and elusive that we know his name only from a letter of Guibert's, had gone. Guibert, who can never have met him since he first went to the Rupertsberg only in 1176, called him 'sober, chaste, and learned in the wisdom of both heart and word'. In his letter to Bovo, Guibert praised Volmar's restraint in his editorial work, clothing Hildegard's words 'however bare and unpolished, in a more presentable dress',[6] a discretion Guibert himself, a few years later, was to exercise more liberally. The *Vita*, compiled by the two monks whose task arose because of Volmar's demise, fails to mention his passing. However, a note added to the *Liber divinorum operum* observes that Ludwig, Abbot of St Eucharius in Trier, showed compassion to Hildegard at this time of trouble 'since he had known this blessed man well, and me and my visions, while I, in my tearful sighs rejoiced over him [Volmar] as one taken up by God'.[7]

Quite apart from causing her sorrow, Volmar's death thrust Hildegard into a fresh and unwelcome dispute with the monks of Disibodenberg, who still had authority over her in appointing priests. Abbot Helenger, who had proved so irksome in the mid-1150s over the independent status of her monastery and properties, had grown no less obdurate with age. Astonishingly, given Hildegard's fame, her age, her achievements – or perhaps inevitably, given the history of her relationship with him – he refused to replace Volmar. Was he paying her back for her autocratic and impatient letter of three years earlier (1170), in response to one from him begging indulgence for his own sloth and the dismal laxity and dereliction into which Disibodenberg was sliding? Her reply had been particularly viperish, accusing him of fecklessness, impiety and instability. To suffer from moral inertia was one of the worst offences in Hildegard's litany of sins. She bristles with sarcasm:

> Sometimes you are like a bear which growls under its breath; but sometimes like an ass, not prudent . . . but rather worn down. In some matters you are altogether useless . . . You are also like certain kinds of birds which do not fly on the heights and yet do not hug the earth, neither excelling nor being subject to harm . . . But when you do get a flash of insight, you pray for a little while, and then you grow weary again, and you do not even bother to finish your prayer, but you take the road which your body knows well,

and you never fully renounce it . . . Poor little woman that
I am, I see a black fire in you kindled against us . . .[8]

Helenger, whose character is here so mercilessly sketched,
must have revelled in his brief moment of revenge. He should
have foreseen, however, that Hildegard would have no intention
of letting the matter rest. She promptly wrote to Alexander III,
still hanging on to the vestiges of papal power despite
Frederick's series of puppet-popes, requesting his assistance.
In a lofty and extended opening eulogy, she urges him to be a
Morning Star to guide the Church, 'which for too long has
been lacking in the light of God's justice because of the dense
cloud of schism'. She then goes straight to the point, without
employing her usual tools of symbol or allusion:

> *Now O gentlest father, my sisters and I bend our knees*
> *before your paternal piety, praying that you deign to regard*
> *the poverty of this poor little woman. We are in great distress*
> *because the abbot of Mount St Disibod and his brothers*
> *have taken away our privileges and the right of election*
> *which we have always had, rights which we have been*
> *ever careful to retain. For if they will not grant us reverential*
> *and religious men, such as we seek, spiritual religion will*
> *be totally destroyed among us. Therefore, my lord, for God's*
> *sake, help us so that we may retain the man we have*
> *elected to that office. Or if not, let us seek out and receive*
> *others, where we can, who will look after us in accordance*
> *with the will of God and our own needs.*[9]

In response Alexander III appointed Hildegard's nephew
Wezelinus, Provost of St Andreas at Cologne, to sort the matter
out, instructing him to ensure that if the monks of Disibodenberg
would not oblige in providing a priest, an appointment would
have to be made from elsewhere. Helenger relented and late in
1174 or early in 1175 sent Gottfried, the chosen monk, to serve

as provost and secretary to the abbess and her fifty nuns. Now the circle begins to near completion. It was this same Gottfried who started work on the *Vita* which has provided the backbone, and much of the flesh, of this entire account. Precisely who instigated the work remains unclear, but the scant evidence points to Hildegard's friend, Abbot Ludwig of Echternach (who had exchanged a series of touching and affectionate letters with Hildegard in 1173–4 and later, it seems, encouraged Theodoric to complete Gottfried's work).

This new state of affairs was short-lived. Gottfried died in 1176, leaving the *Vita* unfinished. Hildegard's brother Hugo, whose name had appeared on the Archbishop of Mainz's crucial document of 1158 when he was cantor of the cathedral there, took over as secretary. Another canon from Mainz acted as provost. Both died within a year of arriving at the Rupertsberg. Thus, in 1177, the French-speaking Guibert of Gembloux received a summons from the abbess and prophet he so admired, with whom he had already corresponded and whom he had visited briefly the previous year. He was to travel from his monastery in Flanders, now Belgium, to the Rupertsberg and take over as Hildegard's secretary, a duty he fulfilled for the last three years of her life.

CHAPTER FIFTEEN

FINAL CRISIS

Having thus set forth these things, we fast approach the end of this work; so let us see also the end of the life of the holy virgin and the signs with which God illumined it, as the sisters . . . have described it.

(*VITA*, III, XXVII)

Guibert of Gembloux, whose asides and embellishments have sounded like grace notes in these pages, was born in Brabant in 1124/5. He attended the monastery school at the abbey of Gembloux, famous for its well-stocked library, learnt Latin and became a monk. There he stayed, with excursions, for the remainder of his life, eventually becoming abbot in 1194 until his death in 1213. In 1157 Gembloux had been destroyed by fire. Guibert and some of the other monks lived on in the ruins, trying to rebuild the abbey and its fragile reputation, with little success. In the next decade his relationship with the monks of Gembloux deteriorated following the appointment of a new abbot, John, in 1160. Guibert detected a whiff of simony in the appointment and had no hesitation in announcing the moral shortcomings of the monastery to anyone who cared to listen. He found an ear among the monks of Villers, a nearby Cistercian foundation, and, not entirely without disloyalty, he established a friendship with them while remaining attached to Gembloux. From this clouded and quarrelsome situation he first wrote to Hildegard in 1175. In this correspondence he, too, raised the infamous matter of the nuns' tiaras and robes nearly thirty years after Tenxwind's tart enquiry (see Chapter 5).

Somewhat brazenly, and with customary flattery, he also offered his ageing and eminent elder a warning about the pitfalls of pride and boastfulness: 'Still saintly lady, I must warn you – not argumentatively, certainly, but reverently – to be cautious and persevering. I know that you have already reached the heights of perfection. All the same, remember that you bear your treasure in a fragile vessel, and that it is not the reeds and twigs (which easily bounce back) but the mighty trees that are uprooted by the winds.'

Was it this very audacity which whetted Hildegard's interest, or was Guibert's keenness in subsequent letters simply too persistent to ignore?[1] Either way, we owe him our gratitude. Hildegard replied at length, her letter providing the invaluable and frequently cited account of her visionary life from childhood into old age. Here, too, she made her famous remarks concerning the way she experienced her visions, stating plainly that she saw them fully awake. In addition, we find her description (recurring in the works) of herself reaching out to the Almighty and being raised up 'like a feather on the breath of God'. As an account of the hardships of old age, this document is surprisingly personal: 'But the constant infirmity I suffer sometimes makes me too weary to communicate the words and visions shown to me, but nevertheless when my spirit sees and tastes them, I am so transformed . . . that I consign all my sorrow and tribulation to oblivion.' Guibert, puffed up and excited by receiving such a full and intimate reply, wrote again at inordinate and obsequious length, promising a visit to the Rupertsberg.

Accordingly, in the autumn of the following year (1176) he visited Hildegard. We know about this meeting from a subsequent letter to Hildegard, in which he describes returning to Gembloux via Villers, where the monks issued him with a catalogue of thirty-five theological questions for him to submit to his illustrious new acquaintance. Impatiently, he followed up with another letter the same year, wondering why Hildegard had failed to reply by return to this lengthy interrogation. Pressed into a response, she pleaded overwork and ill health; her infirmity meant she 'cannot yet refrain from tears' and she was also 'thoroughly taken up with the governing of our monastery'. She promised, nevertheless, that she was working on her replies. Given the bothersome nature of the questions, from banal to immense, her tardiness is understandable. Full answers would have required her to write a lengthy new theological tome as well as draining what surviving energies she had. Three examples of the monks' queries give a flavour:

- In what part of the earth are we to believe that paradise was situated?
- Was it a real fire that Moses saw burning but not consuming the bush?
- What kind of bodies did those angels who appeared to Abraham have, those whom he served with the finest flour, a calf, butter and milk?

That same year, with apparently no respect for Hildegard's age or her other heavy responsibilities as abbess, the relentless Guibert wrote a third letter, once again asking for responses to the questions, demanding that she 'omit nothing', nor for the sake of brevity 'hastily passing over anything that ought to be spoken'. A fourth, praising her womanhood, associating her with the Blessed Virgin Mary and generally soaring on a wing of rhetoric, followed soon after. The monks of Villers themselves bombarded Hildegard with two further copies of their questions lest she had not received Guibert's letter. In a fifth, its tone wordy and breathless, Guibert has heard news of Hildegard's death and begs confirmation or denial, quickly dispatching any thoughts of grief since he knows that 'the luminous soul of that holy woman has been brought up to the Father of lights and has been embraced by His Son, her Bridegroom, Jesus Christ, and is now enjoying eternal brightness.'[2]

Frail though she was, Hildegard was far from dead. Indeed, Guibert's subsequent letter, written in joy at her continuing vitality and expressing a retrospective grief far more elaborate than that shown in his previous letter, continued to pester her for answers to these unwelcome questions, as if his reputation among the monks depended on her dignifying him with a response. He also requested that she might return his previous letters so that their entire correspondence thus far could be collected in one volume, 'to preserve them not only for my consolation but also as a means of exciting divine wonder for His gifts to me in those who will by chance deign to read them',[3] which sounds very like a modern author writing to a celebrity with an eye to publication. That same year (1177), presumably realising that in Guibert she had found a slavish admirer who was also skilled in Latin, grammar and, especially, rhetoric, Hildegard engaged him as her secretary, replacing the late Gottfried. Having had his leave endorsed by Abbot John of Gembloux (who may have welcomed a short respite from this sedulous monk), Guibert arrived at the Rupertsberg in June that year. John of Gembloux wanted him back again almost immediately, but Guibert refused, finding support in Hildegard (no stranger to spats with troublesome abbots), as well as from the diocesan Bishop of Liège and Hildegard's ally, the Archbishop Philip of Cologne.

Not long after his arrival at the women's monastery, Guibert embarked on a newsy and detailed letter to his friend Bovo, a fellow monk at Gembloux. Once again, Guibert's chattiness provides us with singular evidence, in this instance offering an eye-witness account of Hildegard, her relationship with her nuns, their daily activities and the physical circumstances of the Rupertsberg monastery at its flourishing peak. It reads as a summation of her activities in the twenty-seven years since she arrived there and a retrospective account of her working life. He also praises the moral rectitude of this institution compared with his own at Gembloux:

> There is in this place a marvellous contest of virtues to be seen, where the mother embraces her daughters with such affection and the daughters submit themselves to their mother with such reverence that it is hard to decide whether the mother surpasses the daughters in this eagerness or the daughters their mother.

With one accord these holy handmaids of God so cultivate God through lively devotion and themselves by self-command and one another with honour and obedience, that in them you can literally behold the delightful spectacle of the weaker sex triumphing with Christ's help over itself, the world and the devil. For, mindful of the Lord's invitation: Desist! and see that I am God [Ps. 45:11] *they refrain from work or holidays and sit in composed silence in the cloister applying themselves to holy reading and to learning the chant. On ordinary days they obey and apply themselves in well-fitted workshops to the writing of books, the weaving of robes or other manual crafts.*

So by giving themselves to holy reading they acquire the light of divine knowledge and the grace of compunction, and by their engagement in exterior works they banish the idleness which is poison to the soul and curb the levity so apt to arise at idle gatherings from the multiplicity of words . . .

The mother herself, the leader of so great a company, crushes the vice of inflation, so often born of prestigious position, with the profound gravity of humility. In her charity she pours herself out on all, giving the counsels required of her, solving the most difficult questions put to her, writing books, instructing her sisters, putting fresh heart in to the sinners who approach her. She is wholly taken up with it all. Though she is weighed down both by age and infirmity, she is so mighty in the exercise of all the virtues, that many are the things she could say with the Apostle such as: I have become all things to all, that I might save all [I Cor. 1:22]; *and this:* I may be unskilled in speaking, but not in knowledge [II Cor. 2:6] *and this also:* Gladly will I glory in my weaknesses, that the power of Christ may dwell with me for when I am weak then I am stronger and more powerful [II Cor. 12:9–10] *and many sayings of this kind. But at this point, enough of these things.*[4]

Some years later, after Hildegard's death, Guibert attached his own, unfinished life of the abbess to Bovo's letter. He gathered his material from a miscellany of sources, including Gottfried's *Vita*, spoken evidence from the nuns and all the autobiographical passages which Hildegard had, as far as we know, written when Volmar was still alive.

This, however, is to jump ahead. In the last year of her life, Hildegard faced a new crisis. This final trial proved more painful and disruptive than any since her troubled removal to Rupertsberg three decades earlier. It undermined the core precept of her religious observance. Her antagonists were the clergy of Mainz. The battle concerned an interdict placed on her community as a result of the burial of a noble man at the Rupertsberg who had, supposedly, once been excommunicated, possibly as a heretic. The burial of rich local patrons in the monastery grounds had been one of the earliest benefits secured by Hildegard when she first arrived there. The Mainz clergy argued that this man (his name is unknown), having been expelled from the church, could not rest in consecrated ground. Moreover, the nuns were forbidden from singing the Divine Office or celebrating Mass. They demanded that his body be disinterred and removed. Hildegard, unrepentant and un- daunted and calling on the Living Light for guidance, refused. By ironic coincidence, these underling clerics launched their attack when their overseer was away. Christian, Archbishop of Mainz, was in Italy, trying to mediate between Pope Alexander III and Frederick Barbarossa to end the Papal Schism – an event for which Hildegard had longed and prayed for during the past seventeen years and which was, indeed, resolved in 1177–8.

The opportunistic speed with which they acted, and their motives, inexplicable beyond jealous spite towards the eighty- year-old abbess, casts doubt on the validity of their action. Our evidence for this episode is three letters from Hildegard, one to the prelates of Mainz and two more to Archbishop Christian.

She describes exactly what took place. Note her insistence, as always, that her vision occurred 'with wakeful eyes'. Observe, too, her shrewd rhetorical counterpointing of the 'upright' counsel of men and the 'harshness' and 'injustice' of women:

> By a vision which was implanted in my soul by God, the Great Artisan, before I was born, I have been compelled to write these things because of the interdict by which our superiors have bound us, on account of a certain dead man buried at our monastery, a man buried without any objection, with his own priest officiating. Yet only a few days after his burial, these men ordered us to remove him from our cemetery. Seized by no small terror, as a result, I looked as usual to the True Light, and with wakeful eyes, I saw in my spirit that if this man were disinterred in accordance with their commands, a terrible and lamentable danger would come upon us like a dark cloud before a threatening thunder storm.
>
> Therefore we have not presumed to remove the deceased inasmuch as he had confessed his sins, had received extreme unction and communion and had been buried without objection. Furthermore we have not yielded to those who advised or even commanded this course of action. Not, certainly, that we take the counsel of upright men or the orders of our superiors lightly, but we would not have it appear that, out of feminine harshness, we did injustice to the sacraments of Christ, with which this man had been fortified when he was still alive. But so that we may not be totally disobedient we have, in accordance with their injunction, ceased from singing the divine praises and from participation in Mass, as had been our regular monthly custom. As a result my sisters and I have been greatly distressed and saddened.[5]

No feat of imagination is required to see how catastrophic

this ban must have been for Hildegard as her life ebbed away. Death might come at any moment. The double blow of being forbidden to receive the sacrament or to sing the Divine Office could hardly have been more merciless or bullying. In this letter she also proposes at length her philosophy of music (see Chapter 12) and its role in the cosmos, concluding with a warning that anyone who 'without just cause' imposes silence on a church and prohibits the singing of God's praises 'will lose their place among the chorus of angels unless they have amended their lives through true penitence and humble restitution'. She concludes, in ringing tones, that 'this time is a womanish time', a familiar theme throughout her writings. In its state of weakness and reduced virility, the Church must rely on a woman to return it to strength. 'But the strength of God's justice is exerting itself, a female warrior battling against injustice, so that it might fall defeated.'

According to Hildegard in her letter to Archbishop Christian, the dead man in question had been absolved and reunited with Rome; witnesses could easily be found to confirm the fact, the whole of Bingen had turned out for his funeral. Eventually, in March 1179, six months before her death, the interdict was lifted by the relenting Archbishop, who wrote to her from Rome. His action may have been hastened by the knowledge that, were Hildegard to die now, his own reputation would be sullied, his salvation far from guaranteed. Suddenly he was convinced of her innocence, but not without a patronising reprimand (and a nimble request slipped in for her prayers for his 'sinful soul'):

> Dearest lady in Christ, these obvious signs of your holy life and such amazing testimonies to the truth oblige us to obey your commands and to pay especial heed to your entreaties . . . We also hope this sinful soul of ours, made the more acceptable through your saintly intercession, will obtain the mercy of its Creator . . .

> *Hence, with regard to the tribulation and affliction which you and your nuns are enduring because of the suspension of the divine offices, the clearer your innocence in this matter becomes to us, the more firmly we sympathise with you. Nevertheless, the Church held that the man buried in your churchyard had incurred the sentence of excommunication while he was alive, and although some doubt remained concerning his absolution, the fact that you disregarded the outcry of the clergy and acted as if this would cause no scandal in the Church was a very danger-ous act, since the statutes of the holy fathers are inviolable. You should have waited for definitive proof based on the suitable testimony of good men in the presence of the Church. Yet we wholeheartedly sympathise with your affliction, as is only right, and therefore . . . we grant you the privilege of celebrating the divine offices again, on the condition that proof of the dead man's absolution has been established by the testimony of reliable men. In the mean-time, saintly lady, if we have caused any annoyance . . . we earnestly beseech you not to withhold your compassion from one who seeks pardon.[6]*

One might guess that Hildegard's joyful relief was only margin-ally more intense than her irritation at the Archbishop's tone, by turns obsequious and condescending in equal measure.

The monks' *Vita* makes no mention of the interdict, moving rapidly from a catalogue of miracles to Hildegard's demise, and remarking with admirable directness that 'having thus set forth these things, we fast approach the end of this work'. We know nothing of the final months of her life, nor of the exact nature of her final illness. The account of her last moments, unlike that of Jutta's death, reads conventionally and with frustratingly little of the colourful detail the obliging Guibert usually supplied. Disappointingly, though he made amendments to Theodoric's version like an editor determined to leave his mark, his additions are fussy and read as hagiography rather than bedside evidence. Both versions report that the eighty-one-year-old Hildegard had grown weary of 'this present life', especially given her recent battles and struggles. She knew that her end was near, since God had revealed it to her, and told her nuns that it would happen shortly. This is the *Vita*'s account, with Guibert's adornments in roman:

> And thus the blessed virgin *had laboured in a* serious *illness for some time, when in the eighty-second year of her life, on the fifteenth day before the Kalends of October [17 September] she* was freed from the toilsome prison of this life *and went with a happy passage to her heavenly spouse* whom she had longed for with her whole heart. *Her daughters, to whom* after God *she had been all joy and all solace wept bitterly as they took part in the funeral rites of their beloved mother. For though they did not doubt her reward and the favours that would be conferred on them by God through her, yet they* were afflicted with *the most intense grief of heart over her departure,* by which they seemed to lose the unique consolation of her through whom God had visited them. *But God clearly showed even in her passing* through a manifest miracle *how great was the standing she had before him.*

This 'manifest miracle' took the form of two arcs of brilliant and varied colour which appeared in the sky over the room in which 'the holy virgin gave up her happy soul to God'. They widened like broad highways, reaching to the four corners of the earth. A full moon shone, illuminating the apex where the two arcs crossed, its brightness dispelling the darkness of night. What occurred next might have leapt straight from the pages of one of the Blessed Virgin abbess's own visions:

> *Within this light a glowing red cross became visible, at first*

small, but later increasing to an immense size. And all around it were countless circles of varied colour, in which, one by one, small crosses took shape, likewise glowing red, each with circles around it, though these crosses and circles were noticeably smaller than the first. And when they spread themselves over the sky, their width inclined more to the east, and they seemed to bend toward the earth where the dwelling was in which the holy virgin had passed away, and so cast a brilliant light upon the whole mountain.

It is worthy of belief that by this sign God was showing how bright was the splendour with which he was illumining his beloved one in heaven.[7]

CHAPTER SIXTEEN

RELIGHTING THE FLAME

Whereas our beloved daughters in Christ, the abbess and sisters of the monastery of St Rupert at Bingen . . . have petitioned us that, since by the merits of Hildegard of holy memory, abbess of the said monastery, God has deigned to work many miracles . . . [we] ought now to exalt her on earth whom the Lord had honoured in heaven, by canonising her and inscribing her in the catalogue of the saints.

(ACTA INQUISITIONIS, 1228, ADDRESSED TO
THE PRELATES OF MAINZ)

Even before Hildegard was cold in her grave, another miracle occurred. Two men who 'made bold to touch her holy body' were at once restored to health. In the words of the *Vita*, 'Venerable men celebrated her funeral rites' and all about her tomb the air was suffused with 'the fragrance of a wonderful sweetness', a sweet scent which 'filled the lungs and nostrils of many'. Guibert glorifies the heady perfume as having 'the manner of lilies and the most precious scent'. Compared with the eye-witness description of the death of Jutta, Hildegard's passing is kept brief and to the point. She was buried in 'a venerable place',[1] unspecified. Trithemius, a later Abbot of Sponheim (1483–1506), states that she 'was buried in the midst of the choir of the aforesaid monastery of Rupertsberg, before the main altar'. An entry in the chronicles of Sponheim dated 1498, four hundred years after her birth, records that 'the tomb of the holy Virgin Hildegard at Rupertsberg was opened in the presence of the entire community there, and others present for the occasion, one of whom was our Abbot John Trithemius, who by his prayers obtained an arm of the holy Virgin from the *magistra* of the community, for whom she had worked many benefits in the time of their tribulations. These relics were enclosed with others in a certain stone slab.'[2]

Meanwhile, at the Rupertsberg, earnest attempts were made to complete the *Vita* as part of the process of securing her canonisation. Thomas Becket, after all, had been sanctified within three years of his death, admittedly in more shocking circumstances at the hand of an assassin. Speed was of the essence. Thwarted by the death of Volmar and then of Gottfried, the community must have hoped Guibert would continue his task with all speed before further disaster befell. Had Hildegard's great admirer completed his monumental undertaking, we would have a biography of Hildegard unique in scale and detail for its time. Unhappily, he only reached 1141, the point at which her life grew interesting, when she cast off the shackles of silence and strode into the world. In 1180, when Guibert was called back to Gembloux by his abbot, leaving behind his incomplete work, Gottfried's version and Hildegard's own autobiographical notes in all their conflicting muddle, a skilled hand was needed. Eventually, they secured the help of a monk, Theodoric, from Echternach in the nearby diocese of Trier. This busy scribe, archivist and librarian, unlike his predecessors, had almost certainly never met his subject.

As far as one can tell from his more impassive though fluent writing style, he lacked the bumptious charm of Guibert, being a scholar rather than a diarist with an eye for social detail. A child oblate, Theodoric had received a good monastic education. It seems likely that he only took on the job of editor-cum-compiler in response to a request from Hildegard's friend and correspondent Ludwig, Abbot of Eucharius and Echternach. Theodoric started work around 1182, producing an intricate quilt of all the available sources, complete with repetition, parallel versions of the same events and chronological gaps to which Guibert, near the end of his life as already described, added his own emendations and amendments.[3] Theodoric's hand would have written the pithy, relatively matter-of-fact description of Hildegard's death, relying on the nuns' verbatim account as his source. Since he completed the *Vita* in around 1187, nearly a decade after the event, its more detached tone is hardly surprising. Collective memories may have faded.

What happened next, concerning the thorny question of Hildegard's canonisation, is almost impossible to unravel. During the thirteenth century, several attempts were made, drawing on a catalogue of miracles and the evidence of the *Vita*, to win Hildegard a coveted sainthood. All failed, though the matter is not as clear-cut as that implies. Far from it. Several local monasteries commemorated her feast day (by saintly tradition, the day of death, not of birth) after 1179 and throughout the next century. In 1220, just as it might have been waning, her reputation was given a boost by the monk Gebeno of Eberbach, who produced a compendium of her writings, widely copied and read throughout the late Middle Ages, of which several manuscripts have survived. Stressing her prophetic powers, he called it the *Pentachronon seu Speculum Futurorum Tempororum*, or *Mirror of Future Times*. His selections emphasise her role in the late Middle Ages as a Church reformer and apocalyptic thinker. With no authority beyond hearsay and Gebeno's personal opinion, the text ranked her with other (male) saints, including Bernard of Clairvaux and Thomas Becket, which must have done wonders for her reputation.

When is a saint not a saint? Today Hildegard is venerated in Germany, and referred to as Blessed. Yet officially she has still never been canonised. The definition of canonisation is far from scientific. Until the twelfth century, any bishop could authorise the veneration of a departed local holy person in his diocese. Cults abounded. Around 1170 Alexander III tried to establish due process and put a stop to abuse by insisting, in a letter to King Canute of Sweden (regarding his late father, Eric), that no one should be venerated as a saint without papal authority. Thus, after years of laxity, at precisely the time Hildegard's name was up for consideration, the Church was at its most vigilant and fastidious. In the intervening centuries, the lengthy legal rigmarole of sainthood has been refined and revised several times. In 1983 it was simplified yet again and is currently undergoing further streamlining. Without attempting to itemise every detail of a necessarily arcane procedure, it is important to establish what 'canonisation' entails, which helps cast light on Hildegard's nebulous status.

The *Oxford Dictionary of the Christian Church* calls sainthood 'The definitive sentence by which the Pope declares a particular member of the faithful departed, previously beatified, to have already entered into eternal glory, and ordains for the new Saint a public cult throughout the whole Church.' Beatification, the first step towards sainthood (entitling the person to be called 'Blessed'), requires proof of at least one attested miracle or evidence of a life of outstanding charity. Full-scale canonisation requires proof of further miracles both before and after death, or else death as a martyr. Sainthood endows seven benefits on the memory of the recipient as follows:

1 The name is to be inscribed in the catalogue of saints.
2 The new saint is to be invoked in public prayers.
3 Churches may be dedicated in the saint's memory.
4 Mass and the Divine Office are publicly offered to God in the saint's honour.
5 Festival days are celebrated in the saint's memory.
6 Pictorial representations may be made, with the saint surrounded by heavenly light.
7 The saint's relics are enclosed in precious vessels and publicly honoured.

Hildegard seems to score on all but the first and third point. In 1237 Pope Gregory IX rejected an application for her elevation by three canons of Mainz (who had supplied a document now known as the *Acta inquisitionis de virtutibus et miraculis S. Hildegardis*),[4] allegedly as a result of bureaucratic inefficiency. Since many applications for sainthood, like present-day passport forms, were returned first time round on the grounds of incomplete information, the Pope's rejection should not be seen in a sinister light. Moreover, scarcely any women were canonised at this time in the Church's history. Hildegard, though manifestly holy, had not endured martyrdom. It might be argued that beatification was honour enough in the circumstances. The matter rumbled on, without issue, until 1243 when the new Pope, Innocent IV, asked whether this additional information would be forthcoming.

Hildegard was not without her detractors. By now, the brief period in which women had flowered through the monastic life was giving way to the expansion of the universities, in which the female voice was once again silenced. Could a resistance to powerful women lurk behind the critical words in 1270 of an English Franciscan, John Peckham, who refused to believe that Hildegard had ever been endorsed by Bernard of Clairvaux or the Pope. In a powerful indictment (one of few to have been unearthed), he calls the story a lie, 'especially as this woman is known to have handed down many errors in her other reckless scribblings. So until anything persuades me to the contrary, I believe that Hildegard's prophecy proceeded from the devil's cunning.'[5] It is possible, however, that he had been appointed *advocatus diaboli*, the person who officially (and still today) presents the negative case in an application for canonisation.

Additional petitions were made in the next century but to no effect. Again the hiatus appears to have been administrative; it is possible that Rome gave verbal approval to her progress towards sainthood, but no official document ever appeared. In the fifteenth century, Abbot Trithemius of Sponheim to whose abbey some of the Rupertsberg nuns had decamped, kept Hildegard's flame alive with biographical writings, not always reliable but giving a sense of the continuity of the Rhineland monastic tradition in which she played such a key part. He records further communications with Rome. He also reports that spirituality had dwindled in the Rupertsberg monastery, by now scarcely more than a refuge for well-born women. Eibingen fared little better. Despite papal protection having been granted in 1219, with increased sanctioning of its status in 1268, it too fell into decline. In 1505 the Archbishop of Mainz attempted a revival of the foundation, but by 1575 only three women were living there, who then moved to a nearby convent, leaving Eibingen as an informal shelter for nuns from elsewhere in Germany escaping the persecutions of the Reformation.

Despite the collapse of the sisterhood at this time, by a twist of irony it was once again men who kept Hildegard's name alive. In the next decade her name and feast day (17 September) were included in the Roman Martyrology. This new list of saints (building on an outdated version from the tenth century) was compiled by a commission of ten scholars and issued by Gregory XIII in 1584. In 1916, Hildegard's feast day was awarded the official rank of 'memoria', the lowliest of the three categories of 'feast' in the Catholic Church. Only on 21 February 1940 did the Roman Congregation of Sacred Rites (which oversees the uniformity of public worship and canonisation) officially permit her cult in Germany. At the time of the 800th anniversary in 1979, a year after his election as Pope, John-Paul II wrote to the Bishop of Mainz referring to her as 'St Hildegard'. Given that in any circumstance the Pope is the final arbiter over canonisation, what more endorsement is needed? Let the matter rest there.

In 1632, in the Thirty Years War, the Rupertsberg was destroyed by the Swedes and never rebuilt. The surviving nuns (whose exact status is unclear) escaped via Cologne to Eibingen, eventually arriving there four years later, impoverished and travel-worn but with Hildegard's relics and documents pertaining to the Rupertsberg. For the next six years they reportedly lived in penury, subject to further attacks by mercenary troops which again forced them to flee. For the remainder of that century, however, monastic life at Eibingen flourished, with much building over the next century and a low-key identity as a shrine. This calm was about to be shattered by the anti-clerical spirit of the Enlightenment. Spotting an opportunity, the Elector Karl Joseph of Erthal set in motion plans to transform this handsome new building into a secular home for gentlewomen. The nuns resisted but, with the advent of the French Revolution, took the precaution of moving their belongings (presumed to include the relics) to Alzey for safekeeping. The wisdom of this was proved when, in 1802, Eibingen was dissolved and the women evacuated. The monastery became an armoury, the church an arsenal. In 1814 its furnishings and remaining relics were removed to form the interior of a new chapel, the St Rochus, high on a hill behind Bingen. This was visited by Goethe for the 1814 opening. However, in 1889 it was struck by lightning, eradicating the last link with Hildegard's day. By 1817, two-thirds of the Eibingen building itself had been demolished.

Yet while the outward remains of the Blessed Hildegard, as we may confidently call her, and her two monasteries turned to ashes, so her cult began to grow once more. Its roots were deep, like those desert plants that lie dormant for years then burst into spectacular bloom when nourished by rain. The nineteenth-century renaissance of the Benedictine life worked in her favour. In France, Abbot Gueranger (1805–75), who re-established the French Benedictine order, recognised her feast day at the influential abbey of Solesmes (which also, virtually single-handedly, restored the practice of singing medieval chant). In Germany, the Beuron congregation, also Benedictine revivalists, followed suit, which was eventually to lead to the founding, in 1904, of the Hildegard Abbey amid vineyards above Eibingen. The prominent Catholic aristocrat Prince Karl zu Löwenstein provided the money. Benedictine sisters from Prague arrived to settle there on 17 September of that year. Volume 197 of Abbé Migne's *Patrologia Latina*, devoted to her works, was in circulation. He had been aided in the task by Jean-Baptiste Pitra, a devotee of her memory. In 1882, after Migne's death, the faithful Pitra, at one time a monk at Solesmes and later a cardinal and Vatican librarian, published another volume of Hildegard's works in his own edition of Church Fathers, the *Analecta Sanctae Hildegardis*. The selection complements Migne's, adding a further 145 letters (others have since surfaced) and making the bulk of her writings available albeit to a limited medieval Latin-reading public. The situation has improved in recent years through further English and German translations and modern editions.

By now, even as a romantic ruin, the Rupertsberg's days were numbered. In 1801, in the Napoleonic era, the site had been parcelled up and sold off as state property, since when it had deteriorated rapidly. Now a sad romantic shell of its former self, it was about to disappear forever under the dynamite and pickaxes of Prussian urban and industrial advancement. In the nineteenth century, the hill on which it stood became known as Bingerbrück, a suburb of Bingen and a railway interchange very nearly on the scale of Clapham Junction. But if the Rupertsberg lay buried, Eibingen, nevertheless, was stirring

S·HILDEGARDIS·VIRGO·

BINGEN–1179–1929

Invitation to a ceremony celebrating Hildegard of Bingen at Mainz, 1927.

back into life. In 1831, the local community purchased the site, abandoning their parish church in favour of the old monastery church. In 1852 the parish priest, Father Ludwig Schneider – whom we met at the start of this tale – was among those who opened Hildegard's tomb and in 1858 authenticated the bones within. A first feast-day procession took place and Hildegard was made patron of the parish of Eibingen. A new cult was born.

Yet still those bones had not found their final resting place. An eerie photograph dating from 1928 shows Hildegard's skull on the altar of the old Eibingen parish church. Ornate in tiara and as if gagged with a bandanna, it looks faintly, to modern eyes, like a Hammer Horror prop. The previous year nuns at the new Hildegard Abbey up the hill had embarked on the painstaking task of making a faithful copy on vellum of the illuminated manuscript of the authentic Rupertsberg *Scivias.* In retrospect, their work (completed in 1933) has proved of immeasurable value, since the original manuscript was lost during wartime activity in 1945. In 1928, too, another nun of the abbey, Sister Maura Böckeler, published the first modern edition in German of *Scivias*, the start of an abridged series. Did Hildegard's visible presence on that altar give these sisters inspiration in their toils? That may be the last time her relics were seen in their naked state. In 1929, the 750th anniversary of her death, they were wrapped in shrouds and placed in a gleaming reliquary, specially made for the purpose. This lavish bejewelled casket echoes a tradition of twelfth-century metal-work but firmly celebrates a Germanic art nouveau elegance. The monstrance is constructed in the form of a small, ornate building, with a double door which opens at the front for displaying the relics on special feast days. On either side are embossed the names of the cardinal virtues, Justice, Courage, Prudence and Moderation, with four saints depicted front and back. Inside, in addition to the precious vital organs and skull and other remains of Hildegard not meted out to shrines the world over, are small bones of the local German saints Giselbert, Rupert and Wigbert.

Further disaster was to occur. During the night of 3–4 September 1932, a mysterious fire destroyed the parish church, and the remaining seventeenth-century east wing of the Eibingen monastery (that part which had once been used as an armoury) was razed to the ground. The garb which had been found with Hildegard's relics was destroyed, but by some small miracle – not too strong a word – the reliquary was saved. On 14 July 1935, a new church was consecrated. Now the relics of Hildegard of Bingen rest, behind protective glass, on the simple high altar. That Hildegard's bones have survived at all in no small measure reflects the indestructible character of the person whose spirit they once contained and in whose flesh they were once clad.

CHAPTER SEVENTEEN

SHRINES AND ICONS

This nun was one tough sister.

(CHARLOTTE ALLEN, *THE WOMAN'S QUARTERLY*)

Standing today outside the twentieth-century abbey which takes Hildegard's name, within sight of Eibingen and above the busy touristic wine town of Rüdesheim, you can look across the Rhine to Bingen, a short ferry ride away. In one direction the river broadens, the landscape low-lying and flat, the skyline of Mainz just discernible on a clear day. To the north, the Rhine disappears into a rocky wooded gorge and twists away via the famous Lorelei, towards Cologne, Koblenz and the North Sea. This is the Middle Rhine of tourism and legend, of Nibelungen and Wagner, of Schumann and Goethe. The turrets and towers of picturebook castles, of largely nineteenth-century fabrication but with ancient origins, many dating back to Hildegard's day, jostle for attention. Silence never falls. An endless parade of pleasure boats chugs by. Vast barges slide past, some up to 110 metres long, hooting day and night. An estimated 750 trains thunder daily along the railway tracks which hug either side of the river, outstripping the stream of cars on the highway which runs parallel. At Rüdesheim, inhabitants petition for a railway tunnel through the rock to save their small town from death by noise.

Yet still, every September, the cafés, *stuben* and hotels are packed with Japanese and Americans on the wine trail. Local brass bands and accordion players don leather shorts and feathered hats; tourists link arms and line-dance late into the night. All join in loud drinking songs. Now the Iron Curtain is down, English and American visitors come less often, preferring to explore Europe further east. The great Rhine, once one of the most polluted and busiest water routes in the world, with 5,000 vessels registered to navigate it, now ranks among the cleanest. The number of fish has doubled in the last decades of the twentieth century, with forty-two different species recognisable, including eel, roach, bream, pike, perch, rudd and carp. This figure compares well with the thirty-seven identified by Hildegard in the 1150s, and makes her less scientific methods of inquiry, gleaned from local fishermen and her own observations, all the more impressive. Swans glide by, guarding the bank close to the ferry's landing stage. The Binger Loch, with its sandbanks and reefs, remains hazardous today except to natives who know its spirit.

On a hazy day, if you narrow your gaze and shake your imagination, you can blot out the pylons and overhead wires, the oil tanks and chimneys, the ugly modern apartment blocks. Focus instead on the glassy water and the mysterious cluster of low gravelly islands in the direction of Mainz. Trace the serried ranks of vines patterning the south-facing slopes, the soft wooded hills, the spires, churches and castles which dot every promontory. For Goethe, journeying down the Rhine in 1774 and pausing to admire a Hildegard manuscript, the leap of imagination back in time was easier than for us today. In the late eighteenth century, the ruins of the Rupertsberg, destroyed over a hundred years before, were still substantial and awe-inspiring, the façade of the monastery church an imposing sight for those passing by boat. Scarcely a man-made feature remains intact since Hildegard's day. Yet slowly, an approximate, tentative picture emerges of the landscape she might have known, made solid by unchanged geological features: the interlocking valleys and plateau-like hills, the confluence of the Nahe at Bingen and, dominating all, the great Rhine itself.

Whereas Rüdesheim retains a quaint picturebook image, Bingen gives off a lacklustre air of a town forever out of season, the boarding point for a boat trip, criss-crossed by railway lines, level crossings and bewildering one-way systems, a place of business conferences and humdrum shops. Hildegard's name has been used, on street signs, a pharmacist's, a school (on whose premises young English ladies were once taught early in the last century). The cheerless 1981 modernist fountain in the marketplace depicts her preaching to the crowds in 1155. A small New Age bazaar sells joss sticks, stones and crystals at optimistic prices, stuck in a late 1970s hippy era when the seer's cult suddenly sprang to life. A maze of medieval streets survives, their buildings long gone and replaced. The names indicate a rich merchant past. With the exception of a few late-nineteenth-century buildings, complete with *fin de siècle* carving, most of the architecture is featureless; unsightly blocks of concrete, built hastily after the Allied bombs flattened Bingen's bourgeois grandeur. Much of the wartime action seems to have taken place on the exact site of the Rupertsberg. Pre-war photographs tell of another past. The grand Hindenburg Bridge, a feat of 1913–15 engineering which spanned the Rhine just beyond Rüdesheim, was destroyed by those same bombs and has never been rebuilt. Roads still lead confidently towards it, only to end at the river's edge. Once again, those wishing to cross the river here must travel by boat, as Hildegard used to on her trips from the Rupertsberg to her sister house at Eibingen.

How remote Bingen seems from the carnival of commercialism and hyperbole which has turned its most famous daughter, who only bears the town's name by default, into a

German postage stamp marking the 800th anniversary of Hildegard of Bingen's death.

contemporary icon. In 1979, the 800th anniversary year, the artist Judy Chicago included Hildegard among the guests in her pivotal feminist installation, *The Dinner Party*, modern art's virtual equivalent of beatification as a guest at history's imagined banquet of great female souls. Belatedly catching up on the dining theme, newspaper articles in the late 1990s recommended her chant as the ultimate in chic background Muzak to impress your more sophisticated supper guests. In August 1997, the British magazine *The Face*, at that time the epitome of fashion, named her 'the feistiest woman since Boadicea, the smartest since Athena'. Her music has topped the CD best-seller charts and is now available in dozens of different recordings. In Oxford, a distinguished girls' choir takes her name, and at least two British composers have used examples of her chant as a starting point for their own compositions. In the ebbing years of the last millennium, ravers danced to her hymns, complete with backing rhythm track, in the discothèques of Ibiza. A perusal of the Internet unleashes a flood of misappropriation and fabulous invention attached to her name. Alarmingly, even in the course of writing this book, the list of Hildegard sites has doubled.

A few website and essay titles, chosen at random, give a taste: 'Hildegard's fractal antiphon'; 'The flesh of the voice: Embodiment and the homoerotics of devotion in the music of Hildegard of Bingen'; 'Illness and Privilege: Hildegard von Bingen and the Condition of Mystic Writing'; 'Feather, Spark and Mustard Seed'; 'A Theophony of the Feminine'; 'Heavenly Health: When it came to nutrition, medieval nun Hildegard of Bingen was way ahead of her time'; 'Viriditas: Web of Greening Life-Energy'; 'Hildegard: One tough sister'. In 1997, fifty members of the St Aelred and St Hildegard Gay and Lesbian Ministry at the Episcopal Church of the Messiah in Santa Ana, California, entered the Orange County Cultural Pride Parade. To quote their website, they gathered in the parking lot, 'thurifers swinging their incense', and were so resplendent 'with all our flags, banners, pennants and all our Episcopal finery that we won the Pride Award!'[1]

Another Californian, Matthew Fox, a defrocked Dominican priest,[2] has been chastised by Hildegard supporters for incorporating her and her works into his Creation Spirituality, which 'honors women's wisdom' and considers Divinity 'as much Mother as Father'. Scholars issue health warnings about Fox's abridged translations of her writings (made from German into English, instead of from the original Latin). They may object, but his books remain the most readily available on Hildegard and, despite their unscholarly status, give an adequate picture to the general reader. Whether or not you care for his all-embracing theory, which 'promotes personal wholeness, planetary survival and universal interdependence', he has unquestionably helped spread Hildegard's name. His work has spawned a host of similarly inspired publications, many published by Bear and Co. in Santa Fe, whose motto is 'Books to celebrate and heal the earth'. In the media frenzy of late 1999, Hildegard of Bingen appeared in millennium lists of great women alongside Margaret Thatcher, Germaine Greer and Joan of Arc. One writer in the *Times Literary Supplement*, Marina Warner, herself a commentator on Hildegard, chose *Scivias* as her 'Book of the Millennium'.

So far this German town has made agreeably little of its celebrity. Hildegard survives only in the indefinable atmosphere of landscape, not in the detail of bricks or place. It is hard to imagine many of her present-day disciples making the pilgrimage since so little tangible evidence survives. A handsome and thoughtful museum opened in 1998 in a former electricity turbine by the Rhine. The site of the Rupertsberg, merely a street name wedged between road and rail, Rhine and Nahe, is a bitter disappointment, its labelling circumspect to the point of confusion. A much-photographed doorway remains from a part of the monastery built long after Hildegard's day. A crypt and five arcades from the main aisle of the abbey church have been preserved beneath the premises of a local firm, Wurth, locked and inaccessible except with dogged pre-planning through the tourist office. The absence, as yet, of a well-trodden Hildegard heritage route makes the quest all the more rewarding, more archaeological excavation than easy sightseeing.

It takes patience. If you walk from the Rupertsberg along the Nahe towards the ancient bridge named after the pagan Drusus, which pre-dates Hildegard (though rebuilt over the centuries and again after destruction in March 1945), clues present themselves. Hidden in the last of the bridge's seven arches is a tiny Romanesque chapel (only open by appointment), once used by merchants and travellers seeking refuge from brigands or praying for safe deliverance on their journeys. Returning along the bank opposite the Rupertsberg (now a smartly paved embankment lined with sycamores, willows, pyracantha and children's swings), you can apprehend the scale and location of Hildegard's abbey, rising up from the muddy banks of the Nahe, with the woodland and forest behind. Some large-scale maps gratifyingly mark the abbey and monastery garden (*klostergarten*), now buried beneath streets, offices and small modern villas. Above the railway line, the remains of the convent walls, recognisable from drawings, are visible but inaccessible. You risk life and limb from train or car if you venture too near.

The site is best contemplated from the steps of the grand Basilica of St Martin, whose beautiful pure Romanesque crypt is the most direct route back to the twelfth century and which Hildegard must have known. Again we are reminded how wise – or canny – Hildegard was to choose so easily accessible and prominent a position at this junction of rivers, after the relative obscurity of Disibodenberg. The church itself, dating back to the eighth century, has been rebuilt several times (most recently after 1944). A statue of Hildegard made in the eighteenth century can be found in the choir. In 1929/30, Pope Pius XI honoured St Martin's with the status of 'basilica minor' as part of the Hildegard celebrations, presumably to enhance Bingen's reputation, since little other connection with the church appears to exist.

Back across the Rhine above Rüdesheim, the 1904 Benedictine foundation of the St Hildegard Abbey, like its patron, has chosen a powerful and dominating site, visible for kilometres around, but in this case at one remove from the passing traffic of the world. Its twin towers hooded like wimples, this imposing, austere building is made of the distinctive local pink sandstone, warm and biscuit-like in sunlight, dark, dismal and forbidding in rain. The windows are small and prison-like beneath the black slate roof, the beauty spartan. The retrograde Beuron style, borrowing from the language of the Rhineland Romanesque, produced a handful of similar ecclesiastical buildings at the end of the nineteenth and start of the twentieth century, when the Benedictines in particular and the Catholic Church in general were enjoying a surge of vitality. When compared with Meissner's pre-1625 depiction of the Rupertsberg, the cluster of buildings bears a strong resemblance to the monastery Hildegard once built on the opposite bank of the Rhine. These nuns, like Hildegard's before them, have had their hardships. In World War II, the Gestapo requisitioned the abbey for use as a hospital to treat the war wounded, expelling 115 nuns, who were forced to find refuge with other religious orders in the vicinity. Once American troops arrived in Rüdesheim in 1945, the building was restored to its rightful ownership, and to its intended use. For the next decade, however, the sisters continued to provide shelter for those homeless through war, and for refugees fleeing from East Germany.

Only the abbey church, the small shops selling books, wine and Catholic relics, all run by nuns wearing name labels, are generally open to the public. The austere church, though richly ornamented, exudes an air of chastity. Ten elegant art nouveau lamps mark the arcaded nave. A skilful frieze in the Nazarene manner depicting Hildegard's life – from her childhood farewell to her parents as she joins Jutta, to her death – runs along either side, with scenes from the Old and New Testament above. In the apse, a massive head of Christ, made in the style of a Byzantine mosaic, dominates the entire building. You can light a candle in Hildegard's name, or purchase a postcard of one of her illuminations, but the selling of Hildegard is confined to the book shop or the wine shop, where her recipes, her pasta, her muesli, her biscuits are on offer. These items are made with her favourite oat-like grain, spelt.[3] On closer examination, however, you see that the name on the label is that of the abbey, Abtei S. Hildegardis, rather than of the blessed seer herself. These sisters can hardly be accused of hard sell. In fact, they resist it fiercely.

Down the steep hill, less than two kilometres away, through the vineyards, in sight of the abbey, stands the parish church of Eibingen, rebuilt after the fire of 1932. It marks the location of Hildegard's second convent, which she visited twice a week but in which she never lived. No graveyard is likely to contain more Hildegards, some born in one of her anniversary years and named after the saint. Today, this is the heart of her cult, as it survives in purely religious terms within the calendar of the German Catholic Church, officially celebrated on 17 September. A fastidious scholar[4] has queried the accuracy of this date, arguing that in the Julian-Gregorian calendar it was St Ursula's feast day (though by what calculation is unclear), and the coincidence, given Hildegard's musical celebration of that saint and her 11,000 virgins, therefore too great to ignore. In the same context, it has been argued, the poetic numerology of the date, 17.9.1179, surely takes hagiographic chicanery a step too far. Since St Ursula's new feast day (21 October) was suppressed as a result of Vatican streamlining in 1969, the serendipity is somewhat lost on us. Any sequence of figures has its own poetry if you search hard enough. To find a bit of numerical fixing going on should hardly surprise us. Does it matter? Not to those who celebrate her annual festivities. On that day, the church is decorated with a profusion of orange chrysanthemums and peach-coloured gladioli, the courtyard hung with yellow and white bunting. Bell-ringing begins early, while the chilly mist still lingers.

First to arrive is a blind woman, who takes her place near the front for this day-long open-air holy festivity. Soon the rows of long benches, enough for about 1,500 people, begin to fill. Many who come are elderly, alone or in couples, lame or strong-limbed, more women than men. Some wear the black armbands of widowhood. Others are blithe but quiet, bringing flasks, blankets and cushions to ease their vigil. A few tourists combine the wine season with pilgrimage. Two silver-haired sisters, one a nun, sit with a priest, perhaps their brother. A stall selling 'Hildegard candles' does a discreetly roaring trade. Beyond the church confines, a woman with henna-dyed hair and a long shawl has set up shop, like one of Volpone's mountebanks, with a table piled high with potions and lotions, pills and elixirs, pamphlets and recipes promising eternal youth in the name of Hildegard. A few buy, most just look. The silence is broken by the arrival of a busload; its younger congregation spills out noisily into the courtyard, now packed. The bell-ringing stops. Hush descends. A crocodile of choir boys and girls in red cassocks leads a procession of a dozen bishops and priests, gathered from as far away as Scandinavia and South Africa, anointing their way with much swinging of thuribles. Incense mingles with the scent of wood smoke. Adorned in damask and silk, mitres glittering, these men of the church, for they are all men, move like a column of ivory and gold through the crowd and up to an outdoor altar erected under the church porch. On that simple table, moved outside for the occasion, rests Hildegard's reliquary. All eyes focus on the shining casket. The Mass begins.

In the afternoon the main event, a procession through the parish, takes place. A male-voice choir, smart in blue blazers and grey flannels, entertains the waiting crowds with close harmony songs. Neither the songs nor the harmony are by Hildegard. The shutters are down in Eibingen's few shops. Minutes before the procession is due to pass by, villagers in houses lining the route hurriedly make shrines with pots of flowers and plaster models of Hildegard, placed in their windows or on the pavement outside (afterwards removed, curiously, as quickly as they appeared). Bells peal again. The reliquary is hoisted on the shoulders of local men, who carry the mortal remains of the blessed Hildegard round the narrow streets of Eibingen, leading choristers and priests, a few representative nuns, several hundred pilgrims. The glittering coffin-trophy, with its large, brilliant gems glinting in the sun, bobs conspicuously above the crowd, the atmosphere part pageant, part funeral convoy. A mass is said over loudspeakers; the crowds sing the responses as they walk. On returning to the church, the men replace their precious burden on the high altar inside the church. The moment has come. Two small doors at the front of the reliquary are opened by a priest, revealing a metal grille set in glass. Pilgrims file past and kneel to offer a prayer, press a handkerchief to the window, reaching out a hand in supplication, kissing the grille, wiping away a tear.

Through the golden fretwork, a skull wrapped in faded muslin and covered in ruby-coloured stones can be glimpsed, empty eye sockets staring out blindly. Other unidentifiable bones, long and thin like knives and forks wrapped in napkins, lie neatly either side. If you kneel on the altar steps long enough, you can make out two small, curiously shaped boxes, also jewelled and embossed, containing Hildegard of Bingen's heart and tongue. Few writers can be said to come face to face with their subjects in quite this way.

HILDEGARD: PRINCIPAL WORKS

THEOLOGICAL/VISIONARY

Scivias (1141–51) (Know the Way)

Written over a period of ten years and her first major work, this is most easily available to the general reader in (sometimes abridged) translations. It consists of three books, based on a series of twenty-six visions, on the subject of creation, redemption and sanctification. The six visions of the first book show how the world evolved, including the fall of the angels and Adam, the composition of the universe and of the soul, the synagogue (representing the Old Testament) and the hierarchy of angels. The second book, of seven visions, concerns redemption, the coming of the Redeemer and man's struggle against the devil. The third book, written at the time of Hildegard's move to the Rupertsberg, is constructed round an architectural image of salvation and the divine virtues, concluding with the Final Judgement. The literary style is both literal and allegorical, with vivid, often alarming and apocalyptic visual descriptions. While she was writing this book, Hildegard came to the attention of Pope Eugene III, who was attending the Synod of Trier in 1147/48. Also present was Bernard of Clairvaux, a mentor of the Pope and already, the previous year, in correspondence with Hildegard.

The celebrated illuminated edition of *Scivias* is now missing, lost from Dresden in World War II. The reunification of Germany has prompted renewed hope that it may reappear; as yet there is no sign. It was made in Rupertsberg *c.* 1175–80 (some place it much earlier, or later), and is significant in that it is almost certainly the result of close collaboration with

Hildegard herself, just before her death (see discussion in Chapter 12). It resided in the Wiesbaden Hessische Landesbibliothek until its removal to Dresden and subsequent loss. Only black-and-white photographs survive. Fortunately, a faithful illuminated copy was made from the original at the Hildegard Abbey, Eibingen, 1927–33. It is from this copy that coloured reproductions are invariably taken (not always clear in the credits, and a source of some confusion). A separate Rupertsberg manuscript is in the Biblioteca Vaticana. In total ten full copies of *Scivias* exist, in Heidelberg (twelfth century), Oxford (Merton College, manuscript 160, twelfth/thirteenth century), Trier (1487) and elsewhere. The Merton manuscript, probably made at the beginning of the thirteenth century, was in the college before 1360, and was certainly made, unusually, for collegiate rather than monastic purposes.

Liber vitae meritorum (Book of Life's Merits) (1158–63)

Hildegard's second major visionary and theological work is written in the form of a dialogue between the virtues and the vices. Its central preoccupation is with the struggle between man's desires and his respect for a Christian ethical world order.

Of five surviving manuscripts, three were produced at the Rupertsberg scriptorium. The oldest known is the Codex Dendermonde 9, written *c.* 1170 at Rupertsberg and sent to the Cistercian abbey of Villers in Brabant, an establishment friendly to Hildegard towards the end of her life. This codex is referred to in a letter from the monks to Hildegard: 'We have received with joy the book written and sent to us by your holiness, we read it with zeal and we embrace it with affection.' The other two codices, both from Rupertsberg in the late twelfth century, are in Berlin (provenance Benedictine abbey of St James, Mainz) and Trier (provenance Benedictine abbey of SS Eucharius and Matthias, a house known to have had friendly relations with Rupertsberg).

Liber divinorum operum (Book of Divine Works) (1163–73/4)

Her third theological work and last visionary writings is regarded as her most ambitious. It consists of three parts and ten visions, recording the history of salvation from Genesis to Apocalypse and propounding an elaborate cosmological theory. She depicts the world as consisting of three circles conceived in mathematical proportions. A wheel surrounds a circle of luminous fire; beneath it is another circle, of black fire; beneath that a circle of pure ether. The first circle is twice as large as the second, the third as large as both the other two together.[1]

Four manuscripts survive. The oldest known edition is the *De operatione dei*, drafted during her lifetime between 1170 and 1173 at the Rupertsberg scriptorium. It was then passed to St Eucharius's monastery at Trier (today St Matthew's), then to various places in Ghent, where it is today in the University Library. This manuscript provides most information, the research still inconclusive, about the relationship between Hildegard and her secretaries and scribes. In addition, an elaborately illuminated thirteenth-century manuscript known as the Lucca Codex, with ten miniatures illustrating the ten visions, survives in the Biblioteca Statale di Lucca. Each image has a portrait in the corner of Hildegard receiving her visions. It has several variants to the text in older manuscripts but was nevertheless used by Migne in his widely read *Patrologia Latina*.

MEDICAL/SCIENTIFIC

Liber simplicis medicinae (known as *Physica*) and *Liber compositae medicinae* (known as *Causae et Curae*, or *Cause et Cure*), the two books together known as *Liber subtiliatum diversarum naturam creaturarum* (*Book of the Subtleties of the Diverse Nature of Creatures*) (1151–8)

The source of greatest confusion in Hildegard studies and

consequently the area of scholarship as yet least explored. A work on medicine and natural healing written when Hildegard was in her mid-fifties, the original manuscript of which has been lost. Even today the authenticity of the work remains uncertain, but recent scholarly research (especially by Adelgundis Führkötter and Marianna Schrader) tends to confirm rather than refute her authorship, though as recently as 1994 a German scholar, Irmgard Muller, challenged the attribution. The debate continues. Significantly, these works have no visionary element, and in general no theological bias. In this sense, they are truly scientific rather than morally instructive, derived not from divine communication (though Hildegard would have made no distinction) or in a state of heightened awareness or illness, but from observation and inquiry. Like the work of the eleventh-century Persian Ib'n Sin'a, known in the Middle Ages as Avicenna (980–1037), also a mystic and a writer on medical issues, Hildegard's writing here is biological and factual. Nevertheless, *Causae et Curae* starts with an account of the Creation, before proceeding to a discussion of man as a microcosm of the universe, with disorders and diseases accordingly (see Chapters 10 and 11).

i. *Physica*

The title *Physica* only came into use after Hildegard's death. Consisting of nine books, the work describes methods of prevention and cure for a wide range of illnesses, through a detailed analysis of plants, trees, animals, metals, precious stones and elements. Her observations are drawn from scientific writings of the time, many recently translated from antiquity, such as Pliny, Isidore of Seville, Galen and Soranus. Some of the creatures referred to are mythical (as is usual in such works), such as the unicorn, centaur and dragon. She also draws on her own knowledge of local flora and fauna, and on folklore (see Chapter 10).

ii. *Causae et Curae*

Causae et Curae takes the theories cited above further. Only one manuscript is known, from 1300. The work is regarded by modern eyes as a holistic view of the world, with illnesses predetermined by balance and imbalance, all closely linked with Hildegard's theory of cosmology. In common with other encyclopedic works of the period, it opens with the Creation and the structure and composition of the world. Divine creation and human conception together explain the human condition, through a study of the soul as well as the body. Physiology, gender differences and sexual nature are explored, as well as personality and physical and moral deviations. Hildegard may have known the widely dispersed books of Avicenna, which would have been found in many monastic libraries and to whose encyclopedic *Canon of Medicine*, her *Causae et Curae* owes debts, though exact sources have not been identified. The views expressed, which seem striking and outspoken to a modern reader, concur in broad terms with other medical and theological writers of the time. The unique feature of this work is the depth and detail of the study of the sexual differences of men and women, and the means and purpose of reproduction.

Lingua ignota and *Litterae ignota* (Unknown Language and Unknown Writing) (1150–60)

The intention or purpose of Hildegard's invented language of around 900 words with German glossary still foxes scholars. It relates most closely to her medical/scientific works and lists several plant and herb names. It survives in two manuscripts, including the Wiesbaden Riesencodex, part of which can be found in Pitra, pp. 496–502. Five of the words occur in an anthem in *Symphonia*, *O orzchis Ecclesia* (see Newman, *Symphonia*, pp. 316–17). See also Jeffrey Schnapp, 'Virgin Words: Hildegard of Bingen's *Lingua ignota* and the Development of Imaginary Languages Ancient to Modern', *Exemplaria*, 3 (1991), pp. 267–98.

MUSICAL

Ordo Virtutum (The Play of the Virtues) (*c.* 1150)

One of the earliest surviving morality plays and also one of the earliest datable works among Hildegard's extant compositions, consisting of 82 melodies in a relatively direct style. Parts of the *Ordo* form the last section of her visionary prose work *Scivias*. Its language owes a debt to the Song of Songs, Isaiah and the Revelation of St John. The cast required (approx. 20) tallies with the number of nuns in Hildegard's community at the time. The first performance is likely to have been at the consecration of the Rupertsberg in 1152, possibly with Hildegard's secretary, the monk Volmar, in the speaking role of the devil. The music is notated in detail (in the Wiesbaden manuscript) but makes no reference to accompanying instruments. The play depicts the human soul caught between the opposing forces of the virtues and the devil. Eventually the virtues raise the soul up to immortality and defeat the devil.

Symphonie armonie celestium revelationum (*The Symphony of the Harmony of Celestial Revelations* usually known as '*Symphonia*') (1140s/1150s)

77 poems each set to a single melodic line (sometimes grouped together and cited as 71), as follows:

43 antiphons
18 responds
7 sequences
4 hymns
a kyrie
An alleluia
3 miscellaneous

In order of complexity, responds are most elaborate, followed by antiphons with hymns and sequences written in a simpler style. These chants also fall into cycles of local saints (Rupert, Maximinus, Disibod), the Virgin Mary, Angels, Apostles, Martyrs and so on. Two manuscripts survive, both written in early German neumes, from Wiesbaden (Hessische Landesbibliothek M32) and the probably earlier manuscript from the Benedictine Abbey of Dendermonde (1170s). Among the most frequently performed today are *Columba Aspexit*, *O virga ac diadema*, *O Ierusalem – De Sancto Ruperto* and *O splendissima gemma*. See discussion Chapter 12.

OTHER

Letters (1146/7–78)

A correspondence of nearly 400 letters written in Latin has been preserved, exchanged between Hildegard and four popes, emperors, bishops, secular rulers, monks and nuns. Her correspondents came from all over Europe, including modern-day Germany, England, Netherlands, France, Switzerland, Italy and Greece. Most have a predominantly instructional tone, drawing heavily on Scripture, and are primarily didactic rather than personal. In keeping with twelfth-century tradition, these letters were not dated, with no place of dispatch, and did not always give the name of the sender or the person addressed. They were collected at Rupertsberg during and after her lifetime, with clear evidence of later changes by other hands. Some of the answers or recommendations are repeated in different letters. The primary source is the Wiesbaden Riesencodex, produced in Rupertsberg between 1180 and 1190 and edited by Hildegard's nephew Wezelin. Until Lieven van Acker's critical edition, *Hildegardis Bingensis Epistolarium*, in the Corpus Christianorum: continuatio mediaevalis, the only available text has been Volume 197 of Jacques Paul Migne's *Patrologia Latina* and Volume 8 of Jean-Baptiste Pitra's *Analecta Sacra*. A fifteenth-century manuscript of her letters is in the British Library (Add. MS 15102).

Pentachronon (Mirror of Future Times)

An abridged collection of Hildegard's works at her most prophetic and apocalyptic, compiled by Gebeno of Eberbach, taking its title from her prophecies of the five remaining ages of history. Extracts appear in Pitra, *Analecta Sacra*, Volume 8. No complete edition exists.

SISTER ANCILLA

This interview between the author and Sister Ancilla Feerling, a Benedictine nun at the St Hildegard Abbey at Eibingen, near Mainz, took place in October 1999.

How long have you been a nun?
I've been here now for twenty-seven years, always at this abbey.

Why did you take the veil?
It was what we call vocation. I can't really explain it. For every sister living here, it's a personal story. We believe in the call from God, and He does it in so many different ways, just as we are different also.

How old were you when the call came?
I was thirty. I had a normal life, living in the United States. I worked in an office as a secretary for an insurance company.

Were your friends and family shocked?
A few were surprised, not shocked. When you know a person, you can understand. I had a religious life before, but entering a monastic life is always a shock. But I had friends who tried to understand and to support me.

If you had a religious life already, why wasn't it enough for you, as it would be for most people?
For me it was a book I read about the monastic life and all of a sudden I thought: there is something to living a life with God, just for God. You know you have a big urge, you want to do it, but you still think: am I crazy? But if this vocation is true, you have to go forward, and you have to do things you would never have dreamt of before.

What sort of things?
Well, I loved to travel. I loved being independent. I used to think: if one day a partner would come my way, I would give up that freedom. But it didn't happen.

Do you mean marriage?
Yes, marriage. It's not that I was looking for it; I was so free inside. But in my case it was the right time, I was independent, I wasn't hurting anyone or shocking a partner by my decision. It was the 1960s, a time of great change, after the Second Vatican Council, which upset so many in the Church. But I had no doubt.

How did you choose this monastery?
You have to find your house. I was lucky. I was given the address in the States by friends. I didn't want to enter a cloister in the US. I felt too European for that – or too German! I came here and never regretted it.

How many sisters are there?
Now there are fifty-five of us, but when I first came there were almost a hundred.

Why the decline?
When I came there were many old sisters, several of them dying. They were really strong women of the kind we don't have any more. They endured the Second World War and they had to fight for their living. They were stronger than our generation. But they're gone. We've had a good vocation in the last ten or twenty years, but now it's getting less because young girls today have psychological problems, from their family, from their education. They're not brought up to religious faith any more and it's really hard for them to come into a life like ours.

Is there any evangelising drive to attract more women to become nuns?
I think you cannot influence it. Many people come to us here; they are looking for something, they don't know what – stillness,

quiet perhaps. They have many questions. But a vocation is different. It commits you, whatever the place. If people come, they try to adapt, but usually the problems start after a time – either a very short time, and they say, 'Oh no, what have I done?', or perhaps later, after they get the habit, the clothing, and suddenly they get a fright and can't do it. Then when they get to the first vows, they have problems making a decision which is for life. They see outside in the world broken marriages, their parents divorced, they have no ethic of commitment or moral vision. When I came here, our novice mistress told us, 'Look, there are so many women living here – some of them for twenty, thirty, sixty years. They're women living their life, a wonderful, fulfilled life, so you can trust them and make a new beginning, despite all the problems that occur for everyone in the first year.'

Is there a certain type of personality best suited to this life?
Of course we try to find women who are physically and psychologically healthy. Our life is hard. You need good self-awareness. If people are unstable, if they need constant guidance, it won't work. They can't be the kind to hang on to their mother's apron strings. They must know what they want. They can get spiritual help, of course, and you need that to get into this way of life. It doesn't happen in a week or two. It's six years before you take your final vows. In that time it becomes clear whether you can make it or not.

Does that mean six years until you wear your full habit and veil?
No. We get that after about six months or a year, depending on the individual. We have the first petition as postulant. That means you are just like a guest but living inside. You can come or go as you please. We don't lock any doors. If you say, 'I can't stand it', you can go away freely. Then we have the habit; it's the first true commitment. You have the white veil. Only with your final vows do you have the black one.

What form does the robing initiation take?
There is a liturgical ceremony. In my time, we had it in the abbey church so that the public could attend, but now it is done privately in the chapter room, which is in the enclosure inside our monastery. It was such a public occasion, with the character of a confession of belief, a statement that your life is changing, that you will wear the habit of the community you are joining. It's the first step, even though the final vows come later. Yet it began to occur that so many had this great celebration and then left the order, as if nothing had happened, which diminished its value.

Whose choice was it to turn the ceremony into a private event?
It was a decision between the young girls and our novice mistress. It is a trend of our time. They want a simpler ceremony, a more intimate affair with only the monastic family as witnesses. But for me it was important to have everyone there. I had many friends, a big family; I wanted it to be out in the open. I even had the bridal gown when I was 'closed', you know. They don't do that any more. Those days are over.

For you, then, it was a symbolic ritual?
Yes, it really was. I wanted to be a bride once in my life and I really enjoyed that hour. It means more to those close to you too. They see you coming, in your beautiful white dress, and then after the service you change and at last you are a nun like all the others.

Are the final vows still made in public?
Yes, that is really an act before the Church. It's a long ceremony.

How many of you are received at once?
Sometimes it's a double ceremony, but usually just one person. There are not so many vocations now. In the old days you'd have ten or even twenty at once, as in a congregational order. No longer.

Why did you choose the Benedictine order?
Actually, I fell into this order without knowing too much about it. It was important to me to celebrate the liturgy in a festive way. We still celebrate the Divine Office daily, which means seven times a day we are in our choir to sing the Church hours. We still recite it in the Latin language. That was crucial to me too. I love the liturgy. It's what I grew up with. In addition, the Benedictines are an enclosed order. That means we don't have outside activities. We have no hospitals or schools. Our main work is saying the Divine Office, that is, to pray.

Do you regard that as public work, or is it an entirely private occupation?
No, it is public work. We pray and sing for and with the Church. We cannot freely excuse ourselves from these hours, unless of course we are sick, or have a particularly pressing duty. But for Benedictines this is our main work, to keep up with the Office of the Church.

How much is it solitary, how much shared with the community?
It's all done within the community. Of course we have our private hours too, for reading and prayer and adoration. We can do that as much and as intensively as we want.

But you have other tasks too – embroidery, goldwork, cooking, working the vineyards which surround the abbey?
Yes, we make our own living, we work with our hands and we produce things to secure an income. This has changed from former times. When girls came to a monastic life they had to bring a dowry in order to provide their own living. They only did the more beautiful pursuits – singing, copying, writing, making manuscripts – while the so-called lay sisters, who didn't have to keep the Church Office, did the manual work. There were clearly two groups of nuns, a distinct social division, you might say. That's no longer the case.

What about the heavier work, the wine-making for example?
Yes, we do that too. We have sisters who work in the cellar. But we do have help from outside, a man who oversees the making of the wine and cultivation of the grapes. He does the really heavy jobs and digs the earth. But the sisters are out there too, or in the various workshops. I work in our book shop, or sell wine, others work in the goldsmithery, or make candles. These are all things which bring us income, so we are not living off other people. So far we have managed to keep going. But we have to keep up our big house. Just think of the size of the roof, the heating system, the water pipes. This is where our money goes.

Presumably the fact that there are now fewer nuns reduces the abbey's income?
Yes, that's true, and we have old and sick sisters to care for, who cannot contribute to our economy. We have separate quarters for the ill. They are kept in our house until death. In fact, we are like a big family, with different generations. At the moment our youngest is twenty-eight years old, the oldest nearly ninety.

Is there any equivalent of receiving the very young into the monastery, as in Hildegard's day?
It was typical of Hildegard's time that big families gave one or more children over to the Church. But today we don't take girls this young. Times have changed. We ask at least a complete education and some kind of apprenticeship, so that if they leave our house for one reason or another they can start again, get a job. It's not as easy to find a job as it would have been for me thirty years ago.

You said you came to this abbey by chance. Why did your fellow sisters come? Were any drawn by the idea of Hildegard, the abbey's patron?
Not necessarily. Many had known the house since they were young, and visited frequently. If you speak to the sisters here,

Hildegard really comes in a secondary place. Of course it's a big heritage, a heavy tradition. But first of all Hildegard was a Benedictine nun like we are today. This is our chief connection to her. Then of course she's the icon she was in her time, in her century.

Yet you have been here during the time in which a particular interest in her has reawakened.
Well yes, it's interesting. I was given an edition of her book of visions, *Scivias*, by my local pastor when I first came here. I'd never read anything of Hildegard's before. When I arrived, the other nuns were quite astonished that I was reading her. At the beginning of the Seventies no one read Hildegard, even here. They were laughing at me when I got out my *Scivias*. I defended myself by saying it was a gift, and I wanted to get to know the work. I was fascinated by it, but I never studied her works, or knew how to interpret a work from that ancient period. I just read it as a book and Hildegard spoke to me. It was a spiritual help and guide and no more. Then the big boom started in 1979, the 800th anniversary of her death. It all happened in California with Matthew Fox – you know his name? All of a sudden our library was empty. Everybody started reading Hildegard, even in our house!

So it took these Americans to show you what was under your nose?
Yes, and we were not prepared. Suddenly everyone who came here wanted to know about Hildegard and visit places associated with her and know about her work. We were quite embarrassed because we could not answer their questions. Of course she was an important and extraordinary woman, but all this was not primarily to do with her Benedictine life, which is what matters to us.

Who is Matthew Fox?
He was an enthusiast, who started well, but then it went wrong. I believe he was a Dominican monk, who has since been

defrocked. He went more in an esoteric direction. We didn't mind until he started writing about Hildegard, and we thought: this is not *our* Hildegard. He used her for his purposes, which were good in the beginning. But he used her ideas as his ideas and it all got very peculiar. This is what we had to tell many people when they came here, and they were very open and listened to us, that Hildegard is not what they were trying to make her – they all wanted to make her their own, the esoteric and New Agers, the feminists, the ecologists and what have you. They all said, 'She's our woman.' We said Hildegard's task was different.

Did all this attention unsettle the community?
We started thinking about it, because we realised we didn't know too much about her. We had a few sisters here, real good old scholars working on Hildegard. But they did their work silently and the community didn't know too much about it – Adelgundis Führkötter [a Hildegard scholar of international repute], who is now dead, and Angela Carlevarlis, who is Italian, and who is working in her footsteps. But she is already eighty. She hasn't been here with us so very long, perhaps thirty years.

It's Hildegard's music which has brought her particular fame in recent years. Do you perform it much?
Once in a while, on her feast day perhaps. Of course in her jubilee year [1998, the 900th anniversary of her birth] we sang more. We made a CD of her music, sung by the sisters. We were asked to sing in a neighbouring church here, and at Cologne cathedral, but these were exceptional occasions. Normally, it's only about twice a year.

Why not more often?
Why should we? Her music is highly specialised, and it's been taken up by so many ensembles and groups in the past few years. Many of them do it in such an artificial way. Our CD has sold well because people say, well, the sisters must know how

to perform this music as Hildegard wanted it. Though of course we don't know; nobody knows how she sang her songs. We sing it as we do our Gregorian chant and our Divine Office. But this is artful music, not easy to perform and needing great expertise. We aren't a professional group of singers.

Why do so few of you attend Hildegard's annual feast-day ceremony in Eibingen?
We see it as a public event. We send a representative group but we belong to an enclosed order. Normally, we don't leave the monastery. We celebrate her feast day in our abbey church and many people attend. But the Eibingen event has grown larger of late. In former times perhaps just the abbess went, with one of the sisters. Now we say everyone who has time can go down to Eibingen. But we have many duties and we cannot easily abandon them just to have an outing! So many guests come on that day that we are needed here. The shop and café are open. We may have official visitors, too, bishops and so on. It would be impossible, therefore, for many nuns to go.

How is the abbess appointed?
She is elected by the community. It used to be a job for life, but now abbesses are encouraged to retire around the age of seventy.

Does the same jostling for power occur, the same gossip, as usually happens in elections of any kind?
Yes, of course. We are women! We don't change when we go through the big door. Of course there is a sense of pressure, of interest. We always have quite a few candidates. They're nominated. We usually have three rounds of election before the final appointment.

You still have to have a priest to celebrate the sacraments?
We celebrate the daily Eucharist and we need a priest for that, and for confession, and to stand by for last rites and things like that. So far we have always had a priest. But times are getting tougher. We don't know what's coming up.

Do you think this reliance on men, when women's lives have changed so much, is one of the reasons younger women find it hard to enter the Church?

Are you saying do I think there should be a priesthood for women? I am really the wrong person to ask. I still think in a conservative way. I think it's not the role of women to become a priest. If there are ordinations in other churches, I am sure they have their reasons. But I don't think the Catholic Church will agree to it, and if she does one day – it's a concept I cannot even contemplate. To me it's a tradition, a feeling. I cannot argue it logically or scientifically. I don't have the knowledge. But when the priest is standing there in the Lord's place, blessing the sacraments and speaking in Jesus's place – 'This is my body, this is my blood' . . . It's not that women are not equal or not trusted, but that they are different. We have special gifts which we must use in the Church. We are one body, but if our Lord had wanted us to be priests, I think it would have happened before. Ultimately, I cannot consider it. It's not part of Catholic thinking. Even if we get fewer priests in the Church as a result, I am sure there will be different ways of dealing with the problem. Above all we must pray for priests, and not just say, 'Well, we'd better have women.' But I don't know what's going to happen. I think we can rely on the Holy Spirit. He will show us other ways of finding a solution.

The atmosphere of the house is very silent. Is ordinary chat discouraged?

We are urged to think about why we are here. Our time is precious. We should not lose time with things that are unimportant or gossipy. But there are always exceptions, times when you have to say what's in your head immediately. But we are always pulled back to thinking about what's important and to avoid gossip. It's bad for the community. We are living together, so close, twenty-four hours a day. This can destroy a community. We are living a spiritual life, not just an average everyday life like people outside, where people can say what they want. We didn't have to come here. We did it of our own free will, so we have to agree to certain rules, and the house must be quiet. If things need saying, we speak in a soft voice in order not to disturb others. Of course the younger ones find this difficult, but they must respect the places of silence: the cloister, the choir, the official rooms, the refectory. We have our meals in silence, and still have a reading during them from Holy Scripture and Holy Rule. We listen to the news on the radio and then continue with a reading. We have no television, though we do have access to videos to record something, perhaps once or twice a year – the carnival, say. But we never change our hours to watch. It's good that we don't have TV. We all agree to it, and we don't want to lose time, which is so valuable. We are busy with our tasks, but we need time, too, for our spiritual work. We don't miss it.

There must be women, though, who have crises – of sexual denial, of desire to have children?
Yes, there are a few who say, 'Oh I would have loved to have a bunch of children, I would have loved to marry.' But on the other hand, they know why they came here. We have a saying, 'We leave the good for the better'. It's to do with vocation, something which urges you ahead in spite of all that you are seeming to leave behind – in my case, my car, my apartment, my friends and so on. If I'd married and had children, I would have kept those friends. You find new friends, new interests.

What happens when a sister has a crisis of faith?
There are times when we all find it hard to pray, when we hardly know what we are saying, or are very tired perhaps. Often the rhythm and ritual of prayer pulls you through these bad moments, and the community helps; it's a living body. A wife must think about these things too, about her husband and her difficulties, though people change their partners so much nowadays that perhaps the comparison isn't a true one. But if it's more serious than that, we try to recognise where it comes from. Is there something she needs: sleep, or relaxation, or talk? If she needs special help, she will get it, even from the

outside, psychological aid if necessary, or a priest, or an experienced spiritual leader, just to help her back on her feet. It can
occur, of course, that these things will not help and that she
leaves our house.

**Since it takes six years to join, how long does it take to
leave?**
I can leave right away. If I say, 'I must leave', no one will keep
me here. I don't have to jump over the wall.

Does the Benedictine life prepare you for death?
Of course, but not only for death, but also for the life after.
Death is only a station, a point.

**You make it sound straightforward. There must be times
when even faith lets you down?**
Everyone has a crisis about death at some time, whether early
in life or much later. For some people it doesn't arise until the
last hour, the last minute. But spiritual people, who are living
our life, sometimes have more problems with it, because the
more we live in this Christian dimension, the harder the crisis
can be. To me that's something diabolic, that Satan is coming to
get us at our weakest point, that he is really trying to make our
faith crumble. I have seen sisters die in a very hard way, with
great distress. That can be a grace too, although we must get
through this situation. We cannot explain it. It's in God's hands.
There are people who carry crosses of unhappiness or illness
who die easily; others who have lived a calm life of faith who face
torment. A friend, a monk, told me he once experienced the
dying of an old monk who, almost at the end, had a terrible
doubt, asking whether it could all be true – the life that he'd
lived. 'Can it be true what Mary Magdalene said when she saw
the empty grave? Can we believe her?' and so on. He was in
such horror, such agony. Suddenly a faith of two thousand years
was in doubt. My friend said, 'I didn't know what to do. So I
said to him, "We'll say the Creed together, one sentence after
another." Finally, by the end he was peaceful, at least quiet.'

This was a great lesson to me. God must have a reason why He leaves some people in such physical pain, such spiritual agony. But I've also seen sisters die very peacefully. Life goes on for eternity. But we're not meant to live in our physical bodies for eternity. When I see people shortly before death, when the agony is behind them, I am jealous. They can only go forward to light. We have learned to travel to the moon, but what is the moon when you can see the universe? There is always something bigger. So I am looking forward, though I am also afraid. We think of it every day; we must be prepared every minute. Our Lord can come for us any time.

NOTES AND SOURCES

Notes for pages **9–22**.

Chapter One: Birth of Hildegard

1. That of Trithemius, Abbot of Sponheim, *c.* 1500.
2. Chronicles of Disibodenberg, 1095, in Silvas (tr.), *Jutta and Hildegard: Biographical Sources* (Pennsylvania State University, Philadelphia, 1999), pp. 13–14. All subsequent extracts from Disibodenberg chronicles are taken from this source.
3. H. H. Lamb, *Climate Past, Present and Future* (Methuen, London, 1972).

Chapter Two: Childhood and Cloister

1. Silvas, op. cit., p. 40.
2. *Vita Jutta*, in Silvas, op. cit., p. 67.
3. Some evidence suggests it may have been a few days before Jutta's death.
4. Silvas, op. cit., p. 81.
5. Guibert's letter to Bovo, in Silvas, op. cit., pp. 104–5.
6. Guibert's letter to Bovo, in Silvas, op. cit., p. 105.
7. Guibert gives the date of enclosure as 1 November 1112, but insists that Hildegard was only eight, not fourteen. Since he may have been given this account by the elderly Hildegard herself, this compounds the uncertainty over dates. However dim the memory, Hildegard is unlikely to have muddled the ages of eight and fourteen when recalling such a decisive event in her own life. The evidence is inconclusive.

Notes for pages **22–45**.

8. A series of eight stations depicting the life of Hildegard which form a wood-and-plaster-relief altarpiece at the St Rochus Chapel near Bingen.
9. St Jerome, Letter 22, in C. C. Mierow (tr.), *Ancient Christian Writers 33: The Letters of St Jerome* (Westminster, 1963).
10. Quoted in Sharon K. Elkins, *Holy Women of Twelfth Century England* (University of North Carolina Press, Chapel Hills, North Carolina, 1988), which gives a detailed account of the eremitic life.
11. Elkins, op. cit.
12. Eadmer, *Historia Novorum Anglia (History of Recent Events in England)*, tr. by G. Bosanquet, foreword by R. W. Southern (Cresset Press, London, 1964), p. 121.
13. Anselm, *Opera omnia* (T. Nelson, London, 1946–61).
14. It retains some celebrity today as a Middle English set text for English students at Oxford University. A useful English translation with introductory essay has been published by Penguin, tr. and ed. by Hugh White (1993).
15. The year 1106, when Hildegard took the veil, is sometimes given as the year she and Jutta entered anchorage, which would make Hildegard fourteen.
16. Guibert's letter to Bovo, in Silvas, op. cit., p. 109.

Chapter Three: Disibodenberg

1. *Vita Sancti Disibodi*, in J. P. Migne, *Patrologia Latina Cursus Completus*, PL 197, 1101C (Turnhout, Brepols, 1976), written at the request of the Abbot Helenger (1155–79), who must have thought the opportunity of getting the celebrated Hildegard to write the official biography too good to miss.
2. Benedict of Nursia, *The Rule of St Benedict*, tr. by Justin McCann (Sheed and Ward, London, 1970, 1976), p. 16.
3. Curb and Manahan (eds), *Breaking the Silence* (Naiad Press, Tallahassee, 1985).
4. Abbot of Disibodenberg from 1113 until *c.* 1128.
5. *Causae et Curae*, 13.117b, in Berger, *On Natural Philosophy and Medicine: Selections from Cause et Cure* (E. S. Brewer, Cambridge, 1999), p. 100.
6. *Causae et Curae*, 13.116a, in Berger, op. cit., p. 99.
7. *Causae et Curae*, 5.13b, in Berger, op. cit., p. 50.

Notes for pages **46–68**.

8.   Bowie and Davies (eds), *Hildegard of Bingen: Mystical Writings*, tr. by Robert Carver (SPCK, London, 1990), p. 29.

Chapter Four: Visions
1.   *Vita Jutta*, VIII, in Silvas, op. cit., p. 77.
2.   Phil. 1:23.
3.   *Vita Jutta*, VIII, in Silvas, op. cit., p. 79.
4.   Bynum, *Holy Feast and Holy Fast*, p. 323, citing Herbert Musurillo, *The Problem of Ascetical Fasting in the Greek Patristic Writers*, *Traditio*, 12 (1956).
5.   Daniel, *The Life of Aelred of Rievaulx*, ed. and tr. by F. W. Powicke (Clarendon Press, Oxford, 1978), p. 62.
6.   Acta Inquisitions VIII in Silvas op. cit., p. 267.
7.   *Vita*, I, II.
8.   Ibid., I, VIII.
9.   Discussed in detail in Dronke's *Women Writers of the Middle Ages* (Cambridge University Press, Cambridge, 1984, 1996), still the most authoritative introduction to Hildegard's work, using extensive Hildegard extracts.
10.   *Scivias*, Hart and Bishop (tr.) (Paulist Press, New York, 1990), Preface, p. 59.
11.   Mary Lutyens, *Krishnamurti: The Years of Awakening* (Shambhala, 1997). I am grateful to Simon Callow for suggesting the link.
12.   Oliver Sacks, *Migraine, Understanding a Common Disorder*, Picador, London.
13.   Singer, 'The Scientific View and Visions of Saint Hildegard', in *Studies in the History and Method of Science*, Vol. 1 (Oxford, 1917), pp. 1–55. Also Singer, 'The Visions of Hildegard of Bingen', in *From Magic to Science: Essays on the Twilight of Science* (London, 1928), pp. 199–239.
14.   Madeline H. Caviness, 'Hildegard as Designer of the Illustrations of her Works', in Burnett and Dronke (eds), *Hildegard of Bingen: The Context of Her Thought and Art* (Warburg Institute, London, 1998). See also Chapter 12.
15.   *Vita*, II, I.
16.   See I. Herwegen, 'Les Collaborateurs de sainte Hildegarde', *Revue Benedictine*, 21, 1904 and M. Schrader and A. Führkötter, *Die Echtheit des Schrifttums der heiligen Hildegard*

Notes for Pages **69–99**.

      von Bingen. Quellenkritische Untersuchungen (Beheifte zum Archiv fur Kulturgeschichte VI) (Cologne, Graz, 1956). A good discussion in English is by Joan Ferrante in 'Hildegard, Her Language, and Her Secretaries', in Townsend and Taylor (eds), *The Tongue of the Fathers*.

17.   Albert Derolez, 'The Manuscript Transmission of Hildegard of Bingen's Writings: The State of the Problem', in Burnett and Dronke (eds), op. cit.

Chapter Five: Papal Approval

1.   *Vita*, I, IV.
2.   Baird and Ehrman (tr.), *The Letters of Hildegard of Bingen* (Oxford University Press, Oxford, 1994, 1998), Letter I, Vol. I.
3.   In a wise analysis of their friendship, Sister Benedicta Ward has suggested that in her lack of formal education, Hildegard was the model of unfettered spirituality to which Bernard himself aspired. See Ward, *Signs and Wonders* (Variorum, Hampshire, 1992), pp. xxiii, 103–7. See also Bruno James Scott, *The Letters of St Bernard of Clairvaux*.
4.   Baird and Ehrman, op. cit. Vol. II, pp. 190–1.
5.   Caerarius, *Rules for Nuns*, tr. by M. C. McCarthy (Washington DC, 1960).
6.   Baird and Ehrman, op. cit. Letter 52, Vol. I, p. 127.
7.   Ibid., pp. 128–9.
8.   *Scivias*, IV, VI.
9.   Baird and Erhrman, op. cit.

Chapter Six: The Move to Rupertsberg

1.   *Vita*, II, IV.
2.   *Vita*, II, V.
3.   Tr. by R. Vaughan in *The Chronicles of Matthew Paris* (Gloucester and New York, 1984).
4.   *Vita*, I, V.
5.   Ibid.
6.   Charter of Heinrich, Archbishop of Mainz, 1152.
7.   See Suger, Abbot of Saint Denis (1081–1151), *Oeuvres complètes de Suger*, A. Lecoy de la Marche (ed.) (Mme J. Renouard, Paris, 1867).

Notes for Pages **100–127**.

8.   Caerarius, *Rules for Nuns*, tr. by M. C. McCarthy (Washington DC, 1960).
9.   Guibert's letter to Bovo, in Silvas, op. cit., p. 101.

Chapter Seven: The Richardis Affair

1.   *Vita Jutta*, VI in Silvas, op. cit., p. 756.
2.   *Vita*, II, VI.
3.   Bruno Scott James (tr.), *The Letters of St Bernard of Clairvaux* (Cistercian Publications, Kalamazoo, 1998), Letter I, p. 1.
4.   Dronke, *Women Writers of the Middle Ages*, p. 154.
5.   Baird and Ehrman, op. cit., Letter 4, Vol. I, pp. 34–5.
6.   Ibid., Letter 18, Vol. I, pp. 69–70.
7.   Ibid., Letter 18r, Vol. I, p. 70.
8.   Ibid., Letter 12, Vol. I, p. 48.
9.   *Scivias*, V, VI.
10. Baird and Ehrman, op. cit., Letter 64, Vol. I, p. 143.
11. *Scivias*, II, VI.
12. Baird and Ehrman, op. cit., Letter 144r, Vol. II, p. 84.
13. *Scivias*, II, VI.
14. Translation from Peter Dronke, *Medieval Latin and the Rise of the European Love Lyric*, Vol. II (Oxford University Press, Oxford, 1966), p. 481. See also John Boswell, *Social Tolerance and Homosexuality: Gay People in Western Europe from the Christian Era to the 14th Century* (University of Chicago Press, Chicago, 1980).
15. Baird and Ehrman, op. cit., Letter 13, Vol. I, pp. 49–50.
16. Ibid., Letter 13r, Vol. I, p. 51.
17. *Ordo Virtutum*, 147–84, tr. Barbara Newman, *Sister of Wisdom*, pp. 222–4.

Chapter Eight: Imperial and Papal Upheaval

1.   Baird and Ehrman, op. cit., Letter 8, Vol. I, p. 41.
2.   In J. P. Migne, *Patrologia Latina Cursus Completus*, PL 197 (Turnhout, Brepols, 1976), pp. 185–7, and tr. by A. Führkötter *Briefwechsel* (Salzburg, 1965), pp. 84–5.
3.   Baird and Ehrman, op. cit., Letter 78, Vol. I, pp. 172–3.
4.   *Vita*, II, VII.
5.   Ibid., I, VII.

Notes for Pages **128–167**.

6. Baird and Ehrman, op. cit., Letter 75, Vol. I, pp. 162–3.
7. Ibid., Letter 74, Vol. I, p. 159.
8. In Silvas, op. cit., pp. 240–1.

Chapter Nine: Correspondence and Friendship

1. Daniel, op. cit., p. 42.
2. Mews (ed.), *The Lost Love Letters of Héloïse and Abélard* (Macmillan, Basingstoke, 1999).
3. Baird and Ehrman, op. cit., Letter 70, Vol. I, pp. 152–3.
4. Ibid., Letter 201, Vol. II, p. 176.
5. Ibid., Letter 201, Vol. II, p. 176.
6. Ibid., Letter 201r, Vol. II, p. 180.
7. Quoted in Clark, *Elisabeth of Schönau, A Twelfth Century Visionary* (University of Philadelphia Press, Philadelphia, 1992), p. 25.

Chapter Ten: Physician and Healer

1. Throop P. (tr.) *Hildegard von Bingen's* Physica (Healing Arts Press, Rochester, Vermont, 1998).
2. Throop, op. cit., Book VI.
3. Ibid., Book VII, p. 205.
4. Ibid., Book VII.
5. Ibid., Introduction to Book VIII.
6. Strehlow and Hertzka, *Hildegard of Bingen's Medicine* (Bear and Co., Santa Fe, 1998).
7. As cited by Thorndike, *A History of Magic and Experimental Science* (Macmillan, London, 1923), Vol. II, p. 133.

Chapter Eleven: On Sexuality

1. *Scivias*, I, II.
2. Dronke, P., *Women Writers of the Middle Ages* (Cambridge University Press, Cambridge, 1984), p. 175.
3. *Scivias*, II, VI.
4. Radice (tr.), *The Letters of Abélard and Héloïse* (Penguin, 1974), p. 133.
5. *Causae et Curae*, in Berger, op. cit., p. 53. Hildegard uses Latin words which relate to growth but equally have direct sexual meaning. Thus *stirps*, translated as penis, can mean

Notes for Pages **167–183**.

the lower part of the trunk, roots, stem, progeny, origin. Likewise *lumbus* refers to the part of the vine from which the new growth springs, or the loins or the genital organs. *Delectatio* and *libido* are readily understood.

6. Hildegard's generally expressed view, contrary to her male contemporaries, that women's sexual desire is milder than men's is not borne out by this description.

7. Ancient medicine, pre-Hildegard, mentioned the possibility of female orgasm, and Hildegard comes close to a non-specific description (see above). However, the first recorded account only occurs in the fifteenth century in Valscus of Tarentum.

8. *Causae et Curae*, 6.56b, in Berger, op. cit., p. 62.

9. *Scivias*, I, II.

10. Ibid.

11. Aristotle, also newly influential through translation, saw women as defective males, with all the parts outside on a man inside in a woman. He argued that women did not produce seed but 'matter' upon which semen worked.

12. *Causae et Curae* 80a, 80b, in Berger, op. cit., p. 82.

13. *Scivias*, II, VI.

14. Ibid.

15. *Causae et Curae* 105b, in Berger, op. cit., p. 54.

16. A full discussion is found in Riddle, *Contraception and Abortion from the Ancient World to the Renaissance* (Harvard University Press, Cambridge, Mass., 1992), pp. 116–17, 142.

17. Riddle, op. cit., pp. 116–17.

18. See Dronke, *Women Writers of the Middle Ages*, p. 180. Other useful essays are: Joan Cadden, 'It takes all kinds: Sexuality and Gender Differences in Hildegard of Bingen's Book of Compound Medicine', *Traditio* 40 (1984), pp. 149–174, and Scholz, 'Hildegard von Bingen on the Nature of Women', *American Benedictine Review* 31.

19. *Scivias*, I, IV.

20. *Causae et Curae*, 48.

21. Throop, op. cit., p. 147.

Notes for Pages **187–199**.

Chapter Twelve: Harp of God

1. *The New Grove Dictionary of Women Composers* remains the best work in this area and has an introductory essay by Rhian Samuel that sensibly discusses the idea of a feminine tone of voice in musical composition, a source of much debate among feminist musicologists (in which, by inclination, I am reluctant to engage).
2. Hyperion CDA 66039. Christopher Page's forthcoming book, *Music and the Rise of Europe*, promises to make a significant contribution to the debate.
3. From the Wiesbaden Hessische Landesbibliothek MS, available in a facsimile (ed. J. Gmelch, Dusseldorf, 1913), rather than the earlier Dendermonde MS. See note 10.
4. See John Harper, *The Forms and Orders of the Western Liturgy from the Tenth to the Eighteenth Century* (Clarendon Press, Oxford, 1991).
5. Baird and Ehrman, op. cit.
6. See David Hiley, *Western Plainchant* (Oxford University Press, Oxford, 1995), for a full typology, notation and current state of research.
7. Contemporary British composers have been inspired to rework Hildegard's chant, notably Simon Bainbridge in 1999 with his millennial composition *Chant*, and Tarik O'Regan in 2000 with a version of *Columba aspexit* for girls' voices for the Hildegard Choir, Oxford.
8. See Peter Dronke, *Poetic Individuality in the Middle Ages* (Oxford, 1970), and Newman, *Symphonia: A Critical Edition* (Cornell University, Ithaca, 2nd ed., 1998).
9. Newman, op. cit., pp. 212–15.
10. Dendermonde (Villers) Benedictine Abbey MS 9, c. 1175, and, discovered first, the D-WII 2, Riesencodex (Wiesbaden Landesbibliothek), from the 1180s, containing the collected works of Hildegard and compiled during the decade after her death.
11. June Boyce-Tillyard, 'The Eye of a Woman: Hildegard of Bingen at 900', *Musical Times*, Winter 1998, Vol. 139, No. 1865. Dr Boyce-Tillyard runs the Hildegard Network which 'brings together spirituality, the arts, healing and

Notes for Pages **200–230**.

ecology through the vision of the twelfth-century abbess by means of conferences, performances, quiet days and a newsletter'.

12. Richard Witts, 'How to Make a Saint', *Early Music*, August 1998.

13. Led by Professor Alfred Haverkamp of the University of Trier (historical) and Professor Wulf Arlt of the University of Basel (musicological).

14. Annette Kreutziger-Herr, 'Hildegard of Bingen Conference', *Early Music*, February 1999.

15. Otto Pächt, *Book Illumination in the Middle Ages*, tr. by Kay Davenport (Oxford University Press, 1986).

16. Madeline H. Caviness (op. cit.) has argued eloquently for Hildegard's role as artist, but most of her colleagues leave the question open or avoid it.

17. In Delia Graze (ed.), *Dictionary of Women Artists*, Vol. I, 'Hildegard of Bingen' (Fitzroy Dearborn, London, 1997).

18. In 1993 Prince declared that he should only be referred to as 'the Artist formerly known as Prince', as an unpronounceable squiggle 'denoting androgyny', or, simply, as the Artist. On 17 May 2000 he reverted to Prince, announcing, 'I just want to ask God in solitude what he wants from me now.' Had Hildegard lived in the age of mass media, she might have issued the same statement.

Chapter Thirteen: Rhine Travels

1. *Vita*, II, X.
2. Ibid., II, XIII.
3. See Malcolm Lambert, *The Cathars* (Blackwell, Oxford, 1998).
4. *Vita*, III, XXV.
5. Ibid., III, XVIII.
6. Ibid., III, XX, p. 193.
7. Ibid., p. 194.
8. Ibid., III, XXII.

Chapter Fourteen: Last Journey

1. *Vita*, III, XXIII.
2. See L. van Acker (ed.), *Hildegardis Bingensis Epistolarium*,

Notes for Pages 230–257.

Vol. 91A (Turnhout, Brepols, 1993), pp. 443–5. Quoted here from Silvas, op. cit., p. 86.
3. Baird and Ehrman, op. cit., Letter 149, Vol. II, p. 91.
4. Ibid., p. 92.
5. Pitra (ed.), *Analecta Sanctae Hildegardis* (Monte Cassio, 1882; repr. Gregg, Farnborough, 1966), Ep. CXXVII, p. 561.
6. Guibert's letter to Bovo, in Silvas, op. cit., p. 117.
7. See Dronke, *Women Writers of the Middle Ages*, pp. 195, 313.
8. Baird and Ehrman, op. cit., Letter 76r, Vol. I, p. 164.
9. Ibid., Letter 10, Vol. I, p. 45.

Chapter Fifteen: Final Crisis

1. See exchange of letters in Baird and Ehrman, op. cit., Letters 102–109r, Vol. II, pp. 16–49.
2. Baird and Ehrman, op. cit., Letter 108A, Vol. II, pp. 44–7.
3. Ibid., Letter 109, Vol. II, p. 46.
4. Guibert's letter to Bovo, in Silvas, op. cit., p. 102.
5. Baird and Ehrman, op. cit., Letter 23, Vol. I, pp. 76–9.
6. Ibid., Letter 24r, Vol. I, pp. 82–3.
7. *Vita*, III, XXVII.

Chapter Sixteen: Relighting the Flame

1. *Vita*, III, XXVII.
2. Silvas, op. cit., p. 43.
3. Anna Silvas separates the tangled skeins of the *Vita's* authorship and sources, still a matter of exhaustive scholarly inquiry. See also Barbara Newman's illuminating 'Hildegard and Her Hagiographers', in Mooney (ed.), *Gendered Voices: Medieval Saints and their Interpreters* (University of Pennsylvania Press, Philadelphia, 1999).
4. *Proceedings of the Enquiry into the Virtues and Miracles of St Hildegard*, 1233, tr, in Silvas, op. cit., p. 252, or see *Analecta Bollandiana*, 2 (1883), pp. 116–29.
5. John Peckham, 'Tractatus Pauperis', Ch. 16 in C. L. Kingsford, A. G. Little and F. Tocco (eds), *Tractatus Tres de Paupertate* (Manchester, 1910). Quoted by Newman, op. cit.

Notes for Pages **269–279**.

Chapter Seventeen: Shrines and Icons
1. www.beliefnet.com.
2. According to information issued by his University of Creation Spirituality in Oakland, California, Fox was ordained a priest in 1967. 'A liberation theologian, he was silenced by the Vatican and later dismissed from the Dominican order. After dismissal he was received as an Episcopal priest by Bishop Swing of the Diocese of California.' See Appendix II.
3. *The Chambers English Dictionary* defines spelt, disdainfully, as 'an inferior kind of wheat'.
4. Susan Hellauer: note in CD booklet of Anonymous 4: *11,000 Virgins* (1997).

Appendix I
1. Examined by Pozzi Escot in 'Hildegard's Christianity: An Assimilation of Pagan and Ancient Classical Traditions', in Davidson (ed.), *Wisdom Which Encircles, Papers on Hildegard of Bingen* (Medieval Institute Publications, Kalamazoo, 1996).

BIBLIOGRAPHY

The aim of this bibiography is to indicate the primary sources of Hildegard of Bingen's writings, and the principal writings in English. Secondary sources have been listed either as general background or for their specialist interest. In general, journals have not been included unless of particular importance.

(Abbr. CCCM = Corpus Christianorum: continuatio mediaevalis)

Critical editions of Hildegard's works

Hildegardis Causae et Curae, ed. by Paul Kaiser (Teubner, Leipzig, 1903).

Hildegardis Bingensis Epistolarium, ed. by Lieven van Acker, CCCM, 91–91A (to be completed by Monika Klaes) (Turnhout, Brepols, 1991–3).

Hildegardis Bingensis Liber Divinorum Operum, ed. by A. Derolez and P. Dronke, CCCM, 92 (Turnhout, Brepols, 1996).

Hildegardis Bingensis Liber Vitae Meritorum, ed. by Angela Carlevaris, CCCM, 90 (Turnhout, Brepols, 1995).

Hildegardis Bingensis Scivias, ed. by Adelgundis Führkötter and Angela Carlevaris, CCCM, 43–43A (Turnhout, Brepols, 1978).

Lieder, ed. by Pudentiana Barth, M.-I. Ritscher and J. Schmidt-Georg, musical ed. (O. Müller, Salzburg, 1969, 1992).

Ordo Virtutum, ed. and tr. by Peter Dronke, in *Nine Medieval Latin Plays* (Cambridge Medieval Classics, Cambridge, 1994).

Ordo Virtutum, ed. by Audrey Ekdahl Davidson, performance ed. (Medieval Institute Publications, Kalamazoo, 1985).

Sanctae Hildegardis Revelationes, MS 1942, ed. by Anna Calderoni Masetti and Gigetta dalli Regoli, facsimile of *Liber divinorum operum* illuminations (Lucca, 1973).

Sequences and Hymns, ed. by Christopher Page, performance ed.

(Antico Church Music, Newton Abbot, 1983).
Symphonia: A Critical Edition of the Symphonia Armonie Celestium Revelationum, ed. and tr. by Barbara Newman (Cornell University Press, Ithaca, NY, 1988; rev. ed., 1998).
Symphonia harmoniae caelestium revelationum, ed. by Peter van Poucke, facsimile ed. of Dendermonde MS (Peer, Alamire, 1991).
Symphonia harmonie celestium revelationum, ed. by Lorenz Welker and Michael Klaper, facsimile ed. of Riesencodex (L. Reichert, Wiesbaden, 1998).
Wörtenbuch der Unbekannten Sprache (lingua ignota), ed. by Marie-Louise Portmann and Alois Odermatt (Basel, 1986).

For remaining works of Hildegard still awaiting modern critical editions see:

Hildegardis opera omnia, ed. by J. P. Migne, *Patrologia Latina Cursus Completus*, Vol. 197 (Paris, 1855, repr. Turnhout, Brepols, 1976).
Analecta Sanctae Hildegardis, ed. J.-B. Pitra, *Analecta Sacra*, Vol. 8 (Monte Cassio, 1882; repr. Gregg, Farnborough, 1966).

For reproductions of Rupertsberg *Scivias* illuminations see:

Der Miniaturen im 'Liber Scivias' der Hildegard von Bingen, ed. by Lieselotte E. Saurma-Jeltsch (Reichert Verlag Wiesbaden, 1998).

Primary sources

Gottfried of Disibodenberg and Theodoric of Echternach, *Vita Sanctae Hildegardis*, ed. by Monika Klaes, Guibert's Revisions to the *Vita*, pp. 93–106, CCCM 126 (Turnhout, Brepols, 1993).
Vitae domnae Jutta inclusae, ed. by Franz Staab, in Stefan Weinfurter (ed.), *Reformide und Reformpolitik im spätsalisch-frühstaufischen Reich* (Mainz, 1992).
'Annales Sancti Disibodi', ed. by Georgius Waitz, *Monumenta Germaniae Historica*, SS 17 (Hannover, 1861).
Guibert of Gembloux, *Guiberti Gemblacensis Epistolae*, ed. by Albert Derolez, CCCM 66–66A, The Letter to Bovo: Epistola 38, Vol. 66A, pp. 366–79 (Turnhout, Brepols, 1988–9).
Acta inquisitionis de virtutibus et miraculis S. Hildegardis, ed. by Petrus Bruder, *Analecta Bollandiana*, Vol. 2 (1883), pp. 116–29 (also called *Protocollum Canonisationis*, 'The Protocol of Canonisation') (Société Générale de Librairie Catholique, Paris/Brussels, 1883).

Johannes Trithemius, 'De luminaribus sive de Illustribus Viris Germaniae', in *Johanni Trithemi Opera Historica*, ed. by Marquand Freher, Vol. 1 (Frankfurt, 1601; repr. Minerva, Frankfurt/Main, 1966), pp. 123–83.

Selected translations of Hildegard's works and biographical sources

Jutta and Hildegard: Biographical Sources, tr. by Anna Silvas (Pennsylvania State University Press, Philadelphia, 1999).

Gottfried and Theodoric, *The Life of the Holy Hildegard*, tr. from Latin to German by Adelgundis Führkötter, tr. from German to English by James McGrath (Liturgical Press, Collegeville, Minnesota, 1980, 1995).

The Letters of Hildegard of Bingen (two vols), ed. and tr. by Joseph L. Baird and Radd K. Ehrman (Oxford University Press, Oxford, 1994, 1998).

Physica, tr. by Priscilla Throop (Healing Arts Press, Rochester, Vermont, 1998).

Scivias, tr. by Columba Hart and Jane Bishop, with introduction by Barbara Newman and preface by Caroline Walker Bynum (The Classics of Western Spirituality, Paulist Press, New York, 1990).

On Natural Philosophy and Medicine: Selections from Cause et Cure, ed. and tr. by Margret Berger (D. S. Brewer, Cambridge, 1999).

Holistic Healing (Causae et Curae), tr. from Latin by Manfred Pawlik, tr. from German by Patrick Madigan (Liturgical Press, Collegeville, Minnesota, 1994).

Explanation of the Rule of St Benedict by Hildegard of Bingen, tr. by Hugh Feiss (Peregrina, Toronto, 1990).

Play of the Virtues, tr. by Peter Dronke in *Nine Medieval Latin Plays* (Cambridge Medieval Classics, Cambridge, 1994).

Hildegard of Bingen: Mystical Writings, ed. Fiona Bowie and Oliver Davies, tr. by Robert Carver (SPCK, London, 1990).

The Book of the Rewards of Life (Liber Vitae Meritorum), tr. by Bruce W. Hozeski (Oxford University Press, Oxford, 1997).

Selected translations of related sources

Abélard, Peter, *Peter Abélard's Ethics*, ed. by D. E. Luscombe (Clarendon Press, Oxford, 1971).

Abélard and Héloïse, *The Lost Love Letters of Héloïse and Abélard*, ed. by Constant J. Mews, tr. by Neville Chiavaroli (Macmillan, London, 1999).

Abélard and Héloïse, *The Letters of Abélard and Héloïse*, tr. by Betty Radice (Penguin Books, London, 1974).

Aelred, *The Life of Aelred of Rievaulx*, by Walter Daniel, ed. and tr. by F. M. Powicke (Clarendon Press, Oxford, 1978).

Anselm, *The Prayers and Meditations of Saint Anselm*, tr. by Benedicta Ward (Penguin Books, Harmondsworth, 1973).

Benedict of Nursia, *The Rule of Saint Benedict*, tr. by Justin McCann (Sheed and Ward, London, 1970, 1976).

Bernard of Clairvaux, *The Letters of St Bernard of Clairvaux*, tr. by Bruno Scott James, introduced by Beverly Mayne Kienzle (Cistercian Publications, Kalamazoo, 1998).

Bernard of Clairvaux, *On the Song of Songs*, tr. by Killian Walsh and Irene Edmonds, Cistercian Fathers Series, nos. 4, 7, 31, 40 (Cistercian Publications, Kalamazoo, 1971–80).

Christina of Markyate, *The Life of Christina of Markyate*, ed. by C. H. Talbot (Clarendon Press, Oxford, 1959).

John of Salisbury, *The Letters of John of Salisbury, Vol. 1: The Early Letters (1153–1161)*, ed. by W. J. Millor and H. E. Butler, rev. C. N. L. Brooke (Clarendon Press, Oxford, 1986); *The Letters of John of Salisbury, Vol. 2: The Later Letters (1163–1180)*, ed. by W. J. Millor and C. N. L. Brooke (Clarendon Press, Oxford, 1979).

Suger, Abbot of Saint-Denis, *On the Abbey Church of Saint-Denis and its Art Treasures*, tr. by Erwin Panofsky (Princeton University Press, Princeton, NJ, 1946; 1979, ed. Gerda Soergel-Panofsky).

Ancrene Riwle, ed. by E. J. Dobson, Early English Text Society, No. 267 (Oxford University Press, London, 1972).

The Cistercian World: Monastic Writings of the Twelfth Century, ed. and tr. by Pauline Matarasso (Penguin Books, Harmondsworth, 1991, 1993).

The First Crusade: The Chronicle of Fulcher of Chartres and Other Source Material, ed. by Edward Peters (University of Pennsylvania Press, Philadelphia, 1998).

The Song of Roland, tr. by Dorothy L. Sayers (Penguin Books, London, 1957).

Women and Writing in Medieval Europe: A Sourcebook, ed. by Caroline Larrington (Routledge, London, 1995).

Books about Hildegard

Bruck, Anton P. (ed.), *Hildegard von Bingen, Festschrift 1179–1979* (Selbstverlag der Gesellschaft für Mittelrheinische Kirchengeschichte, Mainz, 1979).

Burnett, Charles and Dronke, Peter (eds), *Hildegard of Bingen: The Context of Her Thought and Art* (Warburg Institute, London, 1998).

Davidson, Audrey Ekhahl (ed.), *Wisdom Which Encircles, Papers on Hildegard of Bingen* (Medieval Institute Publications, Kalamazoo, 1996).

Flanagan, Sabina, *Hildegard of Bingen: A Visionary Life* (Routledge, London, 1989, 1998).

Lauter, Werner, *Hildegard-Bibliographie* (Verlag Der Rheinhessischen Druckwerkstatte, Alzey, 1970, 1983, 1998).

McInery, Maud Burnett (ed.), *Hildegard of Bingen: A Book of Essays* (Garland, New York, 1998).

Newman, Barbara, *Sister of Wisdom: St Hildegard's Theology of the Feminine* (University of California Press, Berkeley, 1997).

Newman, Barbara, 'Hildegard and Her Hagiographers', in *Gendered Voices: Medieval Saints and their Interpreters*, ed. by Catherine M. Mooney (University of Pennsylvania Press, Philadelphia, 1999).

Newman, Barbara (ed.), *Voice of the Living Light* (University of California Press, Berkeley, 1998).

Schipperges, Heinrich, *The World of Hildegard of Bingen: Her Life, Times and Visions*, tr. by John Cumming (Burns and Oates, Tunbridge Wells, 1997).

Schmitt, Miriam, 'Blessed Jutta of Disibodenberg: Hildegard of Bingen's *Magistra* and Abbess', *American Benedictine Review*, 40 (2 June, 1989).

Schnapp, Jeffrey, 'Virgin Words: Hildegard of Bingen's *Lingua ignota* and the Development of Imaginary Languages Ancient to Modern', *Exemplaria*, 3 (1991), pp. 267–98.

Scholz, Bernhard W., 'Hildegard von Bingen on the Nature of Women', *American Benedictine Review*, 31 (4 December, 1980).

Steele, Francesca Maria, *The Life and Visions of St Hildegard* (Heath, Cranton and Ousley Ltd, London, 1914).

Strehlow, Wighard and Hertzka, Gottfried, *Hildegard of Bingen's Medicine*, tr. by Karin Anderson Strehlow (Folk Wisdom Series, Bear and Co., Santa Fe, 1988).

Sur, Carolyn Wörman, *The Feminine Images of God in the Visions of Saint Hildegard of Bingen's* Scivias (Edwin Mellen Press, Lewiston, Lampeter, 1993).

Witts, Richard, 'How to Make a Saint: an interpretation of Hildegard of Bingen', *Early Music*, 26 (3 August, 1998).

Secondary sources and related texts

Barber, Malcolm, *The Two Cities: Medieval Europe 1050–1320* (Routledge, London, 1993).

Bowers, Jane and Tick, Judith (eds), *Women Making Music: The Western Art Tradition 1150–1950* (University of Illinois Press, Chicago, 1986).

Brundage, James A., *Law, Sex and Christian Society in Medieval Europe* (University of Chicago Press, Chicago and London, 1987).

Bullough, Vern L. and Brundage, James, *A Handbook of Medieval Sexuality* (Garland, New York, 1996).

Bynum, Caroline Walker, *Holy Feast and Holy Fast* (University of California Press, Berkeley, 1987).

Chance, Jane (ed.), *Gender and Text in the Later Middle Ages* (University Press of Florida, Gainesville, 1996).

Cherewatuk, K. and Wiethaus, U. (eds), *Dear Sister: Medieval Women and the Epistolary Genre* (University of Pennsylvania Press, Philadephia, 1993).

Clark, Anne, *Elisabeth of Schönau: A Twelfth Century Visionary* (University of Philadelphia Press, Philadelphia, 1992).

Cooke, Lynne and Wollen, Peter, *Visual Display: Culture Beyond Appearances* (Bay Press, Seattle, 1995).

Curb, Rosemary and Manahan, Nancy (eds), *Breaking the Silence: Lesbian Nuns Speak Out* (Naiad Press, Tallahassee, 1985).

Dronke, Peter, *The Medieval Lyric*, 3rd ed. (D. S. Brewer, Cambridge, 1996).

Dronke, Peter, *Poetic Individuality in the Middle Ages: New Departures in Poetry 1000–1150* (Clarendon Press, Oxford, 1970).

Dronke, Peter, *Women Writers of the Middle Ages: A Critical Study of*

Texts from Perpetua to Marguerite Porete (Cambridge University Press, Cambridge, 1984, 1996).

Duby, Georges, *The Age of the Cathedrals* (Croom Helm, London, 1981).

Dunstan, G. R. (ed.), *The Human Embryo: Aristotle and the Arabic and European Traditions* (University of Exeter Press, Exeter, 1990).

Gervers, Michael (ed.), *The Second Crusade and the Cistercians* (St Martin's Press, New York, 1992).

Fuhrmann, Horst, *Germany in the High Middle Ages 1050–1200*, tr. from the German by Timothy Reuter (Cambridge University Press, Cambridge, 1995).

Hamilton, Bernard, *The Crusades* (Sutton, Stroud, 1998).

Harper, John, *The Forms and Orders of the Western Liturgy from the Tenth to the Eighteenth Century* (Clarendon Press, Oxford, 1991).

Haverkamp, Alfred and Vollrath, Hanna (eds), *England and Germany in the High Middle Ages* (German Historical Institute, London/Oxford, 1995).

Houts, Elisabeth van, 'Memory and Gender in Medieval Europe 900–1200', in *Explorations in Medieval Culture and Society* (Macmillan, Basingstoke, 1999).

Hunt, Noreen (ed.), *Cluniac Monasticism in the Central Middle Ages* (Macmillan, London, 1971).

James, William, *The Varieties of Religious Experience* (Fontana, London, 1971).

Jezic, Diane and Wood, Elizabeth, *Women Composers: The Lost Tradition Found* (Feminist Press, New York, 1988, 1994).

Jones, Terry and Ereira, Alan, *Crusades* (BBC/Penguin Books, London, 1994).

Lekai, Louis J., *The Cistercians: Ideals and Reality* (University of Kent State, Kent, Ohio, 1977).

Leyser, Henrietta, *Hermits and the New Monasticism: A Study of Religious Communities in Western Europe 1000–1150* (Macmillan, London, 1984).

Leyser, Henrietta, *Medieval Women: A Social History of Women in England 450–1500* (Phoenix Giant, London, 1995, 1997).

McCash, June Hall (ed.), *The Cultural Patronage of Medieval Women* (University of Georgia Press, Athens, London, 1996).

McNeill, John and Gamer, Helena M., *Medieval Handbooks of Penance: A translation of the Principal* Libri Poenitentiales (Columbia University Press, New York, 1938, 1990).

Mooney, Catherine M., *Gendered Voices: Medieval Saints and their Interpreters* (University of Pennsylvania Press, Philadelphia, 1999).

Mundy, John H., *Europe in the High Middle Ages 1130–1309* (Longman, Harlow, 2000).

Murray, Dom Gregory, *The Accompaniment of Plainsong* (Society of St Gregory, Beaconsfield, Bucks, 1950).

Murray, Dom Gregory, *Gregorian Chant According to the Manuscripts* (Cary, London, 1963).

Page, Christopher, *The Owl and the Nightingale* (University of California Press, Berkeley, 1990).

Page, Christopher, *Music and Instruments of the Middle Ages: Studies on Texts and Performance* (Variorum, Hants, 1997).

Pendle, Karin and Peacock, Diane (eds), *Women and Music: A History* (Indiana University Press, Bloomington, 1991).

Riddle, John M., *Contraception and Abortion from the Ancient World to the Renaissance* (Harvard University Press, Cambridge, Mass., 1992).

Rios, Dom Romanus, *Benedictines of Today* (Stanbrook Abbey Press, 1946).

Sacks, Oliver, *Migraine: Understanding a Common Disorder* (rev. and expanded, Picador, London, 1993).

Salisbury, Joyce E., *Medieval Sexuality: A Research Guide* (Garland, New York/London, 1990).

Sarton, George, *Introduction to the History of Science*, Vol. I (Dover Publications, New York, 1931).

Schneider, Edouard, *The Benedictines*, tr. from the French by Johan Liljencrants (Allen and Unwin, London, 1926).

Singer, Charles, 'The Scientific Views and Visions of Saint Hildegard', in *Studies in the History and Method of Science*, Vol. 1 (Oxford, 1951).

Singer, Charles, *From Magic to Science: Essays on the Twilight of Science* (London, 1928; Dover, New York, 1958).

Southern, R. W., *The Making of the Middle Ages* (Hutchinson, London, 1953).

Steele, Francesca Mary, *Anchoresses of the West* (Sands and Co., London, 1903).

Tannahill, Reay, *Sex in History* (Abacus, London, 1989, 1999).

Thorndike, Lynn, *A History of Magic and Experimental Science*, Vol. II (Macmillan, London, 1923).

Townsend, David and Taylor, Andrew (eds), *The Tongue of the*

Fathers: Gender and Ideology in Twelfth-century Latin (University of Pennsylvania Press, Philadelphia, 1998).

Tyerman, Christopher, *The Invention of the Crusades* (Macmillan, London, 1998).

Voaden, Rosalynn (ed.), *Prophets Abroad* (Brewer, Cambridge, 1996).

Waddell, Helen, *The Wandering Scholars* (Penguin Books, London, 1952).

Ward, Benedicta, *Miracles and the Medieval Mind* (rev. ed., Wildwood House, Aldershot, Hants, 1987).

Ward, Benedicta, *Signs and Wonders* (Variorum, Hants, 1992).

Wiethaus, Ulrike (ed.), *Maps of Flesh and Light: The Religious Experience of Medieval Women Mystics* (Syracuse University Press, Syracuse, 1993).

Brief discography

Anonymous 4: *11,000 Virgins Chants for the Feast of Saint Ursula*, Harmonia Mundi HMV 907200 (1997).

Gothic Voices, dir. Christopher Page: *A Feather on the Breath of God: Sequences and Hymns by Abbess Hildegard of Bingen*, Hyperion CDA 66039 (1981).

Oxford Camerata, dir. Jeremy Summerly: *Hildegard von Bingen: Heavenly Revelations*, Naxos: 8550998 (1995).

Schola der Benedikterinnenabtei St Hildegard, Eibingen: 'O Vis Aeternitatis', Ars Musici AM 1203–2 (1997).

Sequentia, dir. Barbara Thornton: *Ordo Virtutum*, 2 CDs, Deutsche Harmonia Mundi 77395 2 (1998).

Sequentia, dir. Barbara Thornton: O *Jerusalem*, Deutsche Harmonia Mundi DES 77353 (1997).

INDEX